TRENDS IN GLOBAL HIGHER EDUCATION

GLOBAL PERSPECTIVES ON HIGHER EDUCATION

Volume 22

Higher education worldwide is in a period of transition, affected by globalization, the advent of mass access, changing relationships between the university and the state, and the new technologies, among others. *Global Perspectives on Higher Education* provides cogent analysis and comparative perspectives on these and other central issues affecting postsecondary education worldwide.

This series is co-published with the Center for International Higher Education at Boston College.

Trends in Global Higher Education

Tracking an Academic Revolution

By

Philip G. Altbach
Center for International Higher Education, Boston College, USA

Liz Reisberg
Center for International Higher Education, Boston College, USA

and

Laura E. Rumbley
Academic Cooperation Association, Brussels, Belgium

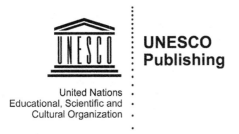

**UNESCO
Publishing**

United Nations
Educational, Scientific and
Cultural Organization

UNESCO PUBLISHING

SENSE PUBLISHERS
ROTTERDAM / BOSTON / TAIPEI

A C.I.P. record for this book is available from the Library of Congress.

ISBN 978-94-6091-338-9 (paperback)
ISBN 978-94-6091-339-6 (hardback)

Published by jointly by the United Nations Educational, Scientific and Cultural Organization
(UNESCO), 7, place de Fontenoy, 75007 Paris, France, and Sense Publishers, P.O. Box 21858,
3001 AW Rotterdam, The Netherlands
http://www.sensepublishers.com

The designations employed and the presentation of material throughout this publication do
not imply the expression of any opinion whatsoever on the part of UNESCO concerning the
legal status of any country, territory, city or area or of its authorities, or the delimitation of its
frontiers or boundaries.
The authors are responsible for the choice and the presentation of the facts contained in this
book and for the opinions expressed therein, which are not necessarily those of UNESCO and
do not commit the Organization.

Printed on acid-free paper

TABLE OF CONTENTS

LIST OF TABLES

Preface

This Trend Report fulfills a simple yet complex purpose—to summarize the main directions in higher education worldwide in the past decade—since the 1998 UNESCO World Conference on Higher Education. The main goal is to provide background analysis and to animate discussion at the 2009 UNESCO World Conference on Higher Education. We, as authors, have no preconceived perspective. Instead, with the contributors who have assisted us in the preparation of this report, we have attempted to provide an objective discussion of central themes. While under no illusion that this report has analyzed everything, we have highlighted what to us seem the most significant forces shaping higher education worldwide. No doubt, some observers will disagree with our choices of themes or points of analysis.

If one retraces higher education back to the time of the 1998 UNESCO conference and reviews the concerns and problems expressed at that meeting, remarkable consistency appears over time. Many of the same challenges remain, but the past decade has intensified the central issues. Higher education has expanded significantly, creating many problems as well as serving much larger numbers of students. At the same time, higher education provides new opportunities for many more students.

Many of the trends examined here have defined higher education over the past half century or more, but our focus is especially on the period since the late 1990s. As shown by the subtitle of this report, *Tracking an Academic Revolution,* higher education has undergone deep changes that will shape the academic enterprise for decades to come. Perhaps the key engines of change consist of the massification of higher education in almost every country, the impact of information and communications technology and its impact on higher education, the "public good/ private good" debate, and the rise of the global knowledge economy and other manifestations of globalization. All of the themes discussed here stem in one way or another from these motivating forces. The

21st century revolution will continue to shape higher education in the coming decades.

This continuing revolution is intensifying. Although issues such as quality, access, and internationalization have preoccupied the higher education community for some time, the discussion has moved beyond awareness to a deeper level of concern with the complexities and implications of these issues. Making higher education more inclusive requires not only moving historically underrepresented groups into higher education but also meeting their unique needs. New mechanisms for cost sharing have appeared and present difficult choices for how the risks and responsibilities will be distributed and whether the programs will reach their intended audience. Quality, instinctively desirable, has proven difficult to define and equally difficult to measure.

This report will not analyze all the forces that influence higher education. Moreover, while we cannot predict all future developments, it can be noted that the trends identified here will likely continue as the main themes in the foreseeable future. For example, the impact of the current global economic crisis on higher education seems at this point unclear, although some appreciable effect is certain to occur.

This report is a collaborative enterprise. The organization and writing was carried out by the three authors, Philip G. Altbach, Liz Reisberg, and Laura E. Rumbley—all members of the Center for International Higher Education at Boston College. This work is derived from text that was commissioned by the UNESCO Division of Higher Education for the World Conference on Higher Education. This book is printed thanks to the permission granted by UNESCO to adapt this work for this publication. The UNESCO Trends in Global Higher Education: Tracking an Academic Revolution is available at: http://unesdoc.unesco.org/images/0018/001832/183219e.pdf.

Our close work with UNESCO staff helped to shape this document and provided important feedback throughout. The UNESCO Institute for Statistics in Montreal, Canada, provided us with all of the statistical information and tables in this report.

We are indebted to Jane Knight, V. Lynn Meek, Marcela Mollis, and Mala Singh, our external evaluators, for careful critiques and constructive suggestions.

We commissioned experts to contribute important substance to many sections of this document. The chapters reflect their ideas as well as our own analysis. Our collaborating authors include:

- Miriam David, professor of sociology of education at the Institute of Education, University of London. She prepared a draft of the section on access and equity.

- D. Bruce Johnstone, Distinguished Professor Emeritus and director of the International Comparative Higher Education Finance and Accessibility Project at the State University of New York at Buffalo. He prepared the section on financing.
- Daniel C. Levy, Distinguished Professor and director of the Program of Research on Private Higher Education at the State University of New York at Albany. He wrote the section on private higher education.
- John Biggs, who has held professorships in Canada, Australia, and Hong Kong and is widely published on teaching and learning in higher education, and Catherine Tang, who was head of educational development at the Hong Kong Institute of Education. They coauthored much of the section on teaching and learning.
- Damtew Teferra, director for Africa and the Middle East at the Ford International Fellowship Program and director of the International Network for Higher Education in Africa. He prepared a draft of the essay on distance education and information and communications technologies.
- Jorge Balán, former senior program officer at the Ford Foundation, is currently a senior researcher at the Center for the Study of State and Society in Buenos Aires. He prepared the section on research.
- Sachi Hatakenaka, formerly on staff at the World Bank, is currently a consultant on higher education. She prepared the essay on university-industry linkages.

Our colleagues at the Center for International Higher Education at Boston College carried out a great deal of work. Kara A. Godwin and Iván F. Pacheco, research assistants at the Center, took part in the research and helped to draft sections of the report. Edith S. Hoshino, the Center's publications editor, provided editorial assistance. UNESCO's higher education staff collaborated with us. Stamenka Uvalic-Trumbic, Chief, Section for Reform, Innovation and Quality Assurance, UNESCO, Education Sector, Division of Higher Education provided helpful comments and cooperation throughout the preparation of the report. Lydie Ruas, Zeynep Varoglu, Yung-chul Kim, and Liliana Viorica Simionescu also helped with aspects of our work. The UNESCO Institute for Statistics in Montreal, Canada, provided the statistical material included here. We appreciate the colleagueship and contribution of its director, Albert Montvans, and are especially grateful for the help provided by Chiao-Ling (Claire) Chien and Yanhong Zhang.

Abbreviations

AACSB	Association to Advance Collegiate Schools of Business
ABET	Accreditation Board for Engineering and Technology
AHELO	Assessment of Higher Education Learning Outcomes
ANIE	African Network for Information Ethics
ANQAHE	Arab Network for Quality Assurance in Higher Education
APQN	Asia-Pacific Quality Network
AUQA	Australian Universities Quality Agency
AUTM	Association of University Technology Managers
AVU	African Virtual University
CAPES	Coordination for the Improvement of Higher Education Personnel (Coordenação de Aperfeiçoamento de Pessoal de Nível Superior)
CD-ROM	compact disc-read only memory
CEPES	European Centre for Higher Education (Centre européen pour l'enseignement supérieur)
CHEA	Council for Higher Education Accreditation
CMC	computer-mediated communication
CNRS	Centre National de la recherche scientifique
DVD	digital versatile disc
EHEA	European Higher Education Area
ENLACES	Latin American and Caribbean Higher Education Area (Espacio de Encuentro Latinoamericano y Caribeño de Educación Superior)
ENQA	European Network for Quality Assurance
EQAR	European Quality Assurance Register
EQUIS	European Quality Improvement System
ERASMUS	European Region Action Scheme for the Mobility of University Students
ESG	European Standards and Guidelines
GATS	General Agreement on Trade in Services

GIQAC   Global Initiative for Quality Assurance Capacity
HEFCE   Higher Education Funding Council for England
ICT   information and communication technologies
IGNOU   Indira Gandhi National Open University
INQAAHE   International Network for Quality Assurance Agencies in
           Higher Education
ISCED   International Standard Classification of Education
MBA   master of business administration
NAFSA   NAFSA Association of International Educators
NAFTA   North Atlantic Free Trade Agreement
NOQA   Nordic Quality Assurance Agency
ODL   open and distance learning
OECD   Organization for Economic Cooperation and Development
OER   Open Educational Resources
PROPHE   Program of Research on Private Higher Education
QA   Quality assurance
QAA   Quality Assurance Agency for Higher Education
R&D   Research and development
RIACES   Ibero-American Network for Quality Assessment and
           Assurance in Higher Education (Red Iberoamericana para
           la Acreditación de la Calidad de la Educación Superior)
RSS   Really Simple Syndication
SEAMEO
RIHED   Southeast Asian Ministers of Education Organisation—
           Regional Centre for Higher Education and Development
UNAM   National Autonomous University of Mexico (Universidad
           Nacional Autónoma de México)
UNESCO   United Nations Educational, Scientific and Cultural
           Organization
UNESCO-
IESALC   UNESCO International Institute for Higher Education in
           Latin America and the Carribbean (Instituto Internacional
           de Educación Superior en América Latina y el Caribe)

1

Introduction: Twenty-First-Century Global Directions

Understanding the changes that have taken place in higher education worldwide in the past half century is a difficult task because of the scope and complexity of those trends. One can, without risk of exaggeration, speak of an academic "revolution"—a series of transformations that have affected most aspects of postsecondary education worldwide. However, comprehending a dynamic process while it is taking place is not an easy task. Arguably, the developments of the recent past are at least as dramatic as those in the 19th century when the research university evolved, first in Germany and then elsewhere, and that fundamentally changed the nature of the university worldwide. The academic changes of the late 20th and early 21st centuries are more extensive in that they are truly global and affect many more institutions and larger populations.

The fundamental forces propelling the contemporary revolution are easy to discern but much more difficult to integrate and comprehend. The central reality of the past half century, or more, involves the massification of higher education. While some systems—for example, in Latin America in the early 20th century—called for mass access and a few countries—mainly the United States and Canada—provided such access in the first half of the 20th century, mass access is a quite recent phenomenon globally. The sociologist Martin Trow (2006) identified three basic stages of higher education development worldwide—elite, mass, and universal access. He argued that most nations, at varying times, will move toward mass or universal participation in postsecondary education, and this is indeed what has happened. While some developing countries still educate fewer than 10 percent of the age group, almost all countries have dramatically increased their participation rates. The "logic" of massification is inevitable, and includes an overall lowering of academic standards, greater social mobility for a growing segment of the population, new patterns of funding higher education, increasingly diversified higher education systems in most countries, and other tendencies (Altbach, 2007, pp. 3–22).

Like many of the trends addressed in this report, massification is not a new phase, but at the "deeper stage" of the ongoing revolution in higher education it must be considered in different ways. Initially, higher education systems struggled just to cope with demand—the need for expanded infrastructure and a larger teaching corps. During the past decade, systems have begun to wrestle with the implications of diversity and to consider which subgroups are still not being included and appropriately served.

A central reality of the 21st century is the emergence of the knowledge economy. The many manifestations of this economy, including the growing centrality of the service sector, new fields like biotechnology, the importance of information and communications technology, and many others enhance the salience of higher education. Growing segments of the workforce require the advanced education offered in postsecondary institutions. Research, much of it carried out in universities, has expanded in scope and relevance. Further, the knowledge economy enhances global mobility of highly trained professionals, and academe plans a central role in mobility.

Demographics will continue as a driving force for development and reform in the coming decades. The patterns and geographical scope will vary, but the basic thrust will remain. In 2008, the Organisation for Economic Co-operation and Development (OECD) identified several key demographic trends for the period to 2030 (OECD, 2008). While these trends were identified on the basis of the OECD-member states (mainly the developed countries), they seem to prevail globally:

- Student participation will continue to expand, as will higher education systems. Only a few countries will see a contraction in student numbers.
- Women will form the majority of student populations in most developed countries and will substantially expand their participation everywhere.
- The mix of the student population will become more varied, with greater numbers of international students, older students, part-time students, and other types.

- The social base in higher education will continue to broaden, along with uncertainty about how this will affect inequalities of educational opportunities between social groups.
- Attitudes and policies relating to access as well as the consciousness among disadvantaged groups will change and become more central to national debates.
- The academic profession will become more internationally oriented and mobile but will still be structured in accordance with national circumstances.
- The activities and roles of the academic profession will be more diversified and specialized and subject to varied employment contracts.
- For many developing countries, the need for ever-expanding numbers of university teachers will mean that overall qualifications, now rather low, may not improve much, and current reliance on part-time staff in many countries may continue (OECD, 2008, pp. 13–14).

While academic systems have been expanding, several other forces have affected higher education worldwide. These trends are all related in a significant way, thus creating a problem of addressing the variables separately. Globalization is not only shaping the world's economy and culture but, without question, is influencing higher education as well. The emergence of a global knowledge system in which communication is instantaneous and research and other information are disseminated globally, the use of English, as the world's main language for scientific communication, and the expansion of information technology are key factors. It may be possible to ameliorate the most negative aspects of globalization, but it is not practical to opt out of the global knowledge system.

Academic mobility is a hallmark of the global age. A truly global market for students and academic staff exists today. At least 2.5 million students study outside of the home country, although reliable statistics are not available for academics teaching abroad.

Information and communications technology composes another global force. The effect on society in general is still unfolding, but without question this aspect of the revolution is one of the more powerful influences on higher education. The impact of technology on science and scholarship, teaching and learning in traditional universities, the possibilities for distance education, and even the internal management of universities has been particularly profound. Without doubt, deep inequalities persist with regard to information and communications technology access, use, and influence.

Dramatic change has occurred in funding higher education and in deliberating how to support mass higher education. In most countries, with the notable exceptions of some East Asian nations, higher education has long been considered a responsibility of the state and thought of as a "public good." University study would benefit the individual, of course, but also society through greater productivity, contributing to national goals, and other factors. The financial pressures resulting from massification, combined with the neoliberal orientation of international funding agencies during the last decade, have tempered the notion of higher education as strictly a public good. The benefits of tertiary education have been emphasized as a "private good," with implications for the allocation of the responsibility for costs. It is becoming obvious that the state alone can no longer afford to educate the growing numbers of students in a mass higher education system and that (given the benefit of education to an individual over a lifetime) students and families need to assume a share of the financial burden. These factors have contributed to both the dramatic rise of private higher education worldwide and to the privatization of public universities.

Although higher education is increasingly affected by global trends, institutions with few exceptions still function within national boundaries. Higher education remains an essentially national phenomenon. Universities function within nations and for the most part serve local, regional, and national interests.

The Global Socioeconomic Environment

We live today in the midst of a profound economic crisis that will have repercussions in society at large and within higher education in ways that are not yet obvious. Many countries and universities will experience financial problems with serious consequences in the short and perhaps the medium term. The crisis is likely to have the following implications:

- Research universities are likely to see significant constraints on their budgets as governments will be unable to provide the resources needed for their continued improvement. In many cases, the priority will be to allocate funds to ensure that access to the higher education system is not dramatically cut.
- In countries where student loan programs exist, either in the public or private sectors, severe constraints on their availability to students may be implemented along with increased interest rates.
- The system will face pressure to establish or increase tuition fees for students.
- Cost-cutting practices at many universities will result in a deterio-

ration of quality. More part-time faculty are likely to be hired, class
sizes expanded, and additional actions.

- "Freezes" on hiring, construction of new facilities, improving
  information technology, and purchasing books and journals are
  likely developments.
- It is possible that the numbers of internationally mobile students
  may temporarily decline as families in such major sending countries as China and India are unable to afford overseas tuition fees
  and other expenses.

How deep the crisis will become or how long it will last is unknown.
However, most experts are doubtful of a quick recovery. Thus, it is likely
that higher education is entering a period of significant cutbacks. There
is no doubt that higher education is entering a period of crisis unprecedented since World War II, and the full impact is as yet uncertain.
At the same time, economic stimulus efforts in some countries have
included funds for research, retraining workers, and other projects that
may assist higher education.

The Revolution of Massification
The expansion of higher education has been the core reality of the sector
in the last half of the 20th century and in the current era. Responding to
mass demand has led to or caused many of the key transformations of
the past several decades. Why has higher education expanded so rapidly
in the past half century? The answers are multifold and related to social,
economic, and political change worldwide. Public demand for access
is perhaps the most powerful force. Higher education has come to be
seen as a necessity for social mobility and economic success in many
countries.

The post–World War II period, has witnessed profound economic
changes across the globe. Many countries have shifted to postindustrial
economies that require more highly educated personnel for many jobs.
Even more traditional economies need a larger number of more highly
educated workers, given changes in technology. The most highly remu-
nerative and prestigious occupations invariably require postsecondary
education qualifications. In the developed countries, the rise of service
industries and the knowledge economy, coupled with social change,
contributed significantly to the demand for access to higher education.

There has been a general expansion of populations worldwide during
much of this period. The "baby boom" in North America and Europe in
the immediate postwar period contributed to greater demand for higher
education. More recently, population growth has characterized the developing world, as well. Additionally, in most of the world, a demographic

shift has taken place from rural areas to the cities. Urban populations tend to have more education and be more focused on highly skilled jobs.

Important social change has also taken place in much of the world. The era of colonialism came to an end, and in the newly independent nations of Africa and Asia populations were empowered to demand political and social development. These new expectations involved access to education at all levels including higher education, which, however, had been limited to a tiny proportion of the age cohort (usually one percent or less).

Meanwhile, women began to assert their right to pursue higher education and were important beneficiaries of massification, first in the developed countries and later elsewhere. In most countries, women had been dramatically underrepresented in the student population. By the 1980s in much of the world women had achieved parity with men and in some countries outnumbered men.

The United States was the first country to achieve mass higher education. By 1960, 40 percent of the age cohort attended postsecondary education. Massification was achieved in Canada shortly after. In western Europe and Japan rapid growth took place in the 1980s, followed by that trend in the developed countries of East Asia (such as the Republic of Korea, among others) soon thereafter. Latin America experienced dramatic growth during this period, as well. Over the past decade, most of the remaining countries in the developing world have experienced similar expansion. China and India, currently the world's largest and third-largest academic systems, respectively, have been growing rapidly and will continue to do so. Indeed, perhaps half of the world's added enrollments will found be in China and India (Altbach, 2009).

Mass higher education has fundamentally transformed the higher education system worldwide. Differentiated academic systems have emerged, with various institutions serving quite different purposes and roles within each country. Historically, only the traditional, research-oriented university, plus a range of nonuniversity postsecondary institutions, existed in most countries. In the past half century, many different kinds of degree-granting institutions have been established to serve diverse populations and purposes. Some countries have borrowed from the experience of the American public university system (Kerr, 2001). Others have pioneered distinctive approaches to differentiation. Most countries now have a small number of research-intensive universities at the pinnacle of the academic system and a much larger number of less-selective universities with more emphasis on teaching than research. A large variety of postsecondary, nonuniversity institutions now serve a mass clientele often emphasizing technical education.

Most countries have also seen the rise of a private higher education sector that is absorbing some of the new demand. Indeed, private institutions enroll a majority of students in a growing number of countries. The challenge of ensuring that the private higher education sector, both nonprofit and the newer for-profit institutions, serves the national interest is significant.

Much of this report is concerned with the ways in which higher education has responded to the challenge of massification (its implications for funding, privatization, access, teaching and learning, etc.) in the past several decades. Without question, the coming period will be dominated by the implications of mass access.

Globalization and Internationalization
Globalization, a key reality in the 21st century, has already profoundly affected higher education. In this report, we are concerned with how it affects universities. We define globalization as the reality shaped by an increasingly integrated world economy, new information and communications technology, the emergence of an international knowledge network, the role of the English language, and other forces beyond the control of academic institutions (Altbach, 2007, pp. 23–48). Internationalization is defined as the variety of policies and programs that universities and governments implement to respond to globalization.

Universities have always been affected by international trends and to a certain degree operated within a broader international community of academic institutions, scholars, and research. But 21st-century realities have magnified the importance of the global context. The rise of English as the lingua franca of scientific communication is unprecedented since the period when Latin dominated the academy in medieval Europe. Information and communications technologies have created a universal means of instantaneous contact and simplified scientific communication. At the same time, these changes have helped to concentrate ownership of publishers, databases, and other key resources in the hands of the strongest universities and some multinational companies, located almost exclusively in the developed world.

It is not possible for higher education to opt out of the global environment since its effects are unavoidable. The local realities of wealth, language, academic development, and other factors all affect the extent to which institutions are motivated and able to internationalize.

One of the most visible aspects of globalization is student mobility. More than 2.5 million students are studying outside of their home countries. Estimates predict 8 million international students by 2020. The flow of international students has reflected national and institutional strategies but also the decisions of individual students worldwide. International students have become "big business," bringing revenues to host universities through tuition payments and other expenditures. These students also add international diversity to an academic environment.

The mobility of international students involves two main trends. One consists of students from Asia entering the major academic systems of North America, Western Europe, Australia, and Japan. The other trend, within the European Union, involves its various programs to encourage student mobility. Globally, international student mobility largely reflects a South-North phenomenon. Additional flows take place from Africa and Latin America to Europe and North America. Currently, English-speaking countries serve as the primary host countries for international students. While during the first stage of the "revolution" the quantitative aspects of student mobility were given more attention, the deeper qualitative implications are now being reviewed. Half or more of international students study for postgraduate degrees and in many cases do not return to their home countries after completing their studies, depriving their home country of these highly trained individuals.

Less information exists about mobility of academic staff, although the academic labor market has increasingly globalized, with many thousands of scholars crossing borders for appointments at all levels. Again, the largest flow is South-North, with North America especially benefiting from an influx of academics from many countries, including a large number from Europe who are seeking higher salaries. The pattern of "brain drain" from the developing world has changed to some extent. Academics who leave their home countries now maintain more contact with their countries of origin and, from abroad, work collaboratively with home country colleagues. Nonetheless, a number of developing countries are still losing many of their best scholars and scientists.

Student and scholar mobility has become a major factor in higher education worldwide. Students seek access to fields that may be lacking in the home system, as well as high-quality degree programs, especially at the postgraduate level. Some countries, most notably Australia and the United Kingdom, see international students as a source of income for the academic system. Many developed countries, hoping that international graduates will *not* return home, increasingly work to adjust immigration laws and offer incentives so that they will remain after degree completion. This concentration of talent in the developed world contributes to international academic inequality.

Universities and academic systems have developed many strategies to benefit from the new global environment and to attract nonresident students. Some universities in non-English-speaking countries have established degree programs in English to attract students from other countries. Universities create partnerships with academic institutions in other countries to offer degree and other academic programs, develop research projects, and collaborate in a variety of ways. Branch campuses, off-shore academic programs, and franchising arrangements for academic degrees represent only a few manifestations of such internationalization strategies (Altbach and Knight, 2007).

The establishment of university branch campuses (usually from a developed country) in another "host" country is a growing phenomenon. Twinning programs, in which universities in two (or more) countries offer joint or dual degrees, is another phenemenon. Most of these programs are taught in English, particularly in such high-demand fields as management studies or information technology. In the Arabian Gulf area a number of foreign universities have been invited by local governments to establish branch campuses. The hosting countries pay most of the costs associated with these arrangements. China only allows foreign institutions to operate within its borders if it has a local partner.

Institutions establishing branches or joint programs are often motivated by a desire for additional revenue, although they are also engaged in raising their international profile and contributing to the internationalization of their home campuses as well. The motivations of the receiving countries are perhaps more complex and include a need for greater capacity at home and a desire to leverage the prestige and resources of a high-quality foreign institution.

A Context of Inequality

The developments discussed in this report also reflect growing inequalities in higher education worldwide, resulting from persistent economic (and other) disparities. This report does not condone such inequalities. It is hoped that a careful analysis of trends and issues will lead to a fuller understanding and contribute to the amelioration of these gaps. Yet, as inequality is part of the global higher education landscape, it must be recognized and examined.

Inequality among national higher education systems as well as within countries has increased in the past several decades. Inequality is seldom the result of foreign policy priorities, foreign assistance programs, or government action. Rather, contemporary inequality is steeped in the wide range of realities facing academic institutions and systems worldwide.

The academic world has always been characterized by *centers* and *peripheries*. Some countries have attained stronger universities than others for a variety of reasons—because of their wealth, long academic traditions, size, language, and other factors. The strongest universities, in developed countries, with research prowess and reputation for excellence, are seen as centers. Institutions dependent on the centers for knowledge and leadership are seen as peripheral.

Tension has grown around the center/periphery dynamic. Developing countries often desire world-class universities on par with the traditional universities at the center. Many people argue that too much emphasis is placed on national and global status and developing countries should be more concerned with serving specific local, national, and regional needs. Yet, the prestige of the centers is strong and unlikely to change in the 21st century; academic inequality will continue to manifest itself in a variety of ways as a result.

What makes an academic system or institution recognized as a center? It is typically a large, research-intensive university. History is significant. Almost all of the world's universities are based on the European or North American academic model, and it is not surprising that European and North American universities have certain advantages and influence (Ben-David and Zloczower, 1962). Academic institutions in non-Western societies confront the challenge of adapting this model to different cultural contexts. Some countries—such as Japan, China, and the Republic of Korea—have been quite successful in blending national and international models.

Universities deemed to be academic centers tend to be large universities with many academic fields, professional schools, numerous academic staff, and a sizable and carefully selected student population (Altbach and Balán, 2007). Large economies and extensive academic systems with many big and diverse universities hold an advantage, particularly because they can support so many talented academics. Some highly ranked universities are indeed located in small countries, such as Switzerland and Denmark, but these are exceptional cases.

Research universities tend to benefit from differentiated academic systems (comprised of different academic institutions with various missions and levels of funding). Even Germany, a once highly homogeneous and democratic academic system, has recognized the need to designate a small number of its universities as central research-focused institutions, moving away from its traditional view that all universities were the same and should be equally funded.

As already noted, all of the world's top-ranked universities are research-intensive institutions, and the academic systems seen as centers are those with strength in research. A university considered to be *world class* is less likely to stress teaching, public service, providing access to underserved populations, or other important social services.

Language plays a role in the center/periphery relationship. Universities that use one of the primary international languages, most often English, dominate the academic community. English-speaking institutions and academic systems tend to produce the largest amount of research and influence the knowledge-communications system. The Internet in many ways has strengthened the major world languages in higher education. In the past half century, the key scientific and academic journals have come to be published in English. Large multinational publishers tend to print most of their books in English, as well. Other world languages, such as Spanish and French, have also benefited, at the expense of less international local languages. Courses and other academic programs are now often offered in English in non-English-speaking environments. Without question, English is at the center, and other languages are moving increasingly to the periphery.

The wealth of nations and universities plays a key role in determining the quality and centrality of a university or academic system. While other factors are meaningful, without abundant resources neither universities nor academic systems can become global centers. This fact, of course, places developing countries at a significant disadvantage and puts special strains on academic systems facing the dilemma of expanded enrollment and the need to support top-quality research universities.

Rankings

A new force in national, regional, and global higher education is created by the many rankings of academic institutions and degree programs. These rankings are criticized but, nonetheless, taken seriously by the public, universities, and at times governments. The classifications are used by individuals to compare places to study and increasingly by governments to make funding decisions. Experts point out common methodological flaws, noting that most ratings rely on highly unreliable reputation surveys, measure only a few variables such as research productivity, analyze internationally noted publications in databases such as the Science Citation Index, which mainly includes only a small number of journals, and others. Rankings compare countries, individual universities, and fields of study, such as management and business administration. In each of these areas, criticism of the rankings is widespread.

International rankings favor universities that use English as the main language of instruction and research, are older, possess a large array of disciplines and programs (e.g., medical faculties), and receive substantial research funds from government or other sources (Sadlak and Liu, 2007). The two primary international rankings—the Academic

Ranking of World Universities of the Shanghai Jiao Tong University
and QS/*Times Higher Education* ranking—practice somewhat different
methodologies, but both emphasize research productivity and quality.
Additional rankings exist in most countries, and efforts are now under-
way to produce European academic rankings. While all of the existing
rankings contain methodological problems, they are nonetheless widely
used, influential, and show no signs of disappearing.

The Tension Between the Public and Private Good
The last several decades have seen a lively debate between different
perspectives on the role of higher education in modern society (Task
Force on Higher Education and Society, 2000). Higher education has
traditionally been seen as a public good—of value to society as well as
to individual students—and thus largely a responsibility of society (the
state) to support and fund. This concept functioned where higher education was mainly public, the academic enterprise was fairly small and
thus not too expensive, and when academe served a small and relatively
elite segment of the population.

   The idea of higher education as a private good—of benefit primarily
to individual graduates and thus to be paid for mainly by the "users"
(students)—is a result of several converging ideas and realities. Neoliberal ideas, which increasingly shaped the policy of international
funding agencies during the last few decades, argue for limited government involvement in all aspects of society and favor leaving services to
markets and private providers. This has affected models for providing
higher education, health care, and other services. Neoliberal thinking
was driven in part by the exploding cost of higher education due to massification but was also predicated on the primacy of the private sector,
regardless of fiscal constraints. Governments no longer had adequate
funds to support a mass higher education system, and in many cases
lacked the inclination to provide public funding and looked for ways to
supplement or even replace state allocations. The growing perception of
higher education as a private good justified charging significant tuition
fees since the student is seen as the primary beneficiary.

   In much of the world, the private-good philosophy, combined with
funding shortages due to massification and the global economic crisis,
has meant that higher education systems and institutions are increasingly responsible for generating higher percentages of their own
revenues. There is no doubt that this trend will continue into the future.
The increased salience of the private-good argument and continuing
shortages of public funds for higher education tend to benefit some
institutions and populations over others. For example, providing access

for disadvantaged groups at one end of the higher education system and building and sustaining world-class research universities at the other reflect public-good endeavors and may be more difficult to achieve in the current climate when universities focus more attention on generating revenue. Similarly, the public-service mission of higher education is put in jeopardy by the tilt toward a private-good orientation.

The broader societal role and the service function of the university are called into question when the private-good argument dominates. More emphasis on cost recovery, higher tuition, and university-industry links distracts from the traditional social role of higher education. Over the centuries, universities have become centers not only of teaching and research but also of intellectual and cultural life. Their libraries are key repositories of a society's intellectual traditions. Some universities sponsor publishing houses and journals. Many universities house theater groups, noncommercial radio and television stations, and in general serve as cultural beacons for society. Universities serve as key intellectual centers, providing a forum for social, cultural, and often political issues. These functions have historically accompanied traditional academic responsibilities and are especially important in environments where there is a dearth of social institutions to provide these forums. This is particularly important in countries with weak societal infrastructures or traditions and few institutions fostering free debate and dialogue.

The Private Revolution and Privatization
The growth of private higher education worldwide has been one of the most remarkable developments of the past several decades. Private higher education has existed in many countries and has traditionally been the dominant force in such East Asia countries as Japan, the Republic of Korea, and the Philippines. While the private sector represents a small part of higher education in most countries, private institutions, many of them for-profit or quasi for-profit, now represent the fastest-growing sector worldwide. The private sector now educates more than half the student population in such countries as Mexico, Brazil, and Chile. Private universities are rapidly expanding in central and eastern Europe and in the countries of the former Soviet Union, as well as in Africa. China and India have significant private sectors as well (Altbach, 2005).

Private higher education has expanded with very little strategic planning in most of the world. Initially, the private sector was often viewed as tangential to higher education, but this conception has changed as private institutions now enroll more students and place more graduates in the labor market. They are no longer separate from the dominant higher education system and are increasingly mainstream. Private institutions are often the source of innovation in the use of technology for instruction. In some countries they have access to public funds.

In general, the private sector is "demand absorbing"—offering access to students who might not be qualified for the public institutions or who cannot be accommodated in other universities because of over-crowding. While some selective private universities exist, in general the private sector serves a mass clientele and is not seen as prestigious.

A related trend is the privatization of the public universities. In most countries, the proportion of state subsidy for public universities has declined. In much of the world, the state provides half or less of the income for public universities. In some American public universities, state funds account for under 20 percent of the total budget, compelling universities to earn additional funds from other sources. Student tuition fees provide the largest source of revenue. Other income sources include research funds, income from the sale of university-related products, consulting and research services, and university-industry linkages. In some cases, such financial sources create conflicts with the traditional roles of the university and contribute significantly to the commercialization of the institution.

A Global, National, and Internal Competitive Environment

In the early 21st century, higher education has become a more competitive enterprise. In many countries, students must compete for scarce places in universities, and in all countries admission to the top institutions has become more difficult to achieve. Academics compete for jobs and work harder to keep their employment in an environment of higher expectations and increased accountability.

There is a growing need for integration with the private sector. Research products, particularly in the natural and biomedical sciences, are more closely linked to the marketplace, and universities compete for private funding. Research is often tied to corporate interests, with the goal of earning profits for the university and the private partner (Fallis, 2007; Washburn, 2005). Universities, as noted earlier, compete for status and ranking and generally for funding from government or private sources.

Globally, countries contend for academic status, international students, and top scientists and scholars. Rankings and league tables have taken on more weight in national higher education policy formulation. Within countries, rankings contribute to a national hierarchy. In some countries a contest exists between the public and private sector.

Competition within an institution is a growing trend. The pressures of accountability and the desire of university leadership for excellence have in many cases pitted one department or faculty against another as they position themselves to acquire limited resources and academic staff.

Competition has always been a force in academe, and in may ways it can help produce excellence and the best performance. But it can also undermine the sense of an academic community, a mission, and traditional values.

The Research University and the Research Environment
Research universities are at the pinnacle of the academic system and enjoy the highest prestige. Their stature is reflected in the world rankings. Research universities produce knowledge, offer advanced academic degrees, and employ the highest-qualified professors (Salmi, 2009). They represent the universities most directly involved in the global knowledge network. Research universities require major expenditures to establish and are expensive to sustain; they must obtain consistent funding over long periods of time. Their facilities—including laboratories, libraries, and information and communications technology infrastructures—should be maintained at the highest international standards.

Research universities typically educate the elites of their societies and provide advanced education for the academic profession and other fields, such as medicine and law. Research universities are, therefore, conceived as special institutions separate from the rest of a mass higher education system. Their goals and missions, international as well as national in character, are linked to both the local academic community and the international knowledge network. While research and teaching form central responsibilities in the university, the research function inevitably serves as the primary role of the top research universities. These key institutions, the only universities in any countries that might be called "world class," require appropriate autonomy, academic freedom, and sustained financial support from national authorities, while they are at the same time part of national higher education systems. While research universities require a special status in national systems, they are also the link to the global knowledge network.

Research universities meet the needs not only of developed countries but also of developing and middle-income nations—for internationally focused institutions that participate in the global knowledge network. Funding for research is more available in developed (compared to developing) countries but is a constant challenge everywhere. Funding has become increasingly competitive. Researchers are often obliged to compete for awards, and not all projects are selected. Support for basic research has become especially difficult to obtain because the cost is high and it is less likely to be supported by industry; state funding is not always available.

Private industry has become more active in supporting applied university-based research although it imposes conditions on the work. Privately sponsored research is generally applied and aimed at producing knowledge relevant to the needs of the funder (Washburn, 2005). University-industry linkages sometimes create tensions between the partners but are often the only way to enable certain kinds of research to be supported.

Ongoing tensions exist between basic and applied research in this complex contemporary research environment. Basic research is in many ways at the heart of the research university and is essential for the advancement of science and scholarship. It is also the foundation for new knowledge and at the heart of doctoral training programs.

Intellectual property is a growing challenge in higher education today and especially in research universities. The fundamental questions of who owns knowledge and who benefits from research are central to this discussion. Universities, seeking to maximize revenues, want to protect intellectual property—research output that leads to patents, licenses, and income—and work produced for the Internet or for publishers. The topic is contentious because it often brings into focus the potential conflicts between the producers of research and knowledge and sponsors who may wish to control the knowledge and its benefits.

The Internet has increased attention on intellectual property issues. Distance education courses, particularly, are a source of income for universities and professors. The question of who "owns" these courses and who may benefit financially from them is a topic of considerable controversy. Similarly, income from knowledge distributed electronically raises issues as well.

The contested ownership of intellectual property reflects the public-good/private-good debate. Many people argue that university-produced knowledge should be available without restriction. Most policymakers, however, believe that the results of research can (and should) provide important income for universities. These issues are hotly debated in academic and policy circles. University-industry linkages have created additional tensions in regard to intellectual property since these agreements—especially in emerging fields like biotechnology—often create problems relating to patents and licenses.

Intellectual property has emerged as an extremely important yet complicated issue. Sophisticated, university-based research is being conducted in an environment filled with pressure to commercialize knowledge. However, at the same time opposing pressure exists to treat knowledge production and dissemination as a public good.

Research universities are the most visible and the most expensive institutions in the academic system. As "flagships," they bring prestige and international visibility to their host country. These universities create and disseminate knowledge and serve industry and commerce.

Students and the Curriculum

Universities ultimately serve students, as institutions primarily devoted to teaching and learning. The role of the university has itself become more complex, and in some cases teaching and learning have moved from the center of academic life toward the margin. Prior to the creation of the German research university in the early 19th century, universities were mainly seen as teaching institutions (Ben-David and Zloczower, 1962). Students constitute a much more diverse population today. In the era of massification, students from a spectrum of socioeconomic backgrounds with a range of intellectual abilities now participate in higher education, complicating the tasks of teaching and curriculum development.

During the past several decades greater societal demands for accountability have prevailed. This has obliged universities to demonstrate that learning is taking place. A greater emphasis is placed on measuring learning outcomes; it is no longer sufficient to measure the "inputs"—what is being taught and how the curriculum is delivered to the students.

Assessing student learning has become one of several important elements of providing greater accountability to an increasingly demanding public worldwide. The National Survey of Student Engagement in the United States is one aspect of the effort to measure the impact of higher education on students. The Organization for Economic Cooperation and Development now seeks to develop ways of measuring what is learned in specific academic disciplines. The assessment of learning is a difficult task, and measuring learning cross-culturally is even more complicated.

The curriculum has also been affected by the dramatic changes in higher education. A more diverse student population with varied interests and goals has raised pressure to differentiate the curriculum and at least to offer qualifications in a wider array of fields and disciplines.

The curriculum has always to some extent been international in character. The most powerful academic systems, such as those of Germany and France in the 19th century and the United States at present, have traditionally pioneered academic thinking and curricular trends (including producing widely used textbooks). The Internet has exerted a strong internationalizing effect in the past several decades. In newer programs, like management studies, the curriculum worldwide has come to be largely American, since the fields were developed in the United States.

In the second half of the 20th century, the rise of English as the main language of scientific communication and the growing number of degree programs offered in English in non-English-speaking countries have also led to curriculum internationalization. While this trend has taken place at all levels of higher education, it is probably the case that postgraduate degrees and certificates are most affected. Not surprisingly, the ideas and practices of the major academic powers, especially those in the English-speaking sphere, tend to be most influential.

The Contradictions of Isomorphism
The need for differentiated academic systems with diverse institutional missions is universally accepted as a response to massification. Yet, the pressure for academic institutions to copy one another—the tendency toward isomorphism— and to rise in the academic hierarchy is very strong (D. C. Levy, 2006). While this trend has a long history, it has intensified in the era of rankings and global competition. It is an artifact of the continuing prestige of the research university, as well as of the expansion in the numbers of universities worldwide. Sixty years ago, sociologist David Riesman criticized the "academic procession" led by the research universities, in which other kinds of universities and colleges sought to emulate these institutions in the United States, at the time the most diversified system in the world (Riesman, 1958).

In the 21st century, the trend toward isomorphism can still be observed and tends to restrict the development of differentiated academic systems. Public authorities need to ensure diverse academic models to serve varied societal needs, while many academic institutions still tend to emulate the research universities at the top of the system. Academic staff often press the university to emphasize research as its key mission, knowing that a research orientation and productivity in this area promise the highest prestige and (often) the best salaries for academics.

If the universities remain the sole decision makers, many more academic institutions would seek to improve their status by becoming research intensive. In most cases, this strategy does not serve the interests of academe in general nor is it widely achievable. Often, it takes governmental "steering" to keep the academic system diversified and institutions within the system serving larger national goals.

In the United States, the well-known California master plan ensures that public higher education meets that state's broader interests by legislating the roles and priorities of the universities and colleges (Douglass, 2004).

The essential problem of isomorphism involves unbridled competition among academic institutions pursuing the same goals. This trend may undermine efforts to develop a system of institutions that is appropriately differentiated, based on the specific needs of a given system—with different goals and responsibilities, patterns of funding, admissions policies, and other characteristics.

The Academic Profession

The professoriate is at the center of the university. Without an effective, well-educated and committed academic profession, universities cannot succeed. Yet, the academic profession is under stress as never before (Altbach, 2003). Responding to the demands of massification with the fast deployment of greater numbers of teachers has resulted in a decline of the average qualification for academics in many countries. Many university teachers in developing countries have only a bachelor's degree. The numbers of part-time academics have increased in many countries, as well. The predominance of part-timers continues in Latin America, where only a small minority of professors has full-time appointments, much to the detriment of higher education in the region.

Many academics are now appointed to full-time "contract" positions that do not offer the promise of a career at their university. In the United States, only half of the new appointments are traditional tenure-track academic positions. Academics are subject to more bureaucratic controls, and their autonomy has decreased. Increased demands for accountability have also meant a great deal of stress for academics in many countries.

Academic salaries rarely compare favorably with compensation for similarly educated professions outside of universities. For many countries, especially in the developing world, salaries barely support a middle-class lifestyle, and in some countries, not at all. The variations in salary among countries are quite significant, contributing to a brain migration to countries that pay more. As an example of the range, average academic salaries in Canada are more than six times higher than in China (Rumbley, Pacheco, and Altbach, 2008).

The global mobility of the professoriate is growing and becoming yet another important trend. Made easier by the growth of English as the international academic language, the Internet, and the relative ease of air transportation, large numbers of academics work outside of their own countries. The many impulses include better salaries and working conditions, academic freedom, stability in academic careers, the lack of high-quality universities at home, a poor domestic academic job market, and other factors. Some countries—including Singapore, the Arabian Gulf nations, some western European countries, Canada, and the United States—have policies in place to lure scholars and researchers from abroad. Not surprisingly, flows tend to be from the developing countries toward more advanced economies.

Information and Communications Technology

It is obvious that academe is influenced (some would argue *transformed*) by the information and communications technology revolution. It has been said that the traditional university will be rendered obsolete by information technology, distance education, and other technology-induced innovation. The demise of the traditional university will, in our view, not take place any time soon. But major change is under way, and it is one of the key parts of the academic transformation of the 21st century.

A few caveats are in order. For more than a decade, many people have argued that Internet-based distance higher education would become a central part of the delivery of knowledge and degree programs. While distance education has become significant, it has moved ahead more slowly than anticipated. Many students, and faculty as well, have been slow to accept it. Providers, nonprofit and for-profit, have had problems developing a successful economic model for distance education, although distance-education-based public universities, such as the Indira Gandhi National Open University in India, have achieved considerable success. Somehow, the distance education revolution always seems to be just around the corner, while it is growing in strength.

In some fields, such as management studies and information technology itself, distance education has become a significant player. The open educational resources movement, ostensibly launched by the Massachusetts Institute of Technology's highly regarded "open courseware" initiative (which has placed many of the materials from its own academic courses on the Internet without charge), is also a significant development.

The Internet has truly transformed how knowledge is communicated. E-mail has become an ubiquitous form of academic communication. Electronic journals have become widespread and in some fields quite prestigious. Traditional publishers of books and journals have turned to the Internet to distribute their publications. Such trends have exacerbated the division between "haves" and "have-nots." Some parts of the world, particularly Africa, remain relatively underserved by high-speed Internet access. The Republic of Korea and Singapore are at the forefront of countries providing access to high-speed Internet service. The traditional "knowledge powers," especially those that use English, have largely maintained their influence.

Conclusion

The goal in this trend report is to examine a sense of the central issues, as well as the contextual factors that have shaped higher education in the past decade, and to present prospects for the immediate future. This introduction has provided the context and overview for these issues. Although many of these trends are not new, the implications of these developments must now be confronted. The remainder of this report discusses these issues in more detail.

The role of higher education as a public good continues to be a fundamental goal and must be supported. This position is emphasized throughout the trend report, given that this aspect of higher education is easily neglected in the rush for income and prestige.

The multiple and diverse responsibilities of higher education are ultimately key to the well-being of modern society, but this expanded function adds considerable complexity and many new challenges. Understanding these factors and the broader role of higher education in a globalized world is the first step to dealing constructively with the challenges that will inevitably loom on the horizon.

2

Globalization and Internationalization

The historically international nature of universities is playing out in new and dynamic ways, while the trend is extending broadly and rapidly across the higher education sector. Pushed and pulled along by the forces of globalization, internationalization presents many exciting opportunities to higher education institutions and systems. At the same time, real risks and challenges are inherent in this complex and fluid environment. At stake are issues of competitiveness and relevance, requiring new kinds of strategic thinking, and acting with regard to the international dimension by all types of higher education actors.

Concepts and Definitions

Although closely related and frequently used interchangeably, the terms *globalization* and *internationalization* in higher education refer to two distinct phenomena. Globalization typically makes reference to "the broad economic, technological, and scientific trends that directly affect higher education and are largely inevitable in the contemporary world." Internationalization, on the other hand, has more to do with the "specific policies and programs undertaken by governments, academic systems and institutions, and even individual departments to deal with globalization" (Altbach, 2006, p. 123).

A give and take between globalization and internationalization has been evident to many higher education observers, but one of the key distinctions between the two concepts is the notion of *control*. Globalization and its effects are beyond the control of any one actor or set of actors. Internationalization, however, can be seen as a strategy for societies and institutions to respond to the many demands placed upon them by globalization and as a way for higher education to prepare individuals for engagement in a globalized world. Indeed, internationalization has been conceived in many quarters as a necessary "process of integrating an international, intercultural, or global dimension in the purpose, functions, or delivery of postsecondary education" (Knight, 2003, p. 2). This process consists largely of two main spheres of action, commonly characterized as "internationalization at home" and "internationalization abroad" (Knight, 2004a).

Internationalization at home typically consists of strategies and approaches designed to inject an international dimension into the home campus experience—for example, by including global and comparative perspectives in the curriculum or recruiting international students, scholars, and faculty and leveraging their presence on campus. Internationalization abroad, on the other hand, calls for an institution to project itself and its stakeholders out in the world. Key examples include sending students to study abroad, setting up a branch campus overseas, or engaging in an interinstitutional partnership.

Beyond the umbrella concepts of internationalization and globalization, a variety of other terms are used—such as, the international dimension, international education, international programming, international and/or interinstitutional cooperation, international partnerships, cross-border education, borderless education, and regionalization. The varied terminology refers to the breadth of experiences in this area and to the distinctive approaches to internationalization taken by different higher education systems and institutions around the world.

Key Manifestations of Globalization and Internationalization
The internationalization of higher education is notable for the multiple ways in which it has manifested itself around the world. Although each local, national, and regional context presents unique characteristics, several broad trends can be identified globally. These developments include mobility of people, programs, and institutions; the rising prominence of collaborative research; evolving curricula as well as approaches to teaching and learning; an increasingly heightened sense of the interconnectedness of the higher education enterprise across the globe; and the growing pervasiveness of the phenomenon of internationalization across institutions and broader systems of higher education.

The mobility of students and scholars has characterized the university since its earliest days in medieval Europe. In the last decade, however, the numbers of students studying outside their home countries have increased exponentially. Although data are difficult to obtain and verify, UNESCO estimates that in 2007 there were more than 2.8 million internationally mobile students, an increase of some 53 percent over the estimated figure of 1.8 million in 2000. By 2025, research undertaken for IDP Pty Ltd in Australia suggests that roughly 7.2 million students may be pursuing some higher education internationally, an increase of 188 percent over the 2006 UNESCO estimate (Böhm, et al., 2002). In some parts of the world, international student mobility has become a central issue in higher education. For example, a recent study on the impact of the ERASMUS student-mobility program, launched in 1987, indicates that the initiative "has had a leading role in internationalisation policies in higher education at national, European and international level[s]" (European Commission, 2008a, p. 4), and affected a wide range of other policies and practices in European higher education.

No less important but harder to track and comprehend are the mobility trends of academics—researchers, scholars, and teaching staff—who spend some period of time working outside of their home countries. The burgeoning number of international agreements between tertiary institutions often includes long- and short-term faculty exchange components. International scholarship and fellowship programs, along with other collaborative projects, move countless numbers of scholars around the globe each year to conduct research abroad, while professional and scholarly meetings and conferences keep many academics on the move abroad. In some cases, academic superstars have been actively recruited from one country to another in an attempt to shore up prestige and academic output in the receiving institutions, while severe human-resource crises have resulted from the large-scale flight of academics (commonly known as "brain drain") from poorer and less-stable countries (notably in sub-Saharan Africa) to more welcoming and resource-rich environments in the North.

International mobility has not been limited to people; the last decade has seen a veritable explosion in numbers of programs and institutions that are operating internationally. It is extremely difficult to gauge the exact number of overseas operations, given the many different manifestations of cross-border provision. These include fully fledged "sister" institutions of existing universities (such as New York University in Abu Dhabi), branch campuses of parent institutions (a common model for many of the foreign players setting up shop in the regional hubs in such places as Dubai, Qatar, and Singapore), and collaborative arrangements (such as the one between the University of Nottingham and Zhejiang Wanli Education Group-University, which allows for the operation of the University of Nottingham Ningbo, China). Also prevalent are single programs or narrow fields of study being offered overseas by one institution or jointly by two or more. This area of activity has also seen significant growth in numbers of new kinds of providers, notably for-profit companies and those operating actively in the online environment. There is also a notable degree of fluidity and uncertainty in this area. A sense of opportunity and also of urgency has been felt by many institutions keen to engage internationally, but the fact that cross-border arrangements come and go with some frequency speaks to the many complexities and challenges inherent in moving programs and other institutional activities abroad. It is also critical to acknowledge that the international flow of educational programming is highly unequal, moving largely in a North-South direction. However, there are exceptions to this rule, including the presence of Pakistani and Indian institutions in Dubai's "Knowledge Village," for example.

The effects of internationalization on higher education can also be seen in the way that the core activities of universities, specifically teaching and research, have been shifting in recent years. The demands of the global knowledge society have placed pressure on higher education to focus more heavily on particular kinds of activities, approaches, and outcomes. Research production in key areas—such as information technology and the life sciences—has risen on national development agendas and for the prestige of individual institutions and has, therefore, become a very high priority for many universities around the world. Much of the world's best research can only be carried out through international collaborative efforts, given the size and complexity of the issues and/or the cost of materials and the investments of time and personnel needed to carry studies through to completion.

Meanwhile, global business trends have put a premium on producing young professionals with particular kinds of credentials and skills. The best example of this may be the American-style MBA (master of business administration) degree, which is now offered in countless countries around the world. At the same time, an arguably global interest in developing students who are skilled communicators, effective critical thinkers, dynamic problem solvers, and productive team members in diverse (increasingly international and intercultural) environments is changing the way that teachers teach and students learn in many contexts, as well as the specific content to which students are exposed. Recent debates on the role of humanities and the liberal arts in East Asia, for example, provide a good example of shifting or expanding curricular considerations in light of globalization and internationalization (Rumbley, 2008).

The last 10 years have clearly witnessed a profound and deepening sense of interconnectedness within the higher education enterprise across the globe. Universities, the knowledge they produce, the academics they employ, and the students they graduate are directly and intimately connected to the global knowledge economy. What happens in institutions and systems in one part of the world has effects far beyond the immediate environment. The international ranking exercises that have taken on such prominence in the last decade are a prime example of how universities no longer operate in a vacuum or even simply in a local or national context but instead sit to a great degree on a world stage.

Ultimately, one of the most critically important characteristics of internationalization to emerge over the last decade is its pervasiveness. The phenomenon is apparent at all levels of the higher education enterprise around the world, affecting individual institutions, regions within countries, and national systems of higher education.

At the institutional level, internationalization can be perceived in the way that large numbers of universities have adopted expanded missions, in many cases embracing service to a community that extends beyond local and national boundaries and aiming to produce "global citizens" with "global competencies." The establishment of international program and support offices and the designation of staff time for these kinds of activities has also become extremely commonplace in tertiary institutions across the globe.

In some countries, internationalization seems quite prominent at a regional level. In Spain, for example, universities in the various autonomous communities—such as Catalunya and Andalucía, to cite just two cases—have banded together to promote their respective regions as destinations for internationally mobile students. In the United States, more than 20 individual states—from California to Oklahoma, Indiana to Massachusetts—have adopted state-level resolutions in support of international education. Although the state-level initiatives in the United States are largely symbolic actions with little to no substantial impact in practice, the symbolism itself is notable evidence of the rising importance of the international dimension.

Meanwhile, internationalization of higher education has reached the national agenda in a wide range of countries. Qatar, Singapore, and the United Arab Emirates stand out as examples of countries taking rather dramatic steps to promote internationalization as a matter of national policy. Their strategies have focused on the recruitment of prestigious foreign universities to establish local campuses, with the goal of expanding access to the local student population and serving as higher education "hubs" for their regions. Economic development and prestige enhancement are often key motivating factors there. Other countries, like the United Kingdom, Australia, and Canada, have adjusted visa and immigration requirements to attract foreign students to their higher education systems, motivated significantly by the desire to maintain economic competitiveness and realize substantial financial gains by enrolling large numbers of full-fee-paying internationals. In the United States, for example, it is estimated that international students and their families contributed nearly $15.5 billion to the US economy during the academic year 2007/08 (NAFSA, 2008). Globally, one estimate indicates that the world's international students represent a $45 billion "industry" (Barrow, 2008).

In addition to income generation, educational, political, and cultural motivations have also become relevant. Many countries in Europe have pursued foreign policy agendas focused on capacity building. These agendas include cooperative activities within the higher education sector, particularly in the developing world and frequently in partnerships that include countries with which there are former colonial ties (notably in Africa and Latin America).

Internationalization has also reached prominence at regional and international levels. The Bologna process and Lisbon strategy in Europe are the clearest examples of international engagement at this level, with the Bologna process drawing more than 40 countries into a "European higher education area" (EHEA). It is hoped that the EHEA will achieve a common, Europe-wide framework of understanding around tertiary education and lifelong learning, with significant cross-border intelligibility of degrees and qualifications, and a high level of quality, attractiveness, and competitiveness on a global scale (Bologna Declaration, 1999). Indeed, the regional focus in Europe appears to have served as the key point of reference for regionalization efforts elsewhere in the world. For example, the Latin American and the Caribbean area for higher education (ENLACES) initiative aims to strengthen cooperation in the region in order to achieve objectives such as

> the harmonization of curricula and institutional reforms, interdisciplinarity, mobility and academic exchange (intraregional mobility of students, researchers and teachers), the implementation of joint agendas for the generation of research with social relevance and priority in the framework of the training needs of human resources at the highest level of scientific and technological innovation, dissemination of knowledge and culture, and offering an increasing range of services to government and productive sectors of our nations. (UNESCO-IESALC, 2008)

A focus on regionalization can also be seen in the establishment of such entities as the African Network for Internationalisation of Education (ANIE) (Teferra and Knight, 2008), and in the development of the African Union Harmonisation Strategy. Similar concepts are being explored in Asia—for example, in November 2008, at the International Conference on Raising Awareness: Exploring the Ideas of Creating Higher Education Common Space in Southeast Asia, organized by the Southeast Asian Ministers of Education Organization-Regional Centre for Higher Education and Development (SEAMEO-RIHED). Furthermore, the 2006 Catania Declaration—signed by education ministers from Algeria, Egypt, France, Jordan, Greece, Italy, Malta, Morocco, Portugal, Slovenia, Spain, Tunisia, and Turkey—puts forth an agenda designed to "activate a structured cooperation in order to promote the comparability and readability of higher education systems" across much of the Mediterranean region (Catania Declaration, 2006, p. 2). The inclusion of higher education in the World Trade Organization's General Agreement on Trade in Services (GATS) regime is another clear reflection of the way in which the international dimension of higher education has achieved a global profile.

Opportunities, Challenges, and Risks

For some analysts, the impact of globalization on higher education offers exciting new opportunities for study and research, no longer limited by national boundaries, while others see the trend representing an assault on national culture and autonomy. It is undoubtedly both. At the very least, with 2.8 million students, countless scholars, degrees, and universities moving about the globe freely there is a pressing need for international cooperation and agreements.

Perhaps the "healthier" consequence of economic globalization and the subsequent pressure on higher education to function internationally has been the necessity for effective (and more transparent) systems of accountability, shared benchmarks, and standards for ethics and quality. Nations can no longer penalize students and scholars who have earned credentials and experience from another country. When individuals cannot enjoy the benefits of education outside of the country where it was acquired, the resulting waste of talent is unacceptable. Yet multiple stakeholders need internationally recognizable benchmarks and standards to properly evaluate unfamiliar foreign qualifications, and these agreements are not reached easily.

At the same time, it is critically important to recognize that some of the forces that currently influence internationalization in higher education are not necessarily compatible with local needs for development and modernization, and opening borders puts diverse motivations for educational development into conflict.

Opportunities
During the last decade, international engagement has risen visibly on institutional and national agendas around the world, even in the face of competing priorities (Rumbley, 2007). There are political, logistical, and educational dimensions to this momentum. The growing ease of international travel and a rapidly expanding information technology infrastructure have opened many new possibilities to higher education. New models for online learning make education and resources more readily available to individuals who reside in locations physically distant from universities. Information technology provides researchers with a broader reach for scholarly collaboration. These expanded opportunities for collegial engagement across borders—whether mediated through technology or not—hold the promise of much-needed capacity-building in research in contexts where this is lacking (Rumbley, 2007). Joint-degree programs, "twinning" efforts, and other approaches to cross-border education—to the extent that these operate in environments with appropriate regulatory and quality assurance oversight—extend the resources of individual universities without significant additional investment, again providing the promise of expanded capacity-building for underresourced institutions and systems.

Stakeholders in a variety of regions across the globe are moving toward a shared language and framework that facilitate the mobility of more and more students during their studies and after graduation. International exposure and experience are commonly understood as mechanisms to provide more graduates and scholars with perspective and insight that will increase their capacity to function in a globalized society.

Internationalization in many contexts has moved from being a marginal, occasional, or ad hoc activity to a more centrally administered, carefully organized, and thoughtful component of institutional action. Indeed, in recent years, there has been real movement in universities around the world from reactive to proactive stances in relation to internationalization. An opportunity now exists for many higher education systems and institutions to move to implement more strategic lines of action in regard to the international dimension. These trends are likely to include very targeted efforts to fashion institutional agreements with strategic partners, leverage the resources of new or existing networks, or develop new approaches to international engagement at more regional rather than global levels. Student mobility is expected to continue as an area of significant dynamism, while growth and innovation in international collaborative research activities also show important potential (Rumbley, 2007).

A widespread focus on internationalization—at individual, institutional, and governmental levels—does present real opportunities for stakeholders to move from rhetoric to action in ways that were not conceivable just a decade ago.

Challenges

The necessity of internationalizing higher education—to keep pace with both economic and academic globalization—presents many challenges at institutional and policy levels.

To be meaningful and sustainable, internationalization requires access to some amount of resources (human and financial) as well as their effective deployment and management. For the world's poorest countries and most resource-deprived institutions, the opportunities to engage internationally can be extremely limited or fraught with worrisome trade-offs. In Africa, for example, the reliance on massive amounts of foreign funding for research and other activities has long placed African universities at a disadvantage on several levels, not the least of which is having to cope with a foreign donor's unpredictable and shifting priorities, as well as serious disconnects between non-local-funder priorities and local needs and interests (Teferra, 2008). The financial dimension of internationalization is also an issue for higher education actors, rich and poor, in the current global financial crisis. Finding and leveraging appropriate resources is a major task moving forward, particularly in contexts where the international dimension is viewed as an optional action area, rather than as an integral component of the academic enterprise and administrative apparatus.

The mobility of higher education programming presents other serious challenges. New providers are crossing national borders with great ease. Some of these initiatives are done at the invitation of the host government, as in the cases of Singapore and Qatar; others are driven (primarily) by the interests of the provider. These new cross-border programs typically follow the structure of the provider's home country and may or may not be compatible with the education system, cultural norms, or labor-market requirements of the host country. It is often the case that neither the host nor home country has the capacity to monitor the quality, ethics, or conditions of the education being provided. These circumstances increase the urgency of international standards, oversight, and qualification frameworks.

Perhaps the most disconcerting characteristic of globalized higher education is that it is currently highly unequal. Philip Altbach's (2004) observation that "existing inequalities are reinforced while new barriers are erected" (p. 7) aptly describes a world in which the influence of Northern, and largely English-speaking paradigms for producing knowledge and setting scientific and scholarly agendas, dominate. The elite universities in the world's wealthiest countries hold a disproportionate influence over the development of international standards for scholarship, models for managing institutions, and approaches to teaching and learning. These universities have the comparative advantage of budget, resources, and talent sustaining a historic pattern that leaves other universities (particularly in lesser-developed countries) at a distinct disadvantage (Altbach, 2004). African universities, for example, have found it extremely challenging and complex to enter the global higher education stage; they barely register on world institutional rankings and league tables (Teferra, 2008), produce a tiny percentage of the world's research output (Gaillard, Hassan, and Waast, 2005), and were long undermined by a powerful global policy discourse that downplayed the role of higher education in development for the world's poorest countries (Teferra, 2008).

The dominance of a specific language or languages for scholarship represents yet another challenge in a globalized world. There is a distinct advantage in using a common language (currently English); learning this one language provides access to most of the world's research and teaching materials. Yet, the use of a single language has inevitably limited access to knowledge and also hinders the pursuit of scholarship in other languages (Altbach, 2004). In places like Africa, the use of nonnative languages also carries with it the heavy history of colonialism and has the potential to affect quality in contexts where faculty, students, and researchers are generally unable to operate with high levels of fluency (Teferra, 2008).

Finally, the students and scholars most likely to take advantage of the range of new opportunities in a globalized higher education environment are typically the wealthiest or otherwise socially privileged. The enormous challenge confronting higher education involves making international opportunities available to all equitably. It is also an urgent necessity to collect and analyze more accurate data on international student and scholar mobility, particularly concerning the developing world. For example, in Africa, "countries are hampered by a crippling lack of data in developing an effective strategy with a clear direction for identifying and supporting international education as an important component of higher education in the current global context" (Mulumba, et al., 2008, p. 509). An open and honest assessment of the dark side of the international student and scholar experience—particularly as concerns racism and xenophobia (Mulumba, et al., 2008)—is also an enormous challenge.

Risks

In terms of a global perspective, "commercialization of higher education," "foreign degree mills," and "brain drain" (Knight, 2006b, p. 63)
stand out as key risks of internationalization. Cross-border education,
specifically, presents particular kinds of threats, including

> an increase in low quality or rogue providers; a decrease in
> public funding if foreign providers are providing increased
> access; non-sustainable foreign provision of higher education if
> profit margins are low; foreign qualifications not recognized by
> domestic employers or education institutions; elitism in terms of
> those who can afford cross-border education; overuse of English
> as the language of instruction; and national higher education
> policy objectives not being met. (Knight, 2006a, p. 65)

However, risk assessment does vary by region of the world and according to the relative strength and standing of specific higher education
institutions and systems. Research suggests that the overall perception
of risk associated with internationalization is higher in the developing
world and that different regions of the world are concerned with different aspects of the phenomenon. For example, Latin America, the
Caribbean, and the Middle East have been identified as parts of the world
that are more sensitive to the possible "loss of cultural identity" through
international engagement, while problems associated with "elitism" as
a side effect of internationalization are more present for developing and
middle-income countries than for more developed economies (Knight,
2006b, p. 66).

It is clear, however, that if current trends of globalization and internationalization continue, the distribution of the world's wealth and talent
will be further skewed. The global migration of talent makes it possible for wealthier nations and institutions to attract and retain human
capital desperately needed elsewhere. Philip Altbach (2004) observes
that 80 percent of the students from China and India who go abroad
do not return home immediately after obtaining their degree, while 30
percent of highly educated Ghanaians and Sierra Leoneans live abroad.
A flow of talent South to North and North to North has continued to
dominate in the last decade. However, exceptions to this rule have also
emerged in recent years. The rising numbers of foreign students opting
to study in places like China, Singapore, Qatar, and Abu Dhabi represent
notable variations on the traditional paradigms of international student
mobility. Furthermore, Pawan Agarwal, et al. (2008) note "a growing
South-South movement which indicates the emergence of regional
hubs." This kind of role is clearly played, for example, by South Africa,

which hosted some 52,579 international students in 2004, of which approximately 68 percent "came from the Southern African region," and a total of 86.6 percent "came from the South or from the developing world" (p. 247). New manifestations of South-South flow among academics must also be acknowledged. A primary example here is the recent recruitment of a large number of Nigerian academics to Ethiopia to help staff a rapidly expanding Ethiopian higher education sector (Semela and Ayalew, 2008).

Still, wealth and power continue to exert powerful influence.

> We are now in a new era of power and influence. Politics and ideology have taken a subordinate role to profits and market-driven policies . . . As in the Cold War era, countries and universities are not compelled to yield to the terms of those providing aid, fostering exchanges, or offering Internet products, but the pressures in favor of participation tend to prevail. Involvement in the larger world of science and scholarship and obtaining perceived benefits not otherwise available present considerable inducements. The result is the same—the loss of intellectual and cultural autonomy by those who are less powerful. (Altbach, 2004, pp. 11–12)

The success of the most prestigious universities in attracting the world's talent cannot be blamed entirely on the influence these universities possess. There are "push factors" as well. Limited access to resources and political constraints may drive scholars from their home country. Governments wishing to retain talent will have to confront the dilemma that results from allowing political expedience to inhibit scholarly activity (Altbach, 2004).

National autonomy in regard to education is certainly at risk and closely related to the concerns about the increasing commodification of higher education. The failure of the most recent round of the General Agreement on Trade in Services (GATS) to sign a treaty that would liberalize "trade" in higher education is most likely only temporary. It is perhaps most clear in the context of GATS that the principles of free trade and the social needs of nations come into conflict. Should a GATS treaty be signed, or regional trade agreements take hold in more substantive ways, it would most likely contribute to the influence of for-profit providers of education and educational services whose products are rarely adapted to local priorities or need and undermine the ability of individual countries to regulate these entities (Altbach, 2004). Given the complexity of issues involved in international trade discussions relevant to higher education—and the myriad stakeholders pursuing different agendas with regard to these matters—an urgent need arises for "the higher education sector [to] be informed and vigilant about the risks and benefits and, more importantly, about the need for appropriate policies and regulations to guide and monitor current and future developments" (Knight, 2006a, p. 65). Failure to develop capacity at a national level to understand and effectively deal with these developments is a serious risk, particularly for less-developed countries.

Nontrade initiatives for international cooperation also present complex side effects, leaving smaller and/or poorer nations potentially more vulnerable in these arrangements. The birth of "a new class of deterritorialized trans-national policy actors" (Rinne, 2008, p. 675) has been noted to create tension with the long-held paradigm of higher education as an enterprise at the service of national interests.

Conclusion

The forces of globalization have exerted an enormous influence over higher education in the last decade, and internationalization has emerged as the primary response to this phenomenon. Barring major unforeseen developments that would derail current trends, the international dimension in higher education appears to be here to stay and will likely continue to rise in prominence on the agendas of individual institutions and national and regional systems of tertiary education around the world. Internationalization presents many new and exciting opportunities for cooperation within the academic enterprise and can be a powerful tool for the enhancement of quality and the insertion of innovation across many dimensions. At the same time, many significant risks and challenges must be faced in a costly, fast-paced, competitive global higher education environment. As with many other aspects of higher education, the phenomenon is playing out against a backdrop of inherent inequity around the world. The need to understand and harness the benefits of internationalization, while minimizing the risks and costs, is of central importance moving forward.

3

Access and Equity

The importance of equal access to higher education was emphasized repeatedly in the declarations that emerged from the 1998 World Conference on Higher Education. UNESCO reaffirmed Article 26(1) of the Universal Declaration of Human Rights, proclaiming "Everyone has the right to education . . . higher education shall be equally accessible to all on the basis of merit." Increasing the participation and role of women in higher education was emphasized, but the declaration included many other factors and conditions that have resulted in inequitable patterns of participation.

Much progress has been made. While many countries have enrolled upwards of 50 percent of the age cohort (and therefore reflect the extent of massification during the last few decades), too many countries still enroll only a small percentage of the cohort. Poorer nations are likely to enroll fewer students than wealthier nations. Additionally, even as enrollment has expanded, participation has rarely been representative of the society as a whole. Within most nations, access to higher education is often still the privilege of specific segments of society.

Many nations have attempted to address inequities with aggressive policies (e.g., affirmative action or reservation policies for admission), innovative financing schemes, and tutoring programs, but it is always clear that these patterns are not easily erased and the challenge remains of making higher education truly accessible to all.

New providers, new delivery methods, the diversity of postsecondary institutions, and the ease of international mobility should, in theory, make higher education available to more people. While this has indeed been the case, the diversity of opportunities has also helped to underscore those pernicious issues that hamper progress.

Massification and Uneven Gains Worldwide

Participation in postcompulsory education has expanded exponentially throughout the world during the last several decades. Globally, the percentage of the age cohort enrolled in tertiary education has grown from 19 percent in 2000 to 26 percent in 2007. Still, while the actual number of participants grows, the proportion of the age cohort varies from region to region and traditional patterns of unequal enrollment persist. Not surprisingly, the most dramatic gains have taken place among upper-middle and upper-income countries. In low-income countries tertiary-level participation has improved only marginally, from 5 percent in 2000 to 7 percent in 2007 (see *Appendix: Statistical Tables,* in this report).

In Africa the challenge is to increase participation for the entire age cohort. With only 5 percent of the age cohort enrolled, sub-Saharan Africa has the lowest participation rate in the world. Countries in the region struggle with limited capacity, overcrowding, limited infrastructure, inadequate management, poor student preparation, and high cost (Bloom, Canning, and Chan, 2005). Distance learning has made higher education significantly more accessible, particularly in rural Africa, but lack of infrastructure and the cost to individuals and institutions to acquire new technology combine to moderate progress.

China and India have recognized the need for increasing their respective pools of talent to support continued economic growth. Yet, China enrolls 23 percent of the age cohort, while India enrolls only 12 percent (see *Appendix: Statistical Tables,* in this report). Demand has grown too rapidly for either country to respond with the necessary infrastructure or with an adequately prepared professoriate.

Despite steady increases in tertiary enrollment in Latin America, participation for the region is still less than half of the enrollment in high-income countries. Cost is still a significant barrier to access. Enrollment in the region struggles against obstacles common to much of the developing world. Although tuition is low (compared to higher-income countries) or free at many public universities in the region, attendance still entails significant private cost (education-related costs, living expenses, opportunity cost) that average 60 percent of gross domestic product per capita. Few countries offer grant or loan programs to make education feasible for lower-socioeconomic sectors of society (Murakami and Blom, 2008).

What Does Access Mean?

In its simplest form, greater access to higher education means making it possible for more individuals to enroll. Despite many policy initiatives in recent years, broader postsecondary participation has not benefited all sectors of society equally. Research has demonstrated that the challenge is complicated by a large number of variables.

Truly providing equal access to higher education means overcoming the social and economic inequities within each nation and the corresponding disparities that result. In a report for the Higher Education Funding Council for England (HEFCE) the authors observed these complexities that challenge the goal of equal access:

> Inequalities in higher education participation are evident throughout the life course and include differences in terms of time (and age), place, gender, ethnicity, first language, parental (and sibling) social class, parental education, type of school attended, housing tenure, health/disability, criminal activity, learning difficulties, family structure and religious background. Multiple social disadvantages can result in initial education and, subsequently, participation in other forms of learning. Parental income and education are particularly influential. Occupational status and family size are also relevant . . . Quality of life factors (such as infant health) are important for understanding disengagement from education rather than participation within it. . . . The question is raised as to whether policymakers should seek to reduce inequality in education directly, or seek to reduce the wider inequalities that are reflected in education. (Gorard, et al., 2006)

These issues are not unique to England by any means. To what extent can access to higher education ever be equal without corresponding policy to address the social conditions that disadvantage some population groups while benefiting others?

Accommodating a more diverse population and broadening access create many new tensions between societies and institutions. Universities are under a great deal of pressure to meet the complex and often contradictory expectations of the societies they serve. Prejudice, discrimination, and disadvantage did not begin within the university. Yet, the university is obliged to address these and other challenges embedded in diverse contemporary societies. In the current economic climate, universities are facing extreme budget pressure precisely when they are being asked to provide new services to address the needs of ever more diverse students. "Today universities are required to promote equity, fairness and justice, on the one hand, and maintain efficiency, quality and public accountability, on the other" (Gupta, 2006, p. 4).

Historically, underserved populations tend to be less well-prepared for higher education than many of their peers. Countries often tend to equate open admission with equal access, but low rates of completion raise doubts about whether access alone is sufficient. Greater diversity also raises concerns about quality and forces societies to address the tension between equity and excellence in admission (Task Force on Higher Education and Society, 2000). The report of the Task Force on Higher Education and Society suggests that higher education must "combine tolerance at points of entrance with rigor at the point of exit" (p. 41).

A commitment to broader participation ultimately requires each society to ensure that all of its young citizens have both the prerequisites (academic and economic) and ongoing support to participate success-fully, as well as equal opportunity to apply their knowledge and skill in the labor market upon graduation. The goals must be understood as more than access, and also attend to opportunities for progress and success (Gupta, 2006). For expanded access to have meaning, systems must be in place to ensure the success of the new populations enrolling.

The unequal distribution of wealth and resources worldwide also determines the extent to which nations can address these problems. The scope and complexity of the challenge are enormous. While advances are being made, there is still much to be accomplished.

Geography

Geography is easily underestimated as a factor that contributes to unequal participation in higher education. Tertiary institutions are not distributed evenly throughout a nation. Rural populations are more likely to be more distant from postsecondary institutions than urban populations. Indigenous peoples are even more likely to live in remote areas, compounding the challenge of improving the participation rate of these groups.

While new technology should, in theory, help bridge this gap, rural areas are less likely to have the necessary modern infrastructure, and rural families are unlikely to have the equipment necessary to par-ticipate in distance programs. Furthermore, traditional-age students (particularly children of parents without postsecondary education) will not possess the discipline and self-motivation to make distance technol-ogy a viable alternative to presential learning (Usher, 2009).

Geography, combined with other factors, contributes to the disadvan-tage of specific populations. For example, aboriginal people in Australia have less access to even secondary schools in their home community, let alone tertiary institutions. Secondary completion was only 32 percent of the age cohort in 1998, complicating the challenge of increasing participation in higher education (Piquet, 2006).

Similarly, in Mexico where the national gross enrollment ratio has grown from 14 percent in 1995 to 26.2 percent in 2005, participation in poor urban areas was only 11 percent and in poor rural areas only 3 percent. Since the early 1990s, the Ministry of Education has invested in the development of additional educational services in underserved areas with some success. Ninety percent of the students that have enrolled are the first in their family to pursue higher education; 40 percent live in economically depressed regions (Brunner, et al., 2006).

Wealthier countries have been able to close the distance somewhat. The rapid expansion of the community college system in the United States put postsecondary institutions within the geographic reach of most of the American population, but this was a result of massive investment. Other high-income countries (the Republic of Korea, for example) still host most of their universities (and certainly their most prestigious) in their major cities (Grubb, et al., 2006). Developing countries do not have the resources necessary for establishing new universities in remote areas. As a result, low secondary school completion rates in rural areas, coupled with the lack of guidance and the expense of relocating (for those students who do complete secondary school and wish to continue), conspire to depress continuance for rural populations.

More to Access Than Meets the Eye

Greater participation rates in higher education do not (by themselves) open the same opportunities equally to all. Research shows repeatedly that disadvantaged populations once enrolled are less likely to continue to degree completion. In addition, these groups also attend particular types of institutions and programs of study. These programs are typically those that offer fewer opportunities for employment and further study.

The small percentage of the age cohort of aboriginal people in Australia who enroll in tertiary education are more likely to be concentrated in basic-entry university programs and vocational education institutions, earning not only fewer but lower-level credentials (Piquet, 2006).

Even where gross enrollment ratios are high, inequities persist. The United States demonstrates impressive enrollment capacity, infrastructure, and funding, but participation by racial and ethnic minorities is disappointing. Although minority enrollment doubled during the last quarter of the 20th century, closer inspection of the data reveals that participation rates for minority students continue to lag behind. Data reported for 2006 show 41 percent of the white age cohort enrolled at a college or university compared to 32 percent of young black adults and 24 percent of Hispanic students (Brainard, 2008). Not only are enrollment rates uneven, but data show a graduation gap, where white students continue to graduate in larger numbers than their minority peers.

Community colleges have made tertiary education more accessible (geographically and economically) to more individuals in the United States since the 1940s, but research shows that the likelihood that community college students will continue on to a four-year degree is largely determined by the socioeconomic status of the student's family, regardless of race or ethnicity (Dougherty and Kienzl, 2006).

A recent comparative study of 15 countries (mainly in the North and mostly upper-income countries) found that the expansion of higher education has allowed larger proportions of all social strata to attend (Shavit, Arum, and Gamoran, 2007). Yet the study also concluded that despite greater inclusion, the privileged classes have retained their relative advantage in nearly all nations.

In France, for example, overall participation in higher education is quite high. Yet, France has a hierarchical system of tertiary education where enrollment in elite institutions often provides access to unique postgraduate opportunities. Despite significant increases in broad-based participation in higher education in general, the elite-postsecondary-track graduates are still more likely to be male and to be children of highly educated fathers (Insee and Dares, 2007).

Opportunities for tertiary-level education have also expanded significantly in the Republic of Korea, but these new places have been opened in lower-status institutions (including those that do not lead to postgraduate education). These new institutions are most likely to absorb lower-income students. Wealthier students have the option and advantage of private tutors to help them prepare for university entrance examinations and, as a result, compete more successfully for limited places in elite universities (Grubb, et al., 2006).

Other developed countries have similar challenges to overcome so as to reach the goal of rewarding merit equitably.

Affirmative Action, Positive Discrimination, Quotas, and Reservation Programs

Widening participation in higher education has been seen as a force for democratization, but this is only the case when participation is representative of the population as a whole. Most countries ration admission to higher education in some way, typically on the basis of an examination. Merit is assumed to make opportunity available equally if all aspirants are evaluated by the same criteria. Yet, because of the many influential variables alluded to above, this is not the case. Traditional beliefs about meritocracy tend to reproduce privilege and exclusion.

Providing higher education to all sectors of a nation's population means confronting social inequalities deeply rooted in history, culture, and economic structure that affect an individual's ability to compete. To address the problem, many countries have implemented policy initiatives to rectify past wrongs. But obliging societies to change behavior and values is no simple matter. Advocates of human rights find themselves challenging cultural and religious traditions that countries may not readily discard. Many conservative Islamic cultures reject the notion that women should have access to the same education available to men. Traditional Indian culture accepts a notion of caste, which does not assume that opportunity will be dispensed equally. Policy does not easily change attitudes.

Nevertheless, programs labeled "affirmative action" or "reservation programs" are being used throughout the world to compensate for patterns of past discrimination. These programs represent "positive discrimination" or "reverse discrimination" (Gupta, 2006); in other words, they give priority to groups once discriminated against over other social groups. These groups reflect differences of gender, race, ethnic groups, economic sectors, and/or religion.

Women have made important strides in gaining access to higher education, but they are distributed unevenly. In the OECD countries (with the exception of the Republic of Korea, Switzerland and Turkey) women now account for more than 50 percent of the enrollment. According to UNESCO data (School Life Expectancy data table), women persist longer in most countries, with the notable exception of the African region. Still, the ratio of women to men tends to be higher in vocational and intermediate degree programs in many member countries, although this appears to be changing (Vincent-Lancrin, 2008a). UNESCO data show that, worldwide, women represent roughly half of the enrollment, but closer inspection shows similar unevenness in their distribution across fields of study. For example, women represented 21 percent of the enrollment in engineering, manufacturing, and construction (average of all reporting countries) in 2000 and only improved to 23 percent of the enrollment in those fields by 2007. In contrast, women represented 65 percent of the enrollment in education in 2000, and this grew to 68 percent in 2007.

Initiatives designed to address inequities are inevitably perceived as unfair by at least one sector of society and invariably controversial. Initiatives in Ghana, Kenya, Uganda, and the United Republic of Tanzania have lowered admissions cutoffs for women to increase female enrollment (Bloom, Canning, and Chan, 2005). This kind of strategy can prove to be a mixed blessing if women, once admitted to university, are perceived as being academically inferior to men.

Simply admitting more women through affirmative action programs overlooks a significant part of the problem. The intersections of gender, poverty, and higher education opportunities have been examined in Ghana and the United Republic of Tanzania. The research has shown that disadvantage is often the result of combinations of characteristics; when gender is intersected with socioeconomic status, participation rates of poorer women are extremely low in both African countries (Morley and Lugg, 2009).

In many societies, social class and status also need to be addressed. Although India has expanded tertiary enrollment significantly during the past two decades, participation has not increased equally across all sectors of society. The Indian government now obliges universities to reserve a set percentage of the spaces in the incoming class for "socially and educationally backward classes" (Gupta, 2006). Modest improvement has occurred, but the gross enrollment ratio of lower castes, rural populations, and Muslims lag behind the general population. Muslims in India are underrepresented in higher education (with a gross enrollment ratio of only 7.6 in 2004) but are not included in the new reservation program (Azam and Blom, 2008). Most (60 percent) of the lower castes gaining access to tertiary study are clustered in less expensive bachelor of arts programs where graduates encounter limited job prospects, reinforcing the premise that increasing participation alone does not achieve social equity (Weisskopf, 2004; Azam and Blom, 2008).

India's initiative to address issues of equitable access highlights many of the challenges of pursuing social integration with policies targeted at higher education. Most of the underrepresented groups in higher education also have a lower secondary-level completion rate. The reservation program places pressures on universities that they are not prepared to address the need either to decrease the number of places available to the "general (non-reservation) students" or increase the total number of places. With limited human resources and budget, expansion is quite difficult.

In Brazil, enrollment in higher education has been skewed toward more prosperous white, able-bodied citizens. State legislatures in Brazil have mandated that universities reserve space for disabled and Afro-Brazilian students. The disabled are often overlooked in discussions of access and equity and are perhaps almost universally underrepresented in postsecondary institutions, certainly the case in Brazil (Lloyd, 2006).

Brazil is a largely mixed-race country, and the challenge of determining who qualifies as Afro-Brazilian has been considerable.

Strategies being tried worldwide are moving more members of under-represented groups into higher education. Yet, without a commitment to cultivate respect and understanding for these relative newcomers, many professors and peers may not welcome these students: "The non-beneficiaries have a general tendency to devalue the accomplishments of the students and faculty belonging to the reserved category" (Gupta, 2006, pp. 13–14).

Completion Rates

Social equity will not be achieved through access to further education alone. In order to fully enjoy the benefits of higher education and to contribute to the society and economy in which they live, individuals need to complete their program of study. True progress depends on high levels of completion for all population groups.

As already noted above, students of color in the United States have a much lower completion rate than white students. In Argentina, where secondary school graduates have free and open access to public universities, the completion rate (based on the ratio of graduating to entering students) is less than 24 percent. The interpretation of access has to go beyond merely getting more students "through the door." Mechanisms to support success are essential, yet they are rarely in place and where they do exist inadequately address the needs of the new diverse populations enrolling.

Only limited data are available about completion rates, especially in developing countries. This is important data for the continued improvement of greater inclusion.

Costs and Financing

The funding of higher education is addressed in a separate chapter of this report but the topic merits some commentary here as well.

Cost remains an enormous barrier to access, obviously affecting some social sectors more than others. As more countries "privatize" public as well as private institutions, more direct cost is being passed along to students. Even where universities refrain from charging tuition or other enrollment fees, students have to bear indirect costs such as living expenses and (often) the loss of income. For students who reside in rural or remote areas, access to higher education may require the additional expense of relocating.

In order to mediate cost as an obstacle many countries offer scholarships, grant, and/or loan programs. These financing schemes (when available) lower the "net cost" of pursuing higher education (Usher, 2006). These programs are demonstrating some degree of success but cannot by themselves remove economic barriers. Financing schemes make good policy, but they are not always embraced by the individuals they are designed to help.

In fact, the price of higher education acts as a serious deterrent in several ways: the price constraint and whether the individual believes that the total price outweighs the benefits of a particular educational choice; a cash or liquidity constraint, where an individual cannot obtain sufficient funds to cover the immediate cost of education; and debt aversion or a reluctance to incur debt in order to obtain an education (Usher, 2006, p. 10). These issues weigh more heavily on students from poorer backgrounds.

Furthermore, although research consistently demonstrates that tertiary education has significant positive impact on the life earnings of an individual, these benefits are not always as apparent (or convincing) to historically underserved populations without family members or other role models who have demonstrated the benefits of higher education. Finally, poorer students are less likely than wealthier students to confidently make long-term investments or to trust long-term outcomes.

Based on research in several countries, the availability of grants (nonrepayable subsidies), as opposed to loans, has been described as an important positive influence on the retention of lower-income students (Usher, 2006). Fear of debt tends to be a greater deterrent for students from poorer backgrounds since there is less financial "backup" in the case of unemployment or underemployment after graduation (a common condition in the developing world).

Many countries offer loan schemes designed specifically for tertiary study that have had success in increasing access. Income-contingent loan schemes (where repayment plans are tied to postgraduation earnings) and other innovative approaches have gained popularity in Australia, New Zealand, and South Africa, and increasingly elsewhere, but are still more attractive to middle- and lower-middle-class students (Gorard, et al., 2006). By tying the repayment schedule to income, students can be more confident of managing their loan burden after graduation in a broader range of circumstances.

Mexico has also introduced loan programs to make the private sector more accessible to a broader spectrum of families. In Mexico, the private sector is absorbing much of the expanding enrollment demand, but since this sector is tuition dependent, cost becomes a serious obstacle to students from low-income families. The national association of private universities (Federación de Instituciones Mexicanas de Educación

Superior) has launched a loan program to bridge the economic gap. But in order to be viable, loans can only be made to families that sign a collateral agreement, a condition that automatically limits the reach of the program (Canton and Blom, 2004). Yet the Canton and Blom assessment demonstrates that the loan program still opens the possibility of postsecondary education to many individuals who otherwise would not have considered it.

Chile has introduced a new loan program that targets students from lower-income families. Although the loan program is not tied to postgraduate income, the payment schedule is adjusted so that students pay less upon graduation and more at subsequent stages of the loan period, based on the assumption that income improves over time. Chile has addressed the problem of collateral by making the tertiary institution the guarantor of the loans for the students it enrolls (Larraín and Zurita, 2007).

Without question, financial assistance is key to expanding access to new populations. Research is still inconclusive on the most effective way to ameliorate cost as a deterrent to low-income groups, but the need to address economic barriers to higher education remains critically important.

Teaching and Retaining More Diverse Students

Expanded enrollment that encompasses historically underrepresented populations presents many new challenges to the institutions enrolling them. As has been noted throughout this report, the previous academic preparation of these new students will be uneven at best, deficient at worst. If the objective of expanded access is to graduate this new cohort as well as to enroll it, then new systems for academic support and innovative approaches to pedagogy will be necessary.

One of the challenges of the diversity lies in the gulf between traditional teaching and the expectations of the new student cohort, with student-learning needs proving to be as diverse as the group itself. Faculty are more inclined to see this as a "student problem" than a teaching problem and expect students to adapt (Gorard, et al., 2006). A number of issues have been observed:

> As universalization progresses, most new students are simply less interested in the kind of education provided by existing higher education institutes or are simply less academically gifted. In order to attract these students, new tactics need to be introduced. (Usher, 2009, p.9)

Mexico has taken the innovative step of creating new "intercultural universities" that are grounded in indigenous philosophies, cultures, languages, and histories (Brunner, et al., 2006). This creates an environment where the new student population is less likely to be received as an "outsider."

Hockings, et al. (2008) have studied how university teaching influences student engagement in classrooms in a range of subjects (biosciences, business, computing, history, and health and social care) in different types of English postsecondary institutions. These researchers explored social, cultural, and educational diversity and difference among the student population and the pedagogic practices that actively embrace or limit the potential for student learning. They suggest that some pedagogies do not engage the diverse interests or meet the needs of all students, while alternative pedagogic approaches appear to create inclusive learning environments and increase academic engagement.

To engage previously underrepresented students and hence retain them, efforts to align the curriculum and teaching approaches to their needs, interests, learning styles, and previous experience will be critical.

Conclusion

There is little question that participation in higher education has expanded dramatically during the last decade. Although there have been greater gains in wealthier nations, the improvement has taken place everywhere and seems to benefit all social strata. The nearly equal participation of women in higher education in so many countries is cause for celebration.

Experience has shown that expanded access to higher education alone does not fully address the issue of social equity. Institutions must consider the conditions required for successful completion as well, which means new services, innovative pedagogy, financing schemes, career advising, and more factors. Successful inclusion also requires strategies to develop respect among diverse cultures studying together.

What has become increasingly apparent is that access to higher education cannot be separated from a host of other social and economic issues. Simple solutions cannot solve complex problems. Ultimately, equitable participation in tertiary education across all sectors of society is inextricably linked to other educational, social, and economic conditions beyond higher education. Rates of completion for secondary education must be improved. Success at the secondary level (like tertiary study) is too often linked to income and parental education and profession(s).

The cost of education must be addressed to enroll and retain lower-income students. Even students who enroll at tuition-free public institutions incur expense that might prove to be a fatal barrier to the successful completion of a postsecondary degree. Making loans available does not necessarily remove financial barriers. Students from lower-income families are more hesitant to assume the risk of debt and more likely to forego income in order to study. Creative solutions will be required to overcome cost as an obstacle to participation.

It has been emphasized that improved access to higher education will not provide advantages to individuals or societies unless corresponding macroeconomic development takes place to ensure productive work for new graduates (Bloom, Canning, and Chan, 2005). Research is limited and, subsequently, not conclusive but indicates that there may be corresponding inequalities that follow disadvantaged groups into the labor market.

As nations attempt to increase participation for underrepresented groups, each initiative seems to reveal additional underlying challenges. As with other aspects of the ongoing revolution in higher education, the goal of access for all populations seems less audacious than it did a decade ago, but the pursuit of the goal has underscored the depth and breadth of the problem. Increased access alone for men and women to higher education will demonstrate limited success unless it is part of a larger, more far-reaching socioeconomic development strategy.

4

Quality Assurance, Accountability, and Qualification Frameworks

By the 1998 UNESCO World Conference on Higher Education, quality assurance was already a concern of nearly all nations, most of which had implemented schemes to evaluate the quality of institutions and programs in higher education. These systems vary enormously in focus, reach, objectives, and impact. Over the last decade, greater attention has been focused on "convergence" or making different national quality assurance schemes and frameworks more comparable or complementary to one another. Increasingly, nations are relying on quality assurance schemes used in other nations as guarantees of quality both to validate the domestic higher education system in its own right and to support all kinds of cross-border activity—student mobility, joint-degree programs, validation of professional qualifications, and others. Cross-border intelligibility can be very useful, but "convergence" also introduces risks and challenges. Nations are often stretched to design quality assurance schemes that reflect international practices, while preserving objectives and practices that take into consideration unique local needs and limitations.

Quality assurance has become a rapidly growing concern in a context of ongoing change in higher education around the world. At the same time, defining and measuring quality usefully has become more difficult. As the higher education landscape has become more complex, so have the expectations of individual institutions. In addition to educating, tertiary-level institutions have assumed (and been assigned) a broader social role—including resolving social inequities, providing appropriately trained labor, contributing to regional and national economic growth, and producing marketable research. Meanwhile, institutions are also obliged to operate more efficiently and transparently. Against these broad and shifting expectations, different constituencies judge the quality of higher education in various ways.

Today, "customers" or "stakeholders" have a considerable influence in determining the perception and measures of quality. Fee-paying students, professional bodies, employers, politicians, and funding agencies are all voicing their particular expectations of what a degree or diploma should represent. New terms such as "transparency," "performance indicators," and "outcome measures" now figure prominently in the discussion. Yet, despite near universal agreement that the quality of higher education must be assured, concern for institutional autonomy, national culture, and the importance of relevance to local contexts further complicate the discussion (OECD, 2004; ENQA, 2007).

Defining exactly what quality looks like is especially problematic in the midst of significant expansion and internationalization. The massive growth in enrollment at the end of the last century and the subsequent diversity of both students and institutions add many layers of complexity to quality assurance efforts. Additionally, globalization, regional integration, and the ever-increasing mobility of students and scholars have expanded the need for internationally recognized standards or benchmarks to help guide the comparison and evaluation of academic and professional qualifications.

Quality in higher education was once assured (in most countries) by the regulation and oversight of provincial and/or national ministries of education. National higher education systems were restricted in size and scope so that national standards were plausible and could be applied efficiently to a limited number of institutional types. The current diversity of institution types and providers—along with increasingly international orientations of these actors—has made this kind of evaluation less practical, while making broader and more flexible criteria necessary. A near universal shift has occurred from *ex ante* regulation (establishing standards and limitations beforehand) to *ex post* evaluation (measuring and evaluating performance after the fact) (Maassen, 1987) with *ex post* evaluation usually being conducted and coordinated by new parastatal agencies (Neave, 1994) taking into consideration expanded criteria for judging institutional performance. The rapidly expanding private sector presents additional challenges to government agencies.

Quality assurance agencies, new and old, responsible for monitoring institutional and program quality, are under pressure from multiple constituencies to address evermore complicated expectations. Preoccupation with quality is now universal, and few countries, if any, have opted out of the quality assurance movement. However, like all issues addressed in this report, the pursuit of quality plays out differently in various regions and countries.

Defining Quality

At some point, every essay that is written about quality assurance addresses the challenge of defining what *quality* actually means in higher education. The general understanding of quality has evolved with each passing decade and continues to adapt to changing contexts and exigencies. At the 1998 UNESCO world conference it was already clear that the range of activities to be evaluated was expansive:

> Quality in higher education is a multidimensional concept, which should embrace all its functions, and activities; teaching and academic programmes, research and scholarship, staffing, students, buildings, facilities, equipments, services to the community, and academic environment. (van Ginkel and Rodrigues Dias 2007, p. 39)

A decade later the definition provided in a UNESCO-CEPES report reflects the increasing complexity of the higher education environment:

> Quality in higher education is a multi-dimensional, multi-level, and dynamic concept that relates to the contextual settings of an educational model, to the institutional mission and objectives, as well as to the specific standards within a given system, institution, programme, or discipline. (Vlasceanu, Grünberg, and Pârlea, 2007)

In practice, the issue of quality is addressed more usefully as a process than an idea. Quality assurance is viewed as a process where key elements of higher education are measured. It is in this process that the concepts of performance, standards, norms, accreditation, benchmarks, outcomes, and accountability overlap to form the foundation of the quality culture emerging in higher education everywhere (Adelman, 2009). The differences in exactly *what* is measured and *how* reflect the way different nations and cultures interpret quality.

The Process of Quality Assurance

Even without a concise definition of quality in higher education, a pattern for evaluating higher education has been established in most of the world. In a break from the past, this new pattern tends to rely on peers rather than government authorities to conduct the evaluation process.

Most quality assurance schemes begin with a self-study or self-review of the institution or program being evaluated. The self-study obliges an institution to undertake a thorough examination of its own practices, resources, and accomplishments with an eye toward measuring performance against mission and identifying ways to improve.

Self-study usually culminates in a report that documents the process and the results. The report is typically considered by a team of external evaluators who visit the institution and write a report of their own, assessing the validity of the self-study.

The process is described by the Australian Universities Quality Agency as a "systematic and independent examination to determine whether activities and related results comply with planned arrangements and whether these arrangements are implemented effectively and are suitable to achieve objectives" (AUQA). The process usually includes an evaluation or inspection of the effectiveness of the internal quality systems.

An important trend in quality evaluation is that institutions are now more often evaluated against their own self-defined mission and less often against an institutional model defined by a regulatory agency. This approach has become increasingly necessary and important with the growing diversity of institutions and delivery systems. The framework that regulators then use for judging the quality of an institution may reflect one or more of the following criteria—quality as excellence, quality as fitness *for* purpose, and quality as fitness *of* purpose, quality as enhancement or improvement.

Another trend has been a modification in the role of government and parastatal agencies. In many cases, the regulatory function of many of these agencies has shifted to a validating role. In other words, as quality has come to be seen as a continuous process of assessment and improvement, coordinating bodies are focusing on whether institutions have adequate mechanisms in operation to support this dynamic process.

This approach to quality assurance as described above forms the underpinnings of most schemes in practice today. But, as they say, the devil is in the details. Evaluations in different systems focus on specific elements of higher education. These processes may be similar, yet the language and terminology of quality assurance are used and often understood differently in each language and culture (Adelman, 2009). In a study undertaken by the European Network for Quality Assurance in 2006, it became apparent that for quality assurance schemes to function across national boundaries the vocabulary of quality needs to maintain its meaning as it crosses cultural boundaries (Crozier, et al., 2006). The report emphasizes that assumptions should not be made lightly as nations move toward new international agreements. Glossaries, such as "Quality Assurance and Accreditation: A Glossary of Basic Terms and Definitions" (Vl sceanu, Grünberg, and Pârlea, 2007), endeavor to clarify the vocabulary of quality. The importance of terminology in reaching shared understandings and agreements cannot be underestimated.

The Limitations of National Programs

External independent mechanisms for evaluating the quality and performance of higher education in the United States have been in place since the early part of the 20th century. This was not the case elsewhere where oversight belonged exclusively to governments until the end of the last century. In the early 1990s, fewer than half of the countries in Europe had established new quality assurance agencies, but by 2004 nearly every country had created an agency charged with the oversight of quality assurance for the higher education sector (Schwarz and Westerheijden, 2004), although with widely varying mandates, responsibilities, and authority. National quality assurance schemes are the essential building blocks of international conventions but are not sufficient by themselves.

At the same time that national programs to monitor quality assurance were being implemented throughout the world, many new cross-border models for higher education were being created. These new models (foreign providers, private nonprofit and for-profit universities, and online delivery) are often excluded from national quality assurance schemes although they account for an increasing number of university students (OECD, 2004; Van Damme, Van der Hijden, and Campbell, 2004). The explosive growth of both traditional institutions as well as new providers in higher education raises new questions in regard to standards of quality in this more diverse environment.

The need for some basis for the comparison of the quality of programs and of qualifications at the international level has become more urgent as a result of the increasing number of internationally mobile students, now projected to reach 7.5 million by 2025 (Verbik and Lasanowski, 2007). Local systems for quality assurance are simply no longer adequate.

National programs to evaluate quality will be essential to international conventions, but they vary considerably in focus and method. Some national schemes are more narrowly focused than others—sometimes evaluating only public universities or specific degree programs. In addition, quality assurance mechanisms are still relatively new in much of the world; institutions and individuals are participating at varying levels of sophistication and experience. National schemes and international conventions are now evolving simultaneously, with each effort influencing the direction of the other.

Managing Mobility

With students and programs moving across borders with increasing ease, a pressing need has emerged for common reference points. The comparability of educational qualifications has become a key issue in international discussions.

National schemes may well build the foundation for quality assurance. However, without incorporating internationally recognized benchmarks and frameworks, there is no means of comparison. As greater mobility is both inevitable and generally considered desirable, international agreements that encourage the mutual recognition of programs and credentials have become more significant. At a practical level, this policy means finding a way to define and validate the level and quality of postsecondary qualifications for individuals who reside and/or work in a country other than where their education was completed.

The Lisbon Recognition Convention in 1997 emphasized that it is a student's *right* to receive fair recognition of his or her educational qualifications within the European region. Lisbon also stressed the importance of national centers staffed with experts who can perform this kind of evaluation (UNESCO, 2004). The increasing diversity of the higher education landscape makes the comparison of qualifications particularly challenging and underscores the need for at least some shared guideposts to allow individuals to enjoy the academic and professional benefits that their credentials merit (OECD, 2004).

Since the late 1970s, UNESCO regional meetings in Africa, Asia, Europe, Latin America, and the Middle East have facilitated the elaboration of conventions that commit signatories to common policy and practice, easing the mobility of individuals within each region. These conventions emphasize the value of shared terminology and evaluation criteria to make mutual recognition of partial or completed studies more efficient and transparent. Additionally, by making national institutions of higher education more widely accessible to students and faculty within each region and increasing the "portability" of diplomas and certificates, higher education can become a vehicle for the retention of talent and, as a result, contribute to regional development.

The Bologna process reflects enormous progress in regard to the integration of higher education in Europe, going further than other regions by creating a common degree structure, qualification frameworks, and implementing new requirements to make the achievement reflected by each level of educational attainment more transparent.

Supranational conventions are continuing to be developed, reviewed, and revised. Ultimately the international recognition of academic and vocational credentials will require new channels of discussion between regions, nations, and institutions, but above all, it will require trust (UNESCO, 2004).

Evaluating Qualifications

As already indicated, higher education can be evaluated in many different ways and at many levels. Institutions can be evaluated in their entirety according to the qualifications of professors, the extent of library resources, research output, and other factors. Professors can be evaluated on the basis of their research productivity or success in securing grants. Students can be evaluated in terms of grades or accomplishments. The evaluation of educational qualifications has special significance in that these credentials serve as a kind of international currency, affording the holder different levels of opportunity depending on how the qualifications are valued.

How educational qualifications are evaluated is a newer dimension of the quality assurance conversation. Historically, the emphasis has been on the content covered in the course of the degree program. In some cases, the broader academic experience is evaluated, taking into consideration complementary coursework and extracurricular activities. New criteria (such as relevance to the labor market) are being added to the assessment of qualifications. Increasingly, attention is being paid to competencies developed in the course of study. In Europe, the Educational Qualifications Framework aims to define qualifications in terms of the depth of knowledge, skills, and competencies they represent. The "Tuning Project" under way in Europe and Latin America and recently launched in three American states attempts to further define these competencies within specific fields of study. Determining what a qualification should represent, once earned, is a fundamental piece of the quality puzzle, but this discussion is still in its early stages.

Finally, there is always the risk of qualifications without any validity whatsoever. With many new providers offering options for postsecondary study, it is sometimes difficult to distinguish legitimate institutions from diploma or degree mills that make credentials available for purchase. Diploma mills have exploited the need of many individuals for easy access to a degree or certificate, given the advantages that advanced study offers in the labor market. The existence of this type of fraud increases the urgency of international mechanisms for quality assurance as they potentially demean the value of educational credentials. Diploma mills all too often blend in with new, legitimate nontraditional providers (CHEA, 2009).

In the interest of educating and protecting stakeholders, UNESCO has launched the "Portal of Higher Education Institutions" online to guide individuals to sources of information to help them distinguish legitimate from bogus documents and institutions.

The Growing Emphasis on Outcomes

Historically, quality assessments relied on quantitative data such as full-time professors with advanced degrees, volumes in a university library, papers published by faculty, or student-professor ratios. In recent years, there has been a growing emphasis on the "outcomes" of higher education. In other words, evaluators are looking for new data and indicators to demonstrate that students have mastered specific objectives as a result of their education. The experience of implementing outcome-based learning is still limited to a small number of institutions in a few countries, but this dimension of evaluation is growing rapidly.

OECD has introduced an initiative to assess learning outcomes on an international scale. The Assessment of Higher Education Learning Outcomes (AHELO) project was launched in 2006 to build the capacity for evaluating teaching and learning. The project is still under development with a target-launch-date in 2016. The approach focuses on the following aspects:

- *Physical and organizational characteristics:* observable characteristics such as enrollment figures or the ratio of male to female students
- *Education-related behaviors and practices:* student-faculty interaction, academic challenge, emphasis on applied work, etc.
- *Psychosocial and cultural attributes:* career expectations of students, parental support, social expectations of higher education institutions, etc.
- *Behavioral and attitudinal outcomes:* students' persistence and completion of degrees, continuation into graduate programs or success in finding a job, student satisfaction, improved student self-confidence, and self-reported learning gains claimed by students or their instructors (OECD).

The desire to measure student learning and learning outcomes requires sophisticated instruments and skilled staff, although there is limited availability of both. There are two primary instruments in use in the United States. The National Survey of Student Engagement surveys students to measure their degree of academic involvement and compiles results to achieve an institutional score that reflects how well the university does at creating a learning environment. The Collegiate Learning Assessment tests general skills such as communication and critical thinking. In this case also, data are compiled to produce an institutional score (Usher, 2009).

While the trend toward a greater attention to learning and learning outcomes has been very positive, there is still only limited attention to teaching quality. Effective and varied pedagogy deserves a more prominent place in the future discussions, as does the impact on teaching quality of such large percentages of part-time professors in so much of the world.

So Many Players
Discussions are taking place at many levels by innumerable international organizations to address the need for a shared understanding of quality. Although an international agency with overarching authority for recognizing and accrediting institutions and programs might be helpful, the politics and logistics of implementing a scheme at this level make it unlikely for the present. Practical considerations suggest (at least for the short term) that evaluation will continue to be managed locally and that adequate information about these processes must be easily available and transparent in order to satisfy the needs of international stakeholders.

There has been a veritable explosion of new agencies taking on roles for different aspects of quality assurance and, as a result, there is a need to evaluate and certify these authorities so as to trust their work in this area. There are unethical agents entering the quality assurance arena as well. "Accreditation mills," like diploma mills, easily confuse stakeholders by mimicking the terminology of legitimate agencies and institutions (Ezell, 2007).

The discussions and negotiations related to the Bologna process placed Europe in the vanguard of coordinating national and regional efforts for quality assurance. The establishment of the European Association for Quality Assurance in Higher Education (ENQA) in 2000 brought together many of the national quality assurance agencies in the region and created an important forum to engage member countries in transnational quality assurance projects.

Membership in ENQA confirms the legitimacy of an agency, but in 2008, European ministers responsible for higher education established the European Quality Assurance Register (EQAR) as an additional mechanism for coordinating the efforts to improve quality within Europe. The registry will offer a list of accreditation agencies that comply with the European Standards and Guidelines for Quality Assurance (ESG).

The six regional accrediting bodies in the United States that accredit postsecondary institutions operate independently and determine their own standards and procedures. Degree programs are accredited separately by professional associations in different fields. The Council for Higher Education Accreditation (CHEA) serves as clearinghouse and umbrella organization for legitimate accrediting bodies in the United States.

Other organizations are attempting to coordinate quality assurance activities on an international level, many with support from the World Bank. These organizations have formed on the basis of common interests or geographical proximity. APQN, the Asia-Pacific Quality Network, was established in 2003 to provide training and support to quality assurance efforts in the region. RIACES, the Ibero-American Network for Quality Assessment and Assurance in Higher Education, was established in 2004 as a forum for cooperation in Latin America and the Caribbean. ANQAHE, The Arab Network for Quality Assurance in Higher Education, was established in 2007 for the same purpose.

Of the new organizations promoting quality assurance activities on an international level, INQAAHE (the International Network for Quality Assurance Agencies in Higher Education) has the broadest reach. Founded in 1991, this network is an assocation of organizations or an umbrella organization, whose members are regional, state, and professional quality assurance agencies. The organization plays several key roles, acting as a liaison between international organizations such as the World Bank, UNESCO, and OECD and their members; providing support to new quality assurance agencies; offering forums where members can share experiences and information; and encouraging cooperation among members (INQAAHE, 2007).

Inevitably, participants in the quality assurance movement end up with multiple memberships in overlapping organizations, which may facilitate international dialogue but may also lead to an excessive number of annual meetings, duplication, and confusion, not to mention budgetary strain.

International Validation and Rankings

"Consumers" of education (students, parents, employers) are demanding some kind of certification of institutions and the qualifications they award. Mechanisms for establishing international comparability of qualifications are still new and largely untested. In the long run, the establishment of qualifications frameworks and endeavors like the

Tuning Project are likely to have enormous international impact. In the interim, some universities look to accreditation agencies based in other countries to validate the quality of their degree programs and provide some level of international credibility.

Despite sensitivities about the importance of national culture in higher education, a number of quality assurance agencies operate outside their countries (or region) of origin with increasing frequency. Specialized program accreditors such as the US-based Association to Advance Collegiate Schools of Business (AACSB) and the Accreditation Board for Engineering and Technology (ABET) as well as the European Quality Improvement System (EQUIS) are now evaluating and accrediting universities throughout the world (OECD, 2004). US regional associations regularly receive requests for accreditation from foreign institutions, and each organization responds differently, in accordance with its own guidelines (Eaton, 2004). The effect of the increasing reach of these agencies is likely to be greater standardization of programs and an endorsement with growing international recognition and influence, with prejudice toward the paradigms used in the North.

In the absence of other forms of international certification, university rankings have helped many individuals to order the vast international higher education landscape. Once only the scourge of the United States, international rankings now position universities through the world on long, eagerly awaited lists. Few educators would defend rankings as a reflection of quality, but where a university falls in the rankings is often interpreted as a measure of its quality by the larger public. Furthermore, rankings have the perverse effect of sometimes persuading university administrators to divert effort and resources to develop characteristics that will affect its position in the rankings and, not necessarily, its quality (Thompson, 2008).

Both the number of published rankings and their influence have grown. The Shanghai Jiao Tong University rankings, first published in 2003, have had (perhaps) the greatest international impact. This ranking emphasizes research output, which gives it greater credibility within the academic community than rankings shaped by student surveys or staff-student ratios. Moving universities into the top level of the Shanghai Jiao Tong rankings has even become a goal of national policy in several countries (Usher, 2009).

Capacity Building
During the last few decades, acceptance of quality assurance schemes has grown considerably. Where they were once seen in many countries as an affront to institutional and national autonomy, there is greater

recognition of the value of this process in meeting the challenges that globalization has presented to higher education.

Yet, as with nearly all aspects of the quality assurance movement, participants and stakeholders must trust the process. This means well-planned and well-executed self-studies, audits, and peer evaluations. As this process is new in so many countries, few people possess the knowledge, skill, or experience to implement it. The shortage of human resources prepared to undertake and manage complex activities, like self-studies and peer reviews, has become a serious challenge to building successful quality assurance programs worldwide.

UNESCO has partnered with the World Bank to create the Global Initiative for Quality Assurance Capacity (GIQAC), which will be another supranational agency that will include members of many of the regional and international quality assurance networks. The World Bank will allocate significant funding during the next few years to provide technical assistance to governments, agencies, and universities (especially in developing nations) to "establish, develop, or reform QA [quality assurance] systems, processes, and mutual recognition arrangements" as well as provide specialized training and support exchanges for quality assurance professional staff (World Bank, 2009).

The Influence of Free-Trade Negotiations
Professional bodies responsible for validating the quality of university programs and, often, licensure have also been actively involved in developing frameworks for the mutual recognition of qualifications, frequently in conjunction with free-trade negotiations. Agreements between nations are encouraged but not always easy to establish. Within the North Atlantic Free Trade Agreement (NAFTA), Canada and Mexico have agreed to recognize engineering qualifications as long as the engineer has the specified education, examinations, and experience; only Texas has approved the agreement in the United States. Requirements for architecture have been recognized by Canada and more American states but not Mexico. Reciprocal recognition between the Canadian Institute of Chartered Accountants and its counterpart institute in New Zealand resulted from agreement on guidelines for professional qualifications and a model curriculum (Knight, 2004b). These agreements are being accomplished very slowly, field by field, country by country.

The General Agreement on Trade in Services (GATS) negotiations are likely to have future bearing on the portability of professional qualifications. These negotiations have been extremely controversial. The encouragement for giving more latitude to market forces to shape higher education could result in more for-profit institutions bypassing nascent international quality-control mechanisms. The terms of fair trade do not necessarily translate into good educational policy or practice, yet pressure on nation states to liberalize "trade in educational services" is likely to increase. Developing countries, unable to meet growing demand for access to higher education, are most vulnerable to the entrance of for-profit providers and least well positioned to regulate their activities (UNESCO, 2004).

Conclusion

Quality assurance in higher education has risen to the top of the policy agenda in many nations. Initially, nations scrambled to set up agencies and establish standards, procedures, and schedules. Many countries are still in this early stage of design and implementation. Countries with more experience are now wrestling with the deeper issues and complexities of quality assurance in higher education. Diversity has certainly created a richer environment of institutions, students, and opportunities, but it presents enormous challenges for establishing appropriate standards or benchmarks that can be compared from one institution to another and from one country to another.

There are risks as well as benefits in the growing quality movement. International practices (often developed in North America and Europe) influence the development of quality assurance schemes everywhere but may not always be the most useful means for evaluating higher education in developing countries. The process must focus on realistic objectives and appropriate goals for each local environment—if not, quality assurance will swiftly become a political or bureaucratic process with limited value.

Much depends on the quality of higher education—with both private good and public good to be gained. Yet quality remains difficult to define and subsequently problematic to measure. Furthermore, quality will have different meanings in different environments.

Postsecondary education has to prepare graduates with new skills, a broad knowledge base, and a range of competencies to enter a more complex and interdependent world. Agencies throughout the world are struggling to define these goals in terms that can be understood and shared across borders and cultures.

Since the 1980s there has been extensive and ongoing discussion within nations, within regions, and across the globe, to find new ways of assuring the many stakeholders involved that quality is being evaluated and monitored. What has resulted at the very least is an explosion of new agencies and a sufficient number of new acronyms—INQAAHE,

GIQAC, ENQA, EQAR, QAA, CHEA, NOQA,[1] among others.

Schemes for quality assurance are now accepted as a fundamental part of providing higher education, but national, regional, and international efforts need to be integrated. One very important question moving forward is whether this integration will lead to the dominance of a "Northern" model for quality assurance that disregards the diverse conditions of higher education worldwide. The need for international cooperation is clear, but the dialogue is really only just beginning.

---

1 International Network for Quality Assurance Agencies in Higher Education, Global Initiative for Quality Assurance Capacity, European Network for Quality Assurance, European Quality Assurance Register, Quality Assurance Agency for Higher Education, Council for Higher Education Accreditation, Nordic Quality Assurance Agency.

5

Financing Higher Education

The financing of higher education in the first decade of the 21st century has been dominated by two phenomena. First, higher education is increasingly important to economies, individuals, and societies striving for democracy and social justice. Second, the cost of higher education is rising significantly. Massification, driven by demographics and the higher percentage of students completing secondary school and desiring higher education, is driving up unit costs for instruction and research. The overall cost pressure is growing at rates beyond which most countries' public revenue streams can keep pace. This is a critical trend, given that public revenue has traditionally accounted for some, if not all, of the higher education expenses in a majority of the world's countries.

These developments would be challenging under the best of circumstances. However, the current global economic crisis exacerbates financial concerns in higher education across the globe. The situation is characterized by slowing economic growth in many developing countries, contracting economies in many high-income countries, and "sharply tighter credit conditions." "Coming on the heels of the food and fuel price shock," and spreading rapidly through tightly interconnected trade and banking channels around the world, the effects of the crisis "are likely to cut into government revenues and governments' ability to meet education, health, and gender goals" (World Bank, 2008). Although the extent, nature, and duration of these circumstances will vary from country to country, higher education around the world is sure to feel the negative impact of these developments.

Worldwide Trends in the Financing of Higher Education

Eight trends sit at the heart of this analysis. Each of these trends has economic, political, and social roots as well as consequences. In turn, these trends, while varying by context, form the setting for higher education's widespread financial austerity and policy solutions. In summary, these trends are:

1. *The increasingly knowledge-based economies of most countries:* higher education in many places is increasingly viewed as a major engine of economic development. In countries with more broadly based innovation systems, these elements are clearly recognized as a key contributor to the advancement of cutting-edge knowledge.

2. *An increasing demand for higher education by individuals and by families for their children:* this increase in demand may go well beyond the capacity that knowledge economies can absorb, even leading to high numbers of unemployed and underemployed college and university graduates. However, the extent of this rapidly rising demand for higher education is due in part to increased competition for good jobs and employers' use of higher education degrees as a screening device for allocating the best jobs.

3. *Unit, or per student, costs that rise faster than inflation rates:* this cost increase is magnified by rising enrollment pressures that drive the total higher education cost in most countries beyond rates of inflation.

4. *The inability of government tax revenues to keep pace with rapidly rising higher education costs:* this failure results from the difficulty most economies face in raising taxes both cost-effectively and progressively, as well as the increasing competition from other political and social public needs.

5. *Increasing globalization:* among many other things, globalization contributes both the increasing demand for higher education and the inadequate government revenue to support it. The declining tax revenue is partly a function of production and capital in one country being transported to areas of lower wage/lower tax jurisdictions.

6. *The increasing reliance in almost all countries on nontax revenues:* known as cost-sharing, parents and/or students are increasingly responsible for tuition and other fees that contribute to higher education revenue requirements. Tuition fees are emerging even in Europe, which was long the bastion of free public higher education, and are increasingly found even in former Communist or Socialist countries. Tuition fees are also ideologically and politi-

cally contested even where they play a relatively minor role in the total expenses incurred by parents and/or students. Tuition fees serve as a flash point in the larger political contests arising from the inability of governments to meet the needs of all the people.

7. *The increasing importance of financial assistance:* student-loan schemes are especially important and more cost-effective for maintaining higher education participation and access in the face of increasing parent and student expenses.

8. *An increasing liberalization—that is, a free market and private-sector orientation—of economies:* this liberalization is leading many governments to respond to higher education's financial challenges by corporatizing and privatizing public universities, implementing new public management tools for public university budgets and financing (Amaral, Meek, and Larsen, 2003; Herbst, 2007), and encouraging private colleges and universities.

The worldwide surge in private higher education over the last several decades is a significant development, and the financing models for this sector have implications for institutional stakeholders, including students and the broader society. In most cases around the world, private tertiary institutions depend on tuition revenue. Tuition dependence means that these colleges and universities must manage their enrollments and expenditures extremely carefully and that they are often financially unable to weather unexpected enrollment downturns. Because they rely on tuition, these institutions often target only those student populations that can afford to pay fees, which can "exacerbate class or other divisions in society" (Altbach, 1999, p. 5).

A small number of cases around the world possess other sources of funding for private higher education apart from tuition. In places where private universities may be owned by individuals or families (such as in Colombia, the Republic of Korea, and Japan), the personal wealth of the owner(s) may be a significant financial resource for such institutions. The United States stands out as an unusual example of a context where private institutions enjoy significant financial contributions from alumni as well as individual and corporate donors. American students attending accredited private colleges and universities may also bring public support with them, in the form of federally administered student grants and loans. Government support for private higher education also exists in India, and to a lesser extent in places like the Philippines and Japan (Altbach, 1999). For the most part, though, private higher education institutions around the world are responsible for generating their own resources (Altbach, 1999). Indeed the active generation of profit is now a critical activity in the corporate and for-profit higher education sectors, which have grown considerably over the last decade in a wide variety of contexts.

Higher Educational Austerity

The immediate effect of these trends on the financing of higher educa-tion (again, varying by country) is a state of austerity in universities, postsecondary education institutions, and national higher education systems. These nearly universal—and growing—higher education con-ditions have affected:

- *Universities and other postsecondary education institutions:* over-crowded lecture halls; restive and otherwise unhappy faculty; insufficient or outdated library holdings, computing, and Inter-net connectivity; a deterioration of physical plants; less time and support for faculty research; and a widely assumed loss in the quality of both teaching and learning as well as research
- *National systems of higher education:* capacity constraints; the inabil-ity to accommodate all graduates who are eligible for and desire further study; faculty "brain drain" as the most talented faculty move to countries with fewer financial troubles; and an inability to compete in the global knowledge economy
- *Students:* tuition fees where there used to be none, in addition to the rising costs of student living; the need to work while study-ing, go into debt, or both, for those fortunate enough to find a place at all.

This downturn has been most crippling in sub-Saharan Africa but is serious throughout the developing countries, as well as in many of the so-called *countries in transition*—such as those emerging from the former Soviet Union. In Europe and Latin America, as well, there is serious overcrowding, and students are unable to find seats in lecture theaters. Teaching is often reduced to didactics and rarely includes dis-cussion and opportunity to ask questions. Other manifestations include the loss of secure faculty positions and faculty morale and students leaving higher education with burdensome levels of debt. These down-ward trends can be seen in countries as affluent as the United States, the United Kingdom, Sweden, and Canada.

Beyond this sheer austerity, and especially noticeable in countries that have moved toward the political right, is a diminution of trust in government and in the public sector generally, including (perhaps especially) public universities. This distrust of government goes beyond insufficient public budgets and results in a loss of the esteem in which public universities were once held.

Policy Solutions on the Cost Side

In response to these financial pressures and demands for accountability, universities and national systems have sought solutions. Solutions on the cost side include increasing class sizes and teaching loads, deferring maintenance, substituting lower-cost part-time faculty for higher-cost full-time faculty, and dropping low-priority programs. These solutions are difficult, academically problematic, and heavily contested, especially by the faculty and their political allies, who frequently reject the claims that public revenues are insufficient and who may not understand the academic priorities of their governments or university leaders. Cost-side solutions are most injurious to participation and accessibility when they limit the capacity of public institutions and force increasing numbers of young men and women into higher-priced (and often lower-quality) private colleges and universities. Some students may be required to pay higher fees than others, even when enrolled in the same public university. Students who lack family resources for private instruction and/or living expenses may be forced earlier into the workforce.

Strategic cost-side solutions, on the other hand, use available resources more wisely to support academic quality, capacity, social equity, and the needs of students, employers, and society alike. The management of governmental agencies and the norms of civil service employment—which prize employment continuity above all else—are generally incompatible with many strategic cost-side solutions to the financial problems common among universities and other institutions of higher education. Typical issues with government agencies include laws, contracts and political considerations that forbid terminating staff, hiring part-time or temporary workers, contracting out services, carrying unspent funds forward from one fiscal year to the next, or shifting available funds from one budget category to another.

A clear shift has occurred in government laws and regulations dealing with public universities in the last decade or two in many Canadian provinces and virtually all American states, in some European countries (notably the Netherlands and the United Kingdom), and very recently in China and Japan—all in the direction of greater managerial autonomy and flexibility. These efforts have frequently transformed public universities from simple governmental agencies into *public corporations,* giving the management new authority and sometimes corporate-style governing boards coupled with new accountability requirements. These new developments for greater managerial autonomy and flexibility— essentially moving toward managerial models associated with private enterprise—are collectively referred to as *new public management* and are designed to maximize the university's teaching and research outputs for the public as well as to provide incentives for maximizing nongovernmental revenue. Universities, for example, rather than the ministry or the state budget office, may be given authority to:

- establish wage and salary policies (formerly reserved for the ministry or parliament and government financial, personnel, and civil service bureaucracies);
- reallocate expenditures from one category to another in response to institutional priorities (formerly generally forbidden);
- carry forward unspent funds from one fiscal period to the next, thus encouraging savings and institutional investment and discouraging spending for no reason other than avoidance of loss or the appearance of an excessive budget;
- enter into contracts with outside agencies and businesses expeditiously and competitively (formerly too frequently politicized and prolonged); and
- receive and own assets and sometimes even borrow and incur debt (not allowed in ordinary government agencies).

Cost-side solutions to financial shortfalls—after deferring expenditures on new plant, equipment, and facilities maintenance—may seek to lower the average per-student costs of instruction by increasing average class size, increasing teaching loads, and substituting lower-cost junior or part-time faculty for higher-cost senior faculty. All such solutions are painful and are typically resisted by faculty and staff and their political allies. However, the gap from the diverging trajectories of higher education costs and available revenues is simply too wide to be closed by further cuts in expenditures alone, even with some of the more radical cost-side solutions like mergers and distance education. Finally, in many or even in most countries, the low-hanging fruit of easy expenditure cuts and other efficiency measures have long since been taken, leaving only the most difficult and educationally problematic solutions on the cost side. In short, higher education in almost all countries must turn to nongovernmental revenues to supplement the increasingly insufficient revenue available from governments.

Policy Solutions on the Revenue Side: Cost Sharing

Revenue supplementation as an alternative to cost cutting and as a preferred route to financial viability may take the form of faculty and institutional entrepreneurship, as in the selling of specialized and marketable teaching or scholarship, the renting of university facilities, or the commercial marketing of research discoveries. It may take the form of fund-raising, appealing to alumni and other donors. Or—and the most sustainable and potentially lucrative—it may take the form of what has come to be known as cost sharing. The term refers to a shift of at least some of the higher educational cost burden from governments, or taxpayers, to parents and/or students (D. B. Johnstone, 1986, 2004, 2006). Cost sharing is thus both a statement of fact—that is, that the costs of higher education are shared among stakeholders—and also a reference to a policy shift of some of these costs from a predominant (sometimes a virtually exclusive) reliance on governments.

Cost sharing is most associated with tuition fees and "user charges," especially for room and board. However, a policy shift in the direction of greater cost sharing can take several forms:

1. *The beginning of tuition (where higher education was formerly free or nearly so):* this would be the case in China in 1997, the United Kingdom in 1998, and Austria in 2001.

2. *The addition of a special tuition-paying track while maintaining free higher education for the regularly admitted, state-supported students:* such a dual-track tuition-fee scheme preserves the legal and political appearance of free higher education while introducing some new revenue. The preservation of the status quo of "free higher education" is particularly important (and is frequently enshrined in a constitution or a framework law) in many transition economies—such as the Russian Federation, most of eastern and central Europe, and other countries that were once part of the former Soviet Union, as well as countries in East Africa with their legacy of African socialism.

3. *A very sharp rise in tuition (where public-sector tuition already exists):* a shift in the direction of greater cost sharing requires that the rise in tuition carried by students and/or parents be greater than the rise in institutional costs generally in order for the government's, or taxpayer's, share to be lessened. This has been the case recently in most of the states in the United States and most of the provinces in Canada.

4. *The imposition of "user charges," or fees, to recover the expenses of what were once governmentally or institutionally provided (and heavily subsidized) residence and dining halls:* this has been happening in most countries, including virtually all the transitional economy countries, and notably and controversially, most of the countries in sub-Saharan Africa, where subsidized living costs at one time absorbed the bulk of higher education budgets. In the Nordic countries of Sweden, Norway, Finland, and Denmark, where higher education remains "free," the expenses to students are exclusively the costs of student living. Student living costs are very high in these particular countries and are "shared" neither by taxpayers

nor (at least officially) by parents. Rather, they are borne mainly or entirely by the students, largely in the form of student loans (costs still shared by the taxpayer in the form of repayment subsidies).

5. *The elimination or reduction of student grants or scholarships:* this strategy is sometimes approached simply by "freezing" grant or loan levels, or holding them constant in the face of general inflation, which then erodes their real value. This began happening to the once generous grants in Britain (which were later abandoned altogether) and has happened to the value of the maintenance grants in most of the transitional countries of the former Soviet Union and eastern and central Europe, as well as in Asia and in many countries in Africa.

6. *An increase in the effective cost recovery on student loans:* several approaches can be taken in this vein. More-effective cost recovery can be accomplished through a reduction of the subsidies on student loans (similar to the diminution in the value of nonrepayable grants). It might also be accomplished through an increase in interest rates, a reduction in the length of time that interest is not charged, or through a cut in the numbers of loans for which the repayments, for any number of reasons, are forgiven. The effective cost recovery might also be accomplished through a tightening of collections, or a reduction in the instances of default (as in the United States in the 1990s).

7. *The limitation of capacity in the low or tuition-free public sector together with the official encouragement (and frequently some public subsidization) of a tuition-dependent private higher education sector:* number of countries—notably Japan, the Republic of Korea, the Philippines, Indonesia, Brazil, and other countries in Latin America and East Asia—have avoided much of what would otherwise have been significant governmental expenditure on higher education by keeping the public sector small, elite, and selective. Much of the cost of expanded participation is thus shifted to parents and students through the encouragement of a substantial and growing private higher education sector.

Although cost sharing may take on these different forms, the imposition of, and/or large increases in, tuition fees provides the greatest financial impact. Tuition fees can be both financially significant, ongoing, and designed to regularly increase, thus keeping pace with the inevitably rising per student costs of instruction. However, a rebate may be needed in the form of grants or discounts to preserve accessibility. Also, unlike most forms of faculty entrepreneurship, tuition fees do not divert faculty from the core instructional mission.

Many observers also assert that higher tuition has the positive effect of improving the quality of teaching and the relevance of the curriculum, providing another key benefit. Yet, tuition fees are also the most politically charged and ideologically resisted form of cost sharing and have therefore become a symbol of the conflict between people who believe that government must continue to provide higher education free of any charge and those who recognized the great unlikelihood of government coming up with annually increasing revenue and who thus accept the imperative of cost sharing.

Competing and Compelling Public Needs
National, global, political, and ideological contexts play a key role in shaping the trends that determine both the financing of higher education and policy solutions for the resulting austerity. At one end of the spectrum, there are groups who accept the appropriateness of governmental control of virtually all institutionalized means of production (including universities and colleges), as well as governmental allocation of resources, the establishment of prices, and the remuneration of workers. High levels of taxation, governmental regulation, and public employment are acceptable, and the emphasis is placed on the income disparities, economic instability, competition, and commercialism associated with markets and capitalism.

Toward the other end of the continuum are the views associated with the desire to diminish the size of the public sector, including publicly owned and financed higher education. Here, government, including both politicians and civil servants, is considered less productive and often self-serving. In keeping with this mistrust of governmental institutions (including public universities) and governmental employees (as well as faculty and staff of these public universities), groups at this end of the political spectrum tend to be more critical of what they perceive to be governmental waste and more insistent on greater measures of accountability. At the same time, there is greater acceptance of the economic instabilities and disparities in income and wealth that follow capitalism as a necessary price for the dynamism and high productivity of private enterprise.

As in any portrayal of a range, most countries, governments, and polities are somewhere near the center but always feel pressures from the extremes. Universities—especially public, but private universities as well—always operate in a country-specific political and economic context as well as in an historical context and in an increasingly globalized international context. The financial problems as well as the possible solutions and their likelihood of adoption all occur within these larger

social and political contexts. Almost everywhere, higher education institutions, systems, and the societies in which they operate are faced with
a complex set of problems that turn on the common issues of inexora-
bly rising per student costs, increasing enrollments, expanded roles for
higher education, more demands for institutional accountability, limits
on governmental taxing capabilities, and lengthy queues of socially and
politically compelling competing public needs. There are many difficult
choices to make and an unquestionable need to identify and implement
workable solutions that make sense for each country's unique social
and political context.

Conclusion

Ultimately, the increasing reach of tuition fees and other forms of
revenue diversification, as well as the pressures for accountability or
institutional autonomy, are mostly attributable to three fundamentally
important aspects of higher education around the world today. First,
a virtually universal higher educational production function accompa-
nies a trajectory of rising unit costs. Second, the increasing demand
for higher education in many contexts exacerbates this rising trajectory of costs, or revenue needs. And third, governmental revenues in
most countries are unable (or at least unlikely) to keep up with these
rising revenue requirements. These factors are now currently playing
out in the midst of a profound global economic crisis, which presents
the higher education sector around the world with challenges to meet
current needs and plan for future developments. Finding ways to sustain
quality provision of higher education, with appropriate access for qualified students at affordable rates for students, families, and other key
stakeholders, will require careful planning that attends to both short-
and long-term needs. Furthermore, these efforts will likely only succeed
insofar as they combine flexibility, innovation, and creative collaboration
among relevant constituents, while sharing a common commitment to
a vibrant and sustainable higher education sector.

6

Private Higher Education and Privatization

At the time of UNESCO's last global overview of tertiary education, private higher education had already surged globally. This expansion has continued, intensifying and spreading to additional regions and countries. Today, some 30 percent of global higher education enrollment is in the private sector (Gürüz, 2008; PROPHE, 2008). Additionally, the extent and importance of the growth of this new sector is attracting more attention (though still insufficient) than it was 10 years ago (Altbach and D. C. Levy, 2005).

Privatization means many things in higher education. While a public university is generally considered to be an institution funded by and responsive to a local, provincial, or national government, private institutions do not reflect a consistent model. Private institutions may operate entirely with private assets or partially with public funds; they may be for-profit or nonprofit; they may be accountable to the host government or operate completely outside of local regulation; they may have owners or investors or operate as foundations. The trend toward privatization also has meaning in the public sector where institutions are being encouraged (if not required) to decrease their dependence on public funds, to be more "entrepreneurial" and competitive, and to demonstrate efficient professional management. Some of these ideas would have seemed ludicrous a few decades ago but are now fundamental to strategic plans and new policy almost everywhere.

Few of the themes of the present UNESCO report can be adequately understood without attention to the private sector of higher education—as most of the growth in higher education worldwide is in the private sector. Private higher education has had a significant impact on the discussions of quality, equity, new learning modes and, perhaps most of all, access. Private higher education is less central to themes of knowledge development, research, and planning; but as governments and international organizations, including UNESCO, increasingly realize the growing role of this sector, they are seeking ways to integrate and shape it more.

The growing importance of private institutions and the tendency to privatize the public sector are key international trends. Indeed, the two types of privatization interrelate and affect one another.

Growth: Regional Dimensions

Well into the 20th century, higher education was overwhelmingly public—in regard to enrollment, legal status, government-centered standardized rules, finance, and dominant normative orientations. In fact, higher education had become more public over a long period of time.

Growth from elite to "mass" higher education obviously occurred first in the developed countries and almost always in the public sector, Japan being the striking exception. But in the developing and postcommunist countries, the transformation occurs mostly in the private sector. It is in that part of the world that private growth is most notable. Fewer and fewer countries (Bhutan, Cuba, the Democratic People's Republic of Korea) host no private higher education. In contrast, as we will see, in many countries an absolute majority of higher education enrollments is found in the private sector.

Looking regionally and working in descending order beginning with the regions with the largest private sector, Asia comes first (PROPHE, 2008). East Asia has the largest concentration of countries with proportionally larger private sectors. Countries with over 70 percent of enrollments in private higher education include Indonesia, Japan, the Philippines, and the Republic of Korea. Malaysia approaches 50 percent. China and much of Southeast Asia (e.g., Cambodia and Viet Nam) remain below 15 percent but are experiencing rapid expansion, although total cohort enrollment rates are still quite low. Thailand and New Zealand are just marginally below 15 percent, Australia around 3 percent. South Asia sees striking private growth, with India above 30 percent (Gupta, Levy, and Powar, 2008) and Pakistan not too far behind. Toward western Asia data are spottier but Kazakhstan and the Islamic Republic of Iran are roughly half private.

Latin America has a longer widespread history than Asia of dual-sector development. By the late 1970s Latin America was already approaching 35 percent private enrollment (D. C. Levy, 1986), and today it is closer to 45 percent. Again, there is variation by country, but now few cases are under 20 percent. Countries with majority private sectors include Brazil, Chile, El Salvador, Guatemala, and Peru. Where the private sector has recently lost share, notably in Colombia, the cause is not numerical slippage on the private side but sudden growth on the public side, largely through elevation of institutions into the "higher education" category. Argentina is alone among major countries and systems in maintaining a large public majority.

Compared to Asia, Latin America has had more stable private higher education shares, but the most striking case of stable shares is the United States—hovering between 20 and 25 percent for decades (compared to roughly 50 percent enrollment in the mid-20th century). US proportional stagnation, juxtaposed to global growth, leaves the present US private higher education enrollment share below the global share, though obviously US private higher education is the most important in the world—with the largest absolute private enrollment and towering above other systems in its graduate enrollment, research activity, and finance.

In central and eastern Europe, Estonia, Georgia, Poland, Latvia, and especially Poland, have passed 20 percent (Slancheva and Levy, 2007). The jump from an entirely public sector to a substantial private sector in the five-year period following the fall of communism marks the most dramatic concentrated growth seen in any region. Still, some countries in this region have not experienced more than a small-percent increase in private-sector enrollment (Wells, Sadlak, and Vlasceanu, 2007). At least as importantly, stagnation has characterized the last 10 years, and some countries have actually had declines in private enrollments. There is a demographic challenge, and as cohort numbers fall, many private higher education institutions could shrink or die off.

Notwithstanding its private precursors (including colonial ones), sub-Saharan Africa has come late to modern private higher education but the growth is notable (Mabizela, Levy, and Otieno, forthcoming). Breakthroughs began in the 1980s, but it was in the 1990s that there was major and widespread growth. Most countries host private institutions, with Anglophone Africa greatly outpacing Francophone Africa. Kenya, Nigeria, Uganda, and others are among the countries with important private sectors, yet most countries' private share remains comparatively small. Kenya, having ascended to one-fifth private, is a rare African example of slippage, not due to demographics so much as public universities taking in "private" paying students (Otieno and Levy, 2007). Nowhere in Africa is the private sector more than one-fourth of total higher education enrollment (Mabizela, 2007). Yet, the sector is growing and garnering more and more attention.

Western Europe remains the developed region with mostly just marginal private–higher education sectors. Privatization in the last 10 and more years has been more about changes within the public sector. Portugal has been the major exception, once reaching the 30 percent range for private share of total enrollment. Spain has some academically prominent private higher education institutions. The Netherlands (majority private) and Belgium (minority private) have long been exceptions, too, but their private sectors have operated mostly with government funds and similar sets of rules. Yet even in western Europe there is change. The United Kingdom's sole private university (1981) may be joined by nonuniversity institutions, as is already the Norwegian case. At another extreme, startling announcements have appeared of philanthropic pledges by wealthy businessmen for Italy and Germany. Germany reflects a regional (and global) tendency that private higher education institutional proliferation exists mostly outside universities. A common but upper-end manifestation is the freestanding MBA (master of business administration).

Beginning to register private higher education enrollment is the Middle East (and North Africa). "American universities" have dotted the horizon in Egypt, Jordan, Lebanon, and elsewhere, with Kurdistan joining this group. Israel was one of the first countries in the region to allow the development of a private sector. Turkey hosted private institutions until the 1970s, when they were closed down; this sector is re-emerging anew only recently. Arab governments plan and promote private universities, often through agreements with European and US universities. Astonishing is the private surge across the gamut of political regimes, as shown by Egypt, Oman, Saudi Arabia, and the Syrian Arab Republic.

Types of Private Higher Education
There has been great growth in private higher education, even considering regional variations. However, private higher education is far from being a homogenous sector. It is important to understand the phenomenon by identifying its major forms. Four categories are elite and semielite, identity, demand absorbing, and for-profit, though there is some category overlap. One can tinker with how to place and regard an assortment of cross-border relationships and private/public partnerships. Restricting the partnership label to formal agreements between private and public higher education institutions shows a tendency for the privates to be colleges, the universities to be public. Salient examples have arisen in China, India, South Africa, and other countries, even if partnerships between domestic and overseas institutions are left aside.

Identity Institutions
In much of the world, most of what we can call identity institutions has been religiously based. In fact, as with many nonprofit sectors, in education and beyond, the first wave of institutions often have religious foundations. Moreover, religious institutions appear more reliably non-profit than are many other private institutions.

For Latin America, Europe, and later Africa, early private universities were usually Catholic. In the United States, the early colleges, such as Harvard and Columbia, were tied to Protestant denominations.

In addition, identity institutions may be based on gender. Although there were once single-sex institutions for men and women, today there are few remaining for men only and a decreasing number of women's institutions.

Although religion defines a major sector within private higher education, two changes have recently modified the picture. One is the increasing mix of religions, including many with evangelical or Islamic orientations. Where Muslims are a minority in the population, private institutions can offer an attractive option; where they are a majority, religion may find expression in the public sector.

A set of values may make institutions with ethnic or religious orientation more attractive. The values of specific populations or subsectors may clash with the general perception of dominant values at public universities. Where these values stress authority, safety, specific ideas of morality and the like, they make institutions more attractive to conservative groups, in particular parents of daughters. Private enrollments tend to be higher for women than men (PROPHE). In fact, women's colleges are another important subtype. There is a longstanding tradition of women's private higher education in the United States and a similar significantly prominent trend in Asia (Purcell, Helms, and Rumbley, 2005).

Elite and Semielite
US tradition notwithstanding, the notion of a widespread nexus between private and elite in higher education is highly misleading. It is important for our global analysis to remember that the US case is unique. The US higher education system is the only one in the world in which private higher education dominates the top tier. Few other systems have any private elite universities. For the two most prominent global rankings of universities, 63 universities make the top hundred in both rankings, and 21 of those are private. However, each of those 21 privates is a US institution. The two rankings are the *Times Higher Education* Supplement World University Rankings and the Shanghai Jiao Tong

Academic Ranking of World Universities. The private non-US institutions beneath the top are mostly European universities with ambiguous private/public status and a couple of Japanese private universities. Relevant, too, in the poor private representation is that the developed world has been overwhelmingly public in higher education (outside Japan and the United States). By the standards used to classify world-ranked elite or "world class" universities (Altbach and Balán, 2007) the private sector outside the United States hardly registers.

The private presence is much stronger in the semielite category. These may be among the leading higher education institutions in their country, as national rankings may show. Below the very top, semielite private universities may compete with a set of good but not top-tier public universities. Bangladesh, Pakistan, Poland, Thailand, and Turkey are just a few national examples where this is the case. There is still a legitimate case to be made that much of Latin America has elite private universities that attract best-prepared students over the public universities, at least in many fields (D. C. Levy, 1986) and even increasingly doing research and graduate education.

Semielite institutions stand between elite and nonelite and thus have above-average selectivity and status. Their salient characteristics appear to include priority on good practical teaching or training and not the kind of research that defines world-class universities (although they may do good applied research). The social-class of students may be quite high, often including accomplished graduates of the secondary system, and also including those capable of paying private tuitions. Some, but not nearly all, semielite institutions, are niche institutions concentrated in a given field of study or on a cluster of related fields, especially business. Most semielite institutions are explicitly and often successfully job oriented.

Semielite institutions are also often economically and politically conservative, Western-oriented, even US oriented. They seek foreign ties and recognition and often teach courses in English. They favor markets and scoff at dependency on the state. Many are quite entrepreneurial and some have serious academic aspirations. They are very private: their income is almost strictly nonpublic, led by tuition; they pride themselves on tight businesslike management, and they aim to serve those pursuing rational self-interest. Given the lack of world-class private higher education (outside the United States), the semielite surge is particularly noteworthy, especially as it appears to fit all regions.

Demand-Absorbing Institutions
Notwithstanding the importance of semielite growth, the largest increase

in private higher education is distinctly nonelite. This is mostly "demand absorbing" as student demand for access to higher education has exceeded the supply of slots available at public and private institutions, even where that supply is also expanding. Contributing to the proliferation of private nonelite institutions has been a lax regulatory environment in many countries. In every country in which private higher education becomes the majority sector (and in many where it becomes a large minority sector), it is this demand-absorbing subsector that has been numerically significant. It tends to be both the largest private subsector and the fastest-growing one.

This private subsector is often comprised of institutions not labeled "university." Furthermore, many private institutions labeled "university" are, rather, technical or vocational institutions, on the border between for-profit and nonprofit.

Demand-absorbing private higher education is commonly denounced aggressively. Much of the denunciation is valid but sometimes applicable to low-level public institutions as well. For scholarship and informed policymaking, however, it is crucial to recognize two subcategories of these nonelite private institutions. The larger subcategory is indeed very dubious in academic quality, seriousness, effort, and transparency. Yet, the other nonelite type is serious, responsible, and usually job oriented (Cao, 2007). This nonelite group has opportunity for both growth and improvement. This type of institution is often well managed and may even show certain traits of some semielite institutions. More empirical study of nonelite institutions is needed. In any event, both the serious and dubious demand-absorbing institutions tend to enroll comparatively disadvantaged students.

For-Profit Sector
Most for-profit institutions could be subsumed into the nonelite category. It is common in Africa that private higher education divides into comparatively substantial religious, for-profit, and demand-absorbing subsectors. These subsectors can overlap as with Mozambique's religious and South Africa's for-profits both being demand absorbing (Mabizela, 2007). For-profits are *not* academically elite institutions, though some may have semielite characteristics. Yet, many for-profits are exploitative institutions, taking advantage of unmet demand and delivering a poor-quality education.

Legally, for-profit institutions constitute a small higher education subsector, but there is notable growth here in all developing regions. Moreover, the for-profits represent the fastest-growing sector within US higher education, already incorporating some 8 to 10 percent of total enrollment, or more than one-third of total private enrollment, though concentrated in programs of just one to two years.

Furthermore, a growing part of the for-profit expansion is taking place internationally and operating across national boundaries. Laureate is the largest international company operating (Kinser and D. C. Levy, 2006) in this area. Most ubiquitous in Latin America, Laureate buys dominant shares of existing universities.

Whitney International and the Apollo Group (owner of the University of Phoenix) also operate abroad. Other for-profits—Kaplan and Corinthian Colleges, for example—find their niche within the United States.

There are other examples of for-profits in addition to large corporate-run universities. A small number of for-profit institutions are family owned and operated. Other types of for-profit activity are emerging, as universities based in the United States, United Kingdom, Australia, and elsewhere establish profitable cross-border partnerships with a private local partner. Universities that may be public in their home country operate as private enterprises abroad.

The for-profit sector reflects many key characteristics of commercial industry—charging fees for service (it is tuition-based) and rarely obtaining any public support. When not family operated, the sector is run mostly on a business model, with power and authority concentrated in boards and chief executives; faculty hold little authority or influence; and students are seen as consumers.

Privatization
Related, but not the same as the rise of private higher education, is the privatization in all sectors of postsecondary education. By privatization, we mean the necessity for institutions and systems to earn income to pay for (at least part of) their operation. Privatization can include, as has been discussed in this trend report, higher tuition fees and other charges to students so that a part of the cost of education is shared by students. This process can also mean earning funds from consulting, licensing, selling intellectual property of various kinds, university and industry collaboration that produces income, renting university property, and many other sources of income. Privatization has become a necessity in many institutions and systems because of budgetary problems created by massification with simultaneous reductions in public investment; it has been legitimized (in part) by the "private-good" arguments for higher education. Countries such as Australia and China have been explicit in asking universities to earn more of their own operating expenses by generating their own revenue. Others have more indirectly made privatization necessary

by inadequately funding the postsecondary sector and forcing institutions to seek alternatives.

Privatization seems to be a significant force in much of the world. Some critics have argued that forcing greater emphasis on revenue-generating activities creates general problems for the traditional roles of higher education, with a negative impact on both teaching and research. Others point to the benefits of academe embracing market forces and opportunities as well as to the need for higher education to pay for more of its costs.

Conclusion

Notwithstanding the salient differences among types of private higher education, some generalizations can be made. It is highly probable that growth will take place in all parts of this sector. Most growth will take place in the developing world but in the developed world as well. Nonelite and functionally for-profit institutions are the fastest growing; semielite types are also expanding in number but on a smaller scale. The potential is less clear for other private models. Private higher education is not the same today as it was 10 or 25 years ago, and it is unlikely to remain as it is today into the future. But many basic types and patterns will persist. Further growth in absolute numbers and even in the portion of total higher education enrollments seems a near certainty.

7

The Centrality and Crisis of the Academic Profession

The growing tension between enrollment demand, constrained budgets, and greater accountability has resulted in a discouraging environment for the academic profession worldwide. No university can achieve success without well-qualified, committed academic staff. Neither an impressive campus nor an innovative curriculum will produce good results without great professors. Higher education worldwide focuses on the "hardware"—buildings, laboratories, and the like—at the expense of "software"—the people who make any academic institutions successful.

To understand the contemporary academic profession, it is useful to examine the status and working conditions of the academic profession worldwide. The academic profession is aging in many countries. In much of the world, half or more of the professoriate is getting close to retirement. In many countries, too few new PhDs are being produced to replace those leaving the profession, and many new doctorates prefer to work outside of academe. Too few incentives for advanced doctoral study and an uncertain employment market for new PhDs, along with inadequate financial support in many fields, deter enrollment and ensure that many students drop out of doctoral programs. Countries with rapidly growing higher education systems are especially hard hit. Viet Nam, for example, requires 12,000 more academics each year to meet expansion goals, and only 10 percent of the academic profession currently hold doctoral degrees. While the profession in the developed countries faces different challenges from those in developing nations, the professoriate faces significant difficulties everywhere.

Like higher education generally and largely as a result of massification, the academic profession has become differentiated and
segmented. It is hardly possible to describe the profession as a whole.
Academics who teach at research universities typically hold a doctoral
degree and have full-time appointments, with some expectation of
career advancement. Those employed at other kinds of universities
and other postsecondary institutions more frequently do not have
the highest academic qualifications, are paid less than their peers at
the top of the system, teach more, and in general have less adequate
working conditions. There are also vast differences among countries, and according to discipline. As sociologist Burton Clark noted,
academics occupy "small worlds, different worlds" (Clark, 1987). Academic salaries are highest in the wealthier countries and lowest in
the developing world. A recent study noted that average salaries are
in some cases as much as eight times higher in North America and
western Europe than in China and India, and some developing countries have salaries below them (Rumbley, Pacheco, and Altbach, 2008).
Working conditions, career structures, and access to good laboratories
and libraries also vary significantly in different tiers of the academic
system within a country and among nations as well.

Global examples of the current state of the academic profession will
illustrate contemporary realities. These examples are chosen to highlight significant themes.

The Rise of the Part-Time Profession

To be most effective, professors need to be truly engaged in teaching
and research. A significant proportion of profession members must
have full-time academic appointments and devote attention exclusively
to academic responsibilities and to the universities and colleges that
employ them.

The full-time professoriate is in retreat. Latin America is the home-
land of the part-time "taxicab" professor, rushing between teaching
jobs or between class and another profession. Except for Brazil, and a
few smaller universities elsewhere on the continent, in almost all Latin
American countries up to 80 percent of the professoriate is employed
part time. Paid a pittance, they have little commitment to the university or to students. It is not surprising that there are almost no Latin
American universities among the top 500. In addition, research productivity is a modest feature. In the United States, only half of newly
hired academics are full time on the "tenure track"—that is, scholars
who can hope for a career in higher education. The rest are part-time
"contingent" faculty who are paid poorly for each course and have few

benefits. A new class of full-time contract teachers has grown in recent years as a way for universities to ensure flexibility in staffing. Traditional tenure-track academic appointments tend to be most common in the upper-tier colleges and universities, thus increasing inequalities in the academic system as a whole. While most western European academics are full time, part-time and temporary staff are growing in number.

In many countries, universities now employ part-time professors who have full-time appointments at other institutions. Many eastern European countries, China, Viet Nam, Uganda, and others are examples of such a higher education sector. Academic salaries are sufficiently low, and the universities expect that faculty will earn extra funds to supplement their own incomes and in some cases to subsidize the university's own budget. At some Chinese universities, professors are expected to practice consulting and other outside work as part of their academic duties. In other cases, universities set up additional degree-granting colleges and ask the faculty to perform extra teaching at those schools, enhancing university revenues and individual salaries at the same time. It is also the case that professors at state universities in much of the world help to staff the burgeoning private higher education sector by "moonlighting."

The decline of a real full-time professoriate is undermining high-quality higher education. If professors cannot devote their full attention to teaching and research, working with students outside of the classroom, and participating in the governance of their universities, academic quality will decline. As the British say, "penny wise and pound foolish."

Deteriorating Qualifications

It is possible that up to half of the world's university teachers have only earned a bachelor's degree. No one knows for sure. What we do know is that the academic profession is growing rapidly, and facilities for advanced-degree study are not keeping up—nor are salary levels that encourage the "best and brightest" to join the professoriate. In China, the world's largest academic system, only 9 percent of the academic profession has doctorates (although 70 percent do in the top research universities). Thirty-five percent of Indian academics have doctoral qualifications. In many countries, significant parts of the profession have a bachelor's degree, and some have not even attained that basic degree. In most developing countries, only academic staff at the most prestigious universities hold a doctoral degree—usually under 10 percent of the total. The expansion of graduate (postgraduate) programs has been identified as a top priority worldwide, but expansion has been slow because the demand for basic access is so great. It is the case that qualified academics are not being produced fast enough to meet the demand.

Inadequate Compensation

It is no longer possible to lure the best minds to academe. A significant part of the problem is financial. Even before the current world financial crisis, academic salaries did not keep up with remuneration for highly trained professionals everywhere. Now, with tremendous financial pressures on higher education generally, the situation will no doubt deteriorate further. A recent study of academic salaries in 15 countries shows full-time academic staff can survive on their salaries (Rumbley, Pacheco, and Altbach, 2008). However, they do not earn much more than the average salary in their country. Relatively few of the most qualified young people undergo the rigorous education required for jobs in the top universities.

Highly trained individuals frequently flee to higher-paying jobs in other professions or, in the case of developing countries, leave for academic or other jobs in Europe or North America. While the "brain drain" is a complex phenomenon, it is clear that the exodus of many of the most experienced academics from, for example, sub-Saharan Africa to South Africa, Europe, and North America has caused severe personnel problems in African universities.

The Bureaucratization of the Professoriate

In years past, even if academics were not well paid, they held a good deal of autonomy and control over their teaching and research as well as their time. This situation has changed in many academic systems and institutions. In terms of accountability and assessment, the professoriate has lost much of its autonomy. Assessment exercises and other accountability measures require a lot of time and effort to complete. The pressure to assess academic productivity of all kinds is substantial, even if much of that work is in fact quite difficult or impossible to measure accurately. Much criticism has been aimed at the British Research Assessment Exercises, which many claim have distorted academic work by overemphasizing certain kinds of academic productivity.

Universities have also become much more bureaucratic as they have grown and increased the accountability to external authorities. Accountability is both appropriate and necessary in contemporary academic institutions and systems and is not necessarily inimical to the community of scholars. Often, however, heavy bureaucratic control is deleterious to a sense of academic community and generally to the faculty's traditional involvement in academic governance. The power of the professors, once dominant and sometimes used by them to resist change, has declined in the age of accountability and bureaucracy. The pendulum of authority in higher education has swung from the academics to managers and bureaucrats, with significant impact on the university.

A Global Academic Marketplace
Just as students are internationally mobile, so, too, are academics. There are no accurate statistics concerning global flows of academic talent. The numbers are quite large. In general, academics go from developing countries to North America, western Europe, and Australasia. There are also significant flows from sub-Saharan Africa to South Africa, from South Asia to the Middle East and Africa, from Egypt to the wealthier Arab countries, and from the United Kingdom to Canada and the United States. A key motivator in this flow is salary, but other factors such as improved working conditions, and particularly research infrastructures, opportunities for advancement, academic freedom, and others may also be involved.

At one time, this phenomenon was labeled a brain drain, but in the era of relatively easy air travel and the Internet, many internationally mobile scholars keep close contacts with their home countries. These diasporas can play a significant role by keeping in contact with the academic communities in their home countries and sharing research and experience. Yet the fact remains that the global flow of academic talent works to the disadvantage of the developing world. There are some small signs the situation is changing. More Chinese scholars are choosing to return home after sojourns elsewhere, for example. Universities in Singapore, Hong Kong, China, and elsewhere are attracting Western academics with high salaries and favorable working conditions.

Conclusion
The challenges to the academic profession are complex and very much tied to broader criticisms of the professions generally in many countries. Some of the problems are directly linked to mass higher education and the financial and other challenges massification has created. It is not difficult to identify the path to a restored academic profession—and thus successful higher education systems. The academic profession must again become a profession—with appropriate training, compensation, and status. This means that academic programs, to provide master's and doctoral degrees, must be significantly expanded. The rush toward part-time teachers must be ended and, instead, a sufficient cadre of full-time professors with appropriate career ladders appointed. Salaries

must be sufficient to attract talented young scholars and to keep them in the profession.

In a differentiated academic system, not all professors will focus on research—typically the gold standard in terms of prestige and status. Most academics mainly teach, and their workloads should reflect this. It would also be impossible to return to the days of unfettered autonomy and little if any evaluation of academic work. Yet, accountability and assessment can be done in ways that are appropriate to academic work rather than punitive exercises.

If there is any good news in this story it is that more professors enjoy what they are doing and feel a loyalty to the profession. The 1992 international Carnegie study of the academic profession found surprisingly high levels of satisfaction, and a 2008 changing academic profession global survey found much the same result. Academics feel a commitment to teaching and research, enjoy the autonomy they have to determine their own work, and like interacting with students and colleagues. Despite their problems, academic life has significant attractions. The challenge is to ensure that the academic profession is again seen by policymakers and the public as central to the success of higher education.

8

The Student Experience

Students constitute the most central stakeholder group in higher education around the world. Over the last decade, major shifts have occurred in the size, demographic makeup, needs, aspirations, and expectations of the student population across the globe. These developments have exerted significant pressure on individual institutions and entire systems of higher education in many countries. Efforts to respond to new student realities have resulted in a wide range of institutional and systemic adjustments that have changed—and continue to change—the size, shape, and very nature of higher education. These developments, in turn, have affected the student experience of higher education, presenting students worldwide with a new and particular set of challenges and opportunities. Some half-dozen fundamental issues stand out as central to an understanding of the interplay between students and higher education over the last decade. These include:

- Demographic changes
- Diversification of the student body
- Transformation of higher education institutions/systems
- Rising demands for relevance
- Increased calls for cost sharing
- Globalization and internationalization

While many of these topics are discussed at length in other chapters of this report, they are explored in this chapter through the particular lens of the student experience. Taken together, these issues speak to an evolving higher education experience for students, as well as a changing environment for systems and individual institutions as a result of new kinds of student needs and shifting enrollment numbers.

Demographic Changes

Over the last decade, the world population is estimated to have grown from approximately 5.9 billion (US Bureau of Census, 1998) to more than 6.7 billion (US Bureau of the Census, 2008). Today, "more than 1.5 billion people are between the ages of 10 and 25," representing the "largest-ever generation of adolescents" (United Nations Population Fund, 2007, p. 3). As young people have moved in increasingly large numbers through primary and secondary levels of education, there has been a sustained increase in student enrollment in higher education over the last decade. This has held true in both absolute and relative terms and comes as a result of a variety of demographic and systemic factors, as well as overt policy decisions and national development aspirations. The most recent UNESCO figures estimate that there are some 150.6 million tertiary education students globally. This is roughly a 53 percent increase over UNESCO's 2000 estimate of 98.3 million tertiary students worldwide. The gross enrollment ratio figures for this same time frame reflect upward trends as well. UNESCO data suggest that globally, the gross enrollment ratio for tertiary education has grown by 37 percent over the period from 2000 to 2007. Most of the most dramatic growth in overall youth numbers over the last decade has occurred in the developing world, while particularly robust increases in higher education enrollment have been seen in regions such as East Asia and the Pacific, central and eastern Europe, and Latin America and the Caribbean.

Common consequences of the rapid and sustained demand for tertiary education in recent years have been the creation of new institutions, the expansion of existing ones, the introduction and extension of distance-learning options, and the growth of a private higher education sector to supplement the educational opportunities provided by the public sector. Real benefits have accrued to students in many of these contexts. Expanded possibilities for higher education enrollment, in general, and a sense of choice in terms of institutional size, type, and location are some of the most obvious examples of an improved situation for students in higher education systems that have grown and diversified in the last decade.

At the same time, difficulties and disadvantages have also plagued rapid expansion in many quarters. Growth in systems has often occurred in ad hoc ways, resulting in less-than-optimal deployment of limited resources, short-term solutions to long-term challenges, and uneven benefits for stakeholders.

Quality has also been a central concern in such environments. In some cases, the creation of new institutions has outpaced capacity to monitor and assure quality. In other cases, extremely large, "massified" institutions—grown exponentially to accommodate expanded student numbers—have not been able to maintain traditional standards in a resource-stretched context. The *Global Student Statement to the UNESCO World Conference on Higher Education +10* (in 2009) specifically highlights the link between access and quality, asserting

> quality is a distinguishing characteristic that provides a guide for students and higher education institutions. High quality and accessibility should be two sides of the same coin. Accessible higher education that is not high quality is worthless and high quality education that is not widely accessible is meaningless. (p. 2)

Meanwhile, the expansion of student numbers in many countries has presented a major challenge for systems where the tradition has been to provide access to free or highly subsidized tertiary education. In financial terms, this has become an unsustainable model, placing pressure on systems to fundamentally restructure the "social contract" between higher education and society at large. In many cases, emotions—particularly among students—have run extremely high around this subject, creating not insignificant political challenges and social tensions. The highly divisive, nine-month, student-led strike at the National Autonomous University of Mexico (UNAM) in 1999 offers an important example of a powerful student response to fee increases; it also reflects the real way in which broader political and economic issues can play out in higher education institutions (Maldonado-Maldonado, 2002).

While growth and massification of higher education have been the norm in many countries, the situation in the world's more developed countries is quite different, although challenged by demographic changes in its own right. A rapidly aging population in the North forces higher education systems and institutions there to consider new and different student paradigms. These societies have faced fluctuations in traditional-age student numbers and have also begun to respond to the new and unique demands of lifelong learning. The European Union's Lifelong Learning Programme, which has allocated "nearly 7 billion for 2007 to 2013," aims to enable "individuals at all stages of their lives to pursue stimulating learning opportunities across Europe" (European Commission, 2008b). Nontraditional learners (particularly older individuals) and international students are coming to play an increasingly important role in the higher education systems of many developed countries. In addition, the growing diversification of societies in

North America and much of Europe due to immigration patterns also demands a serious rethinking of pedagogies, curricula, and research agendas. By necessity, these must now take into account a wider range of cultural, racial, linguistic, and overall "identity" factors at play in tertiary institutions.

Diversification of the Student Body

Broadly speaking, evidence suggests that higher education systems around the world are increasingly serving a more diverse group of students. In general, this development is a source of great encouragement and hope for those who see fundamental connections between higher education and positive personal and professional outcomes for individuals, as well as enhanced economic, social, and political developments for nations with a broad base of highly educated workers. However, traditionally underrepresented groups continue to face serious challenges. Underrepresented groups may be understood to include, among others, ethnic, racial, cultural, and linguistic minorities; "the poor, those living in places far from major urban centres . . . people with disabilities, migrants, refugees, those deprived of their freedom" (*Declaration of the Regional Conference on Higher Education in Latin America and the Caribbean*, 2008, p. 4); women and working adults. In many parts of the world, involvement in higher education by these groups still does not reflect the full scope of their numbers in the broader society. Nor are these students assured equal access to the same kinds of institutions (the most prestigious, for example) as students from the more dominant groups in society, graduating at the same rates, or accruing the same benefits as a result of their tertiary education experiences.

Where progress toward broader social inclusiveness has occurred, diversification of the student body has placed a complex new set of demands on higher education institutions and systems around the world. Central to this discussion is the need to reconsider the fundamental questions of what is taught, when, and how and what constitutes quality in higher education. There have been widespread calls to incorporate new approaches into teaching and research, as well as new curricula and administrative structures that respond more appropriately and effectively to the unique identities of the new kinds of students pursuing higher education. Program structure and delivery are deeply implicated in this changing context, as are the perspectives and experience of the faculty responsible for delivering instruction and intellectual guidance, the staff tasked with supporting bureaucratic activities and student services, and the administrators charged with providing institutional leadership.

Institutional transformation—whereby universities evolve to provide meaningful opportunities for many different forms of knowledge and ways of learning—is seen by some as an ideal objective in the face of a diversifying worldwide student population (*Declaration of the Regional Conference on Higher Education in Latin America and the Caribbean*, 2008). Indeed, the 2009 *Global Student Statement to the UNESCO World Conference on Higher Education +10* calls unequivocally for "Education for All!" (p. 1), and urges that greater attention be given to the provision of "adequate support measures, specifically designed to adapt to the needs of the individual learner" (p. 1). The political challenges of this kind of commitment are considerable, however. Even in contexts where there may be a consensus that greater social inclusiveness in higher education is a positive value, implementation of real changes at institutional and national levels can rub up against deeply held beliefs about "meritocracy, national cohesion, and democracy" (David, 2009). As greater numbers of nontraditional students are actively recruited or otherwise find their way into tertiary education around the world, the importance of responding to the unique needs of new kinds of learners will prove to be increasingly central to the higher education enterprise.

Transformation of Higher Education Institutions/Systems
As the tertiary student population has grown in size and complexity in much of the world over the last 10 years, the landscape of higher education institutions has, in many contexts, expanded and evolved in response to the changing student population. Primary developments in this area have been the dramatic growth in the private higher education sector, the increasing popularity of professionally oriented programs (notably in the fields of business and information and communications technology), and the more widespread provision of higher education opportunities with flexible formats for working adults. Also important have been the trends to establish new universities and/or to modify existing institutions by expanding their size and scope, elevating non-universities to university status, or merging multiple institutions. All of these developments may in some way be seen as responses to increased calls for access and/or perceived needs to better serve a new generation of learners with particular educational needs and aspirations.

The growth in numbers of private higher education institutions, and their increasing share of worldwide tertiary education enrollment, has been a remarkable feature of the last decade. Much of this activity has been fueled by student demand for access in general and for access to certain types of programs and fields of study in particular, accompanied by an inability of the public higher education sector to keep pace with these demands. In some parts of the world, students have become frustrated with failing public institutions that are prone to overcrowding, substandard facilities and services, and political and bureaucratic gridlock (including prolonged strikes and closures). They have therefore turned, in many instances, to private higher education in search of a more stable and viable educational experience. In other contexts, private higher education has served to fill a void for minority groups seeking a more comfortable or welcoming environment. This has been especially true for female students or those coming from particular religious traditions or ethnic/racial backgrounds in societies where the minority student population has found it difficult to integrate into the mainstream higher education sector. The rise in recent years of religiously affiliated private universities in Nigeria (Obasi, 2006), for example, provides some insight into this trend.

The shifting needs and interests of students have also contributed to an increase in popularity of many professionally oriented programs and institutions. Characterized as a "vocationalization" of higher education in many corners of the world, student enrollment globally in the business, information and communications technology fields, and other similarly "practical" areas of study have changed the higher education landscape. An explosion in the last decade of master of business administration (MBA) program offerings around the world is a prime example of this trend, with countries like China rapidly introducing Western-style business schools in the last 15 years (Lavelle and Rutledge, 2006). In the case of the MBA surge, students in ever-greater numbers have been seeking a competitive credential that enhances employment opportunities, while institutions have looked for ways to increase tuition income and prestige. In many ways, this has been mutually beneficial for students, institutions, and social stakeholders such as employers. However, there have also been problems associated with such trends. Notable among these is lack of locally relevant teaching materials (such as case studies for Chinese MBA programs), and questionable quality assurance oversight in a context of rapid expansion in order to meet the "market demand" for these specific credentials (Lavelle and Rutledge, 2006). In countries with limited resources to apply to the higher education sector, concerns may emerge about the preservation of less-popular programs in fields such as the arts and humanities, where employment outcomes are ostensibly less promising.

Partly as a way to accommodate the increase in number and types of students served (and in some cases as a way to actively attract new learners), some higher education systems have undertaken broadly based efforts to split, merge, or otherwise retool institutions in their systems or add brand new universities to the mix. In many cases, this has occurred in the context of a national reform agenda. The student-related objectives embedded in such agendas have ranged from providing more and better choices for the student population, to simply keeping up with the growing number of learners or the expanding interests of students in particular fields of study. New institutions may bring with them real opportunity, innovation, and excellence. However, Damtew Teferra (2007) notes that "expansion and quality are often in constant counter-play, especially so where resources are in short supply." Overly ambitious or narrowly conceived reform or expansion efforts may sacrifice quality and prevent a clear focus on the achievement of broader objectives, to the ultimate detriment of the student population.

The transformation of higher education systems and institutions over the last decade has represented a notable effort to achieve some convergence of evolving student needs and tertiary education interests and capacity. Yet, the complexity of issues and factors involved has made for a most-challenging environment and an uneven range of outcomes in this area.

Relevance

In the rapidly changing global economic environment of the last decade, "relevance" has become a key consideration in higher education in many corners of the world. Students have exhibited an increasing tendency to want educational experiences that are directly relevant to their personal and/or professional interests and objectives, particularly as related to employability. Practically oriented programs and fields of study, as well as pedagogical approaches stressing "real world" applications, have seen an appreciable rise in popularity. At the same time, new demands on higher education have made it increasingly important for the tertiary education sector in many countries to demonstrate its social and economic relevance to the societies served. To this end, many universities have moved to provide the kinds of applied academic and professional programs that are both sought by larger numbers of students and considered fundamentally linked to economic expansion. In other countries, an emerging interest in liberal arts and humanities, as well as interdisciplinary studies, has been noted. Here, the development of more versatile, well-rounded graduates has been a key objective.

Evolving approaches to teaching are also quite important to the discussion of relevance. Key developments here have been the introduction of new program options, such as part-time programs, online study possibilities, and courses that allow students to acquire credit for current or prior professional experience, among others. These innovations seek to more effectively meet the needs of contemporary students, many more of which are balancing work and/or family obligations, returning to schooling after a break of some years, or pursuing lifelong learning interests and goals. In countries where the focus has long been on rote learning, emphasis has shifted in recent years to developing students' analytical and critical thinking skills, as well as a clearer understanding of *how* to learn. Along with curriculum and pedagogy, research has also been an important factor in the move toward relevance. In this area, some tertiary institutions and systems have focused more on expanding research capacity and developing entrepreneurial activities as a means to commercialize valuable technologies, and contribute to the advancement of national development agendas.

From the perspective of the student experience of higher education, each of these trends has brought with them a complex set of benefits and drawbacks. The expanded ability to develop key skills and access programs in preferred fields of study is a very positive trend for those students who, a decade before, might have had to settle for enrollment in courses that led to few real employment options or in which they had limited interest. At the same time, unregulated access to particular fields of study can lead to overenrollment, which, in turn, can adversely affect the quality of programs and the student experience within them. Clustering of large numbers of students in specific areas can be detrimental to learners seeking individual attention and guidance, stretching already limited resources to accommodate oversized cohorts. After graduation, employment prospects can be scarce for those coming out of overenrolled programs. This is problematic not only for individuals but also for societies facing workforce surpluses in some areas and shortages in others. Meanwhile, it is true that the rush to expand applied research activities has generated revenue and prestige for some institutions and provided students with new opportunities to be exposed to cutting-edge research within the context of their studies. The downside of this trend, however, is the potential for a focus on research to undermine teaching activities. This shift may occur if the research function of an institution is privileged in such a way—financial, political, or otherwise—that a sizable proportion of time, talent, and resources is diverted away from the teaching function. There is also the problem of the migration of resources and prestige away from fields of study considered less relevant to personal financial advancement and broader economic development, which are nonetheless very important to the cultural life of a society.

Cost Sharing

The demographic trends that have brought larger numbers of students into postsecondary education have led to a corresponding financial strain on higher education around the world. To fill the gap between supply—heavily subsidized if not wholly publicly funded in many countries—and growing demand for postsecondary access, many higher education institutions and systems have moved to introduce or raise tuition and student fees. In many parts of the world, this represents a profound change in both policy and practice, with a direct impact on students and their families. These effects can be seen in both positive and negative lights.

In terms of positive effects, being obligated to pay for some portion of the costs associated with higher education does give individuals a quantifiable stake in the higher education process and outcome. Students (independently or actively encouraged by their fee-paying families) may focus more energetically on the process of moving swiftly and successfully through the higher education experience, decreasing the time to degree, and increasing the overall efficiency of the system. In contexts where students have tended to languish for years in tuition-free systems—sometimes even earning small salaries in the form of student stipends—the incentives to graduate (particularly in countries of high unemployment) have been limited. Cost sharing in some instances has rendered inertia more uncomfortable and costly, arguably reducing the attractiveness of life as a "career student." The shifting of some of the burdens of cost onto students and their families can also be understood to have empowered these groups to some extent, transforming them into consumers of higher education with a choice, in many more countries, of where to spend their tuition monies.

At the same time, cost sharing also presents important challenges. Most obviously, the imposition or raising of tuition and fees can have a serious exclusionary effect, erecting real barriers to access among students with limited resources. It also has the potential to ghettoize poorer students in particular kinds of institutions or fields of study based solely on socioeconomic, rather than academic, factors. Meanwhile, although the responsiveness of tertiary institutions to the demands of fee-paying students can yield dynamic and innovative results, there are concerns that these efforts can be shortsighted, ultimately undermining student choices as well as the public good ethos of much higher education around the world. For example, those institutions and/or systems that put a premium on programs able to generate their own revenue through tuition and fees may eliminate programs unable to meet this threshold. Areas of study with low enrollment numbers, often in more obscure or highly specialized fields, are vulnerable in such contexts. Also difficult to sustain in these circumstances are more expensive areas of study, such as medicine and the sciences, which require costly laboratories and supplies. The scope of students' educational possibilities may be narrowed, which may have a detrimental effect on the long-term vibrancy of a given institution, tertiary system, or broader society. Furthermore, whereas cost sharing can be an empowering force for students in some cases, in others it can cultivate a distinctly utilitarian, consumer-oriented approach to higher education. In this setting, the focus is overwhelmingly on the private-good aspects of the enterprise rather than the more expansive concerns for the development of students as citizens or for the public good.

The move toward increased cost sharing by students and their families represents an extremely important shift in the student experience of higher education around the world over the last decade. The *Global Student Statement to the UNESCO World Conference on Higher Education +10* (2009) urges "a deep investment in the higher education of students globally," and states that "higher education needs to be . . . a fundamental right for all," regardless of a student's ability to pay (p. 1). However, fiscal and economic realities the world over make it likely that cost sharing will continue to be an issue of concern for higher education and exert an influence on the student experience in a variety of ways across the globe.

Globalization and Internationalization
The student experience of tertiary education has been affected by globalization and internationalization, most notably through the expansion of student mobility, the growth in cross-border provision of education, and the emergence of international university rankings and the quality assurance movement. Enormous benefits have accrued to many students as a result of these developments, although the student experience of internationalization and globalization has also been fraught with difficulties and inequities for many.

Opportunities for students to spend all or part of their higher education careers outside of their country of origin or residence have risen dramatically in the last 10 years. Although it has proven to be exceedingly difficult to get reliable data on international student mobility, indications are that the worldwide flow of students has grown appreciably over the last decade. UNESCO estimates that there were some 1.8 million internationally mobile students in 2000, which grew to over 2.7 million in 2007. Furthermore, the potential for significant growth over the coming decade is quite realistic (Verbik and Lasanowski, 2007). At the same time, while it is difficult to assess personal, professional, and academic outcomes in any systematic or large-scale way, a preponderance of anecdotal evidence suggests that the benefits of international study for most students are quite positive—enjoyable, meaningful, and often life changing. Only a small portion of the world's tertiary students experiences these benefits, however. Given the costs involved in overseas study, most internationally mobile students—with the exception of small numbers benefiting from special funding and scholarship programs—are full fee-paying students coming from privileged socioeconomic backgrounds. They represent select segments of the student population in the home country—Caucasian women in the United States, for example, or male graduate students in much of the developing world, for another. This information suggests an uneven access to international study opportunities exists, which perpetuates other inequalities among students, at both local and global levels.

The arrival of foreign higher education providers in various parts of the world has also been a positive development. These entities have in some cases given students new options for study in contexts where the local supply of tertiary education could not meet demand and also introduced new programs, materials, and pedagogical approaches that bring an informative international dimension to the teaching and learning processes. But in some instances, unscrupulous foreign providers have offered substandard academic services or perpetrated outright fraud, operating as nothing more than "degree mills." An uncertain quality landscape for students enrolling in unregulated cross-border providers, as well as the potential for foreign providers to impose inappropriate curricula or teaching methodologies, forms just some of the ways in which internationalization can harm more than help the student experience. The inability of students to gain recognition at home for degrees earned abroad at high-quality institutions or to gain meaningful employment in the home country after studying overseas or in international institutions operating locally further complicates the experience of higher education's international dimension for the world's students. Raising public levels of awareness about institutional regulation, accreditation, and levels of quality, as well as credential recognition issues, is extremely important in this context. The UNESCO Portal on Higher Education Institutions is an example of an international effort to provide students, families and other stakeholders with access relevant information in order to make informed decisions (UNESCO, n.d.-c).

The emergence of international university rankings and the quality assurance movement also represents a mixed blessing. Students receive obvious benefits in the push to raise the levels of quality and competitiveness. Resources pumped into these efforts have, in many cases, raised the level of academic quality (at least in some areas) and enhanced institutional prestige in others, providing students with better academic experiences and more widely recognized credentials. Students have suffered, however, in contexts in which the effort to obtain certain international league-table standings, or a particular quality assurance agency endorsement, has not been in alignment with real student needs. The failure of institutions or systems to adequately serve local students, by pursuing ambitious (and not always appropriate or realistic) internationally oriented agendas, is yet another example of how internationalization can harm the student experience of higher education.

The evolving global and international dimensions in tertiary education have exerted important effects on higher education systems and institutions around the world, some enormously positive, and others more worrisome. These developments have and will continue to affect the ways in which students experience tertiary education, as globalization continues apace and many aspects of internationalization expand and mature in the coming decade.

Conclusion

Shifts in student numbers, characteristics, needs, and interests have had an enormous impact on higher education around the world over the last 10 years. Student concerns will continue to demand attention in the coming decade as the variables associated with this key stakeholder continue to fluctuate across the globe, exerting a range of direct and indirect influences on the size, scope, quality, and nature of the higher education enterprise worldwide. How best to accommodate and effectively serve an increasingly large and more diverse tertiary student population will be a central consideration for policymakers and institutional leaders moving forward. Effective responses to enrollment growth and diversification will require careful attention to individual, institutional, and systemic needs, as well as local and global contexts. The student experience in the 21st century will likely be characterized by more years of engagement with education over the course of a lifetime, as well as greater options in terms of what, when, and how to study. In most parts of the world, students will increasingly need to finance their studies from personal resources. This may negatively affect the time to degree for many students, but it may also encourage new and different kinds of learning as students combine formal education with work and other activities. Students and their families will require more detailed and comprehensive information on the relative merits of different study options as the higher education sector expands and evolves in many countries and the incidence of cross-border delivery grows. Finding ways to protect students' rights and enhance their roles in governance and decision making will be especially important if higher education is to respond effectively to changing student profiles and needs the world over.

From a global perspective, the student experience of tertiary education appears poised to take on greater complexity than ever before, presenting considerable challenges and opportunities for the higher education sector around the world in the coming years.

9

Teaching, Learning, and Assessment

University systems have changed profoundly in the last 10 years. Larger and more diverse student populations, a growing interest in professional education and lifelong learning, the privatization of higher education, financial constraints, enhanced attention to quality and accountability, and evolving tendencies for postsecondary institutions and national systems to situate themselves in international and global contexts are just a few of the major trends of the last decade. Individually and collectively, these developments have exerted pressures on the core functions of higher education, including teaching and learning. These changes have had impact on how and what students learn and the way that knowledge, skills, learning, and teaching are assessed.

While it is difficult to generalize globally, the mission of the majority of institutions in most countries today is to teach less of the basic disciplines and offer more in the way of professional programs to a wider range of students than in the past. Greater attention is also being paid to students' need to develop skills, knowledge, and attitudes so as to operate effectively in more complex, fluid, and ambiguous environments. Students must be primed to engage in learning activities across many more phases of their lives, and institutions must be prepared to meet the needs of a wide range of nontraditional learners. A profound challenge, inherent in the need to effectively accommodate both teaching and research functions, will engage higher education systems and individual institutions.

Even though these important changes are taking place, relatively little research exists on the status and role of teaching and learning in higher education around the world. Analysis about assessment is slightly more prevalent due to the education community's heightened awareness of accountability and quality assurance, particularly in Europe and the United States. Overall, however, teaching, learning, and assessment in the context of global higher education require significantly more research to make better judgments about current trends and their impact on individual countries and institutions. This chapter summarizes what is known based on expert opinions, observations, and the available scholarly literature.

A recent and far reaching example of shifting teaching, learning, and assessment paradigms can be seen in the Bologna process, which is attempting to achieve real interchangeability between universities across Europe and beyond. The primary objectives of the Bologna process are to bring compatibility and quality assurance across Europe's many and varied higher education systems, while promoting transparency, mobility, employability, and student-centered learning. All of these developments require potentially enormous changes in how academics and institutions understand and approach teaching and assessment. Further, they encapsulate broader global trends to develop a clearer understanding of what constitutes meaningful higher education "inputs" and "outputs." These discussions have generated a great deal of excitement in many quarters but also represent real challenges and concerns for many stakeholders around the world.

Teaching in the Traditional University

Twenty years ago, universities in most parts of the world were much more highly selective than they are today, accepting relatively small percentages of secondary school leavers. A high proportion of the subjects taught included the basic science and arts disciplines. Given that academic reputations were built on research, however, it follows that research, not teaching, was the top priority. Teaching usually meant lecturing to very bright and highly motivated students. Assessment was usually norm-referenced to determine which students were the most effective at remembering and understanding what they had been taught, and students were graded accordingly. Poor results were attributed to student deficits such as lack of motivation or talent, rarely to poor teaching.

In most university contexts around the world, oversight of teaching was left to departments, which often gave individual teachers a virtually free hand to teach as they liked. Academic appointments and promotions were and still are, for the most part, made on the basis of research output, not teaching proficiency. When recognized, teaching excellence was often showcased through competitive awards to individuals, which only confirmed to many that teaching was a gift possessed by the rare few, not a skill to be cultivated. Among those universities fortunate enough to have teaching development and educational technology centers—mostly outside of the developing world—workshops provided opportunities to improve teaching and assessment but were attended only on a voluntary basis and by more self-motivated teachers. The prevailing conception of teaching emphasized what teachers did, not what students learned.

Until fairly recently, teaching meant "covering" a body of *declarative* knowledge—that is, knowledge that could be "declared" in books or in lectures—while assessment measured how well students received that knowledge based on their ability to regurgitate it on examinations. Less thought was given to *functional* knowledge—that is, knowing how to apply theory to practical situations. In sum, traditional university teaching was knowledge centered rather than student centered. Although underresearched in a global context, today an emerging dialogue focuses on the need for more student-centered approaches to teaching, the "inputs," and more meaningful assessments regarding student learning, the "outputs."

Factors Transforming University Teaching
Massification has produced—and continues to do so—an enormous impact on universities today. Student intake is much higher than before, approaching 60 percent of school leavers in many parts of the developed world (and even higher in some countries). The larger student population is also more mature in age and more international, with diverse abilities and motivations. Postsecondary education is thus oriented toward vocational and professional instruction, with a focus on functional knowledge. Given the pressures of massification and the evolving educational outcomes, lecturing about declarative knowledge can no longer be the default teaching method. Several other important developments stand out as key drivers of change in the areas of teaching, learning and assessment.

Teaching and Learning Theory and Outcomes-Based Approaches
Research about student learning (Biggs, 1993; Marton, Hounsell, and Entwistle, 1997; Prosser and Trigwell, 1999) and the "scholarship of teaching and learning" in general (Boyer, 1990) have provided a philosophy, a technology, and an impetus for universities to design more effective teaching and assessment. Teaching models have evolved from the primitive "blame the student" approach (meaning that a failure to learn is due to the student's lack of talent or effort), to the teacher-cen-

tered scenario of acquiring "tricks of the trade" to initiate good teaching, and to the most up-to-date student-learning research that defines good teaching by examining whether students achieve desirable and pre-defined learning outcomes. Ideally, this approach involves engaging students actively in the learning process. Theoretical developments that prioritize learning outcomes have led some participants in the higher education community to shift from a teacher-centered input model, to one that is student centered and based on outputs. Good teaching, in other words, would focus less on what *teachers do* and primarily on what *students learn*. This paradigm shift is playing out dynamically in some learning environments but is encountering obstacles in others.

Public-Good Versus Private-Good Considerations
Shifts in the debate about whether postsecondary education is more a public good or a private good have altered some stakeholder relation-ships with higher education around the world. As indicated in the financing chapter of this report, in recent years the responsibility for financing higher education has, in many places, shifted largely to indi-vidual students and their families. This trend reflects a growing sense that the personal benefits of obtaining a degree may be as important as (or even more so than) the societal benefits of an educated popula-tion. With increasing numbers of students paying more money for their education (in both cash-strapped public institutions and in the growing private higher education sector), students have higher expectations of the education supplier and the "product" they receive (Campbell, 2008). The complex side effects for education include the fact that universities, to survive in an increasingly competitive "knowledge market," must look at the quality and relevance of their teaching activities in ways they never have before.

Quality Assurance and Institutional Accountability
Governments have in recent years insisted on greater accountability from higher education, which has included new emphasis on quality assurance. Initially, quality assurance meant retrospective managerial assessments that operated irrespective of teaching theory or research findings on what constituted good teaching (Liston, 1999). In the last 10 years, however, quality assurance agencies have increasingly used a theory-based lens to define effective, or good, teaching and assessment. Example organizations include the Quality Assurance Agency in the United Kingdom, the University Grants Committee in Hong Kong, and the Australian Universities Quality Agency. If used reflectively across the whole institution, quality assurance mechanisms can bolster teaching

and learning, rather than simply maintain the status quo (Biggs, 2001). Meanwhile, in some (but certainly not all) cases, demand from students, governments, employers and other stakeholders has forced universities to take leadership responsibility for teaching rather than leaving it to department heads and individual professors. Excellent reasons, related to education outcomes, support universities having some centralized influence over teaching (D'Andrea and Gosling, 2005). Developments in the theory of teaching, and of outcomes-based approaches to student learning in particular, have provided the means by which universities can construct new approaches to teaching and assessment, new resources for teaching and learning, and new outcome standards that ensure high-quality teaching across all departments.

Emerging Curricula and a Shifting Sense of Education's Purpose
In recent years, there has been renewed conversation about the purpose of education, particularly in light of the recognized role higher education plays in developing human resources for a growing global economy. In this process, questions are being raised about the curriculum. Social leaders and educationalists (particularly outside of the United States) are asking whether a traditional professional focus, which prepared students for work in the industrial economy, is adequate in the evolving and ambiguous knowledge economy. Professional education, sometimes called specialization or vocational education, typically refers to curricula that focus on preparing students for a specific career like law, medicine, business, or engineering. New conversations are emerging, however, about the value of and potential need for liberal education. Sometimes referred to as general education, liberal education (or liberal learning) emphasizes a broad interdisciplinary curriculum focused on creativity, critical thinking, cultural awareness, problem solving, and communication skills. The knowledge economy is more often requiring a workforce of generalists who are adaptable, know how to learn, and can "manage and assimilate greatly expanded quantities of information" (Task Force on Higher Education and Society, 2000, p. 83). Although not in great numbers, liberal education institutions and programs are starting to appear around the world, where they have previously not existed. In places like the Russian Federation and eastern Europe, which have witnessed changing political and economic structures in recent years, as well as in other emerging democracies, liberal education is being considered as a means for developing a critical and participatory citizenry. Questions about curriculum and higher education's purpose are particularly salient in developing regions where emerging economies require both specialists trained for science and technical professions as well as strong

leaders with generalist knowledge who are creative, adaptable, and able to give broad ethical consideration to social advances. It will be important to think carefully about how teaching, learning, and assessment might need to change if liberal education emerges as a trend worldwide.

Competition and Cooperation Between Teaching and Research Functions
Teaching and research are unquestionably two core functions of the academic enterprise around the world. These functions are understood and managed today in various ways across institutions and national systems, presenting complex challenges as well as new opportunities. The traditional prestige associated with research has been amplified in recent years by the focus of highly influential ranking systems and league tables on research activity and output. Money and attention often flow to institutions that excel in research, placing teaching-oriented institutions at a disadvantage for attracting funding and nonfinancial support. However, producing a skilled labor force is more than ever a critically important function of higher education. Thus, the teaching function cannot be disregarded in the race to achieve research prestige. Meanwhile, the rising relevance of research in professional graduate education and interdisciplinary fields (which typically focused more exclusively on teaching) is serving as a catalyst for enhanced engagement between research and teaching functions in new and different areas.

These and other developments in higher education have suggested a paradigm shift in university teaching in some countries over the last 10 years, and they are beginning to exert pressure for change on a more global scale. Where evolution in philosophy and approaches to teaching, learning, and assessment have emerged, some notable changes are occurring, particularly among universities that accept institutionwide responsibility for teaching and assessment. These changes include a focus on approaches based on outcomes, to student learning and attention to the complex interplay between curriculum innovation and approaches to teaching, learning, and assessment.

Teaching as an Institutional Responsibility
There is potential momentum building for institutions to assume centralized oversight for teaching-quality practice and development. Although it is too early to call this centralization a trend, it has been most prevalent in North America and Europe, as well as discernible in Australia and in select Asian contexts like Hong Kong China, (SAR). In these settings, many universities have developed policies and procedures that enhance the quality of teaching and assessment across all departments in the institution. A variety of strategies have been used to advance this

agenda. Perhaps the most prominent among these has been the establishment of teaching and learning development centers. Ideally, these centers play an integral role in the university's teaching and learning structure, providing universitywide staff development in line with the institution's approach to teaching, student learning outcomes, and best practices revealed through the scholarship of teaching and learning. The strength of these facilities depends on whether they are frequented by not only the enthusiastic teachers but by a wide range of faculty and instructors seeking to improve their classroom work. However, because research institutions (and in some cases their promotion and reward systems) focus on research rather than teaching, little incentive is provided for instructors to develop their skills or be concerned with teaching quality. For this reason, centers are most effective in improving teaching quality and assessment if endorsed by the central administration or when teaching quality, assessment, and learning outcomes are made an institutional priority. With proper support and institutional culture, teaching and learning centers can provide critical resources for all teaching staff across all departments, assist departments in solving classroom and curriculum challenges, provide programming for new faculty and instructors, and assist with course design and evaluations.

In many contexts, teaching and learning centers are also requested to advise their institutions on questions of policy and operational procedure affecting the quality of teaching and learning across the university. Specific examples include designing student feedback instruments that are sensitive to nontraditional teaching methods and approaches to student learning. This approach can be a critical component to improving learning outcomes, given that most general-purpose feedback questionnaires assume that the lecture/tutorial is the default teaching method. Teaching and learning centers can also help guide university policy in the area of student assessment, for example, by articulating research-supported rationales for helping institutions move away from norm-referenced to criterion-referenced assessment. This shift is fundamental to outcomes-based teaching and learning but is frequently resisted by traditional academics and administrators who persevere with the belief that grade allocation should follow the bell curve.

In some contexts, teaching and learning centers also play an important role for students. Many centers include tutoring services or learning-skills-development workshops that help students recognize how they learn and encourage students to take responsibility for their own learning in and outside of the classroom.

Technology can play an interesting and essential role in an institution's centralized approach to teaching and outcomes-based handling of student learning. For example, faculty may be required to use e-learning platforms such as BlackBoard or WebCT. This process—painful though it may be for many individuals—typically forces teachers to think more reflectively about course design, delivery, and assessment. It can stimulate creative new ways to engage students and to incorporate highly contemporary materials, while sensitizing faculty to the range of new challenges and possibilities inherent in the application of educational technologies. On a global scale, however, enhancing teaching and learning by using expensive technology often requires costly equipment and expertise that magnifies the digital divide between developed and developing parts of the world. These opportunities, therefore, are significantly more accessible to more resource-rich higher education sectors and geographic regions.

In short, institutionwide approaches to teaching and assessment, including making teaching a centralized priority and the possibility of curriculum changes (mentioned earlier), are increasingly recognized as able to create more dynamic contexts for enhanced student learning. Already, some tertiary institutions around the world are developing strategies to facilitate such environments. However, to be most effective, a coherent theory of teaching and learning, preferably rooted in notions of outcomes-based student learning, is essential, as this provides a clear framework for making decisions and policies about teaching and learning, from the level of the individual classroom through to the president or rector's office.

Outcomes-based Approaches to Student Learning

Outcomes in higher education are crucial on a variety of levels and for a variety of reasons. Most fundamentally, it is critical for interested stakeholders—students, educators, employers, and governments, among others—to recognize and appreciate the relevant added value from public and private investment in higher education. In many cases, the relative value of what is produced by higher education is assessed in terms of the commercialization of new knowledge and innovative technology, specifically through research. However, also of critical importance is understanding what students take away from the postsecondary experience—what and how well they learn and how the skills and knowledge they acquire serve their individual interests as well as a broader set of societal objectives.

Teaching and learning outcomes can be understood in two ways. One model, sometimes called "outcomes-based education," refers to institutional or systemic outcomes defined for the needs of external audiences. Averaged student performances, for example, are designed

to meet accreditation requirements and the requests of external stakeholders like employers and policymakers (Miller and Ewell, 2005).
Many US institutions now collect data and have established performance outcomes. However, there are no connections made between
these externally driven managerial concerns and the quality of teaching
within institutions.

Therefore, a second and critically important understanding of outcomes is captured by the notion of "outcomes-based approaches to
student learning," which specifically concerns program and course outcomes and the enhancement of teaching and learning both in and, in
some cases, outside the classroom (National Committee of Inquiry into
Higher Education, 1997). Outcomes in this sense date back to the mid-
20th century (Tyler, 1949) but did not gain traction until the mid-1980s
when it became clearer that "If students are to learn desired outcomes
in a reasonably effective manner, then the teacher's fundamental task is
to get students to engage in learning activities that are likely to result in
their achieving those outcomes" (Shuell, 1986, p. 429).

Embedded in this statement is a powerful design for teaching that
draws on two important principles:

1. The idea deriving from constructivist psychology that knowledge is
   not transmitted by a teacher but is constructed by students through
   their own learning activities
2. Outcomes need to be stated upfront and be aligned with both
   teaching methods and assessment strategies

When teaching, including course design and curriculum development, is based on student learning and involves identifying pedagogy
that will produce stated learning outcomes, it is accordingly called
"constructive alignment" (Biggs, 1996; Biggs and Tang, 2007). This
approach represents a crucial shift in teaching, away from declarative knowledge to functional knowledge. By articulating in advance
intended learning outcomes, appropriate teaching and learning
activities are built, followed by meaningful assessment tasks that
directly address the outcomes and the degree to which the teaching
and learning activities facilitate or hinder progress against the desired
outcomes.

Constructively aligned teaching systematizes what good teachers
have always done—stating upfront and making transparent what they
intend their students to learn, using teaching that helps the students
attain those outcomes, and assessing students in terms of how well
they attained the outcomes, while remaining open to learning outcomes that emerge organically during the critical exchange between
students and instructors.

Conclusion

It is clear that over the last 10 years, real momentum for change in university approaches to teaching and learning has emerged in at least some parts of the world. The challenges of producing those changes across systems, institutions, and disciplines, however, are significant. The traditional research-based university will still exist, but privatization, massification, and commodification greatly increase the need for prioritizing teaching, learning, and assessment and for effecting changes that are is anchored in credible scholarship and proven strategies.

Teaching and research always played a central role in the traditional university, although the prestige associated with these functions has been decidedly unequal. Contemporary circumstances are highlighting important teaching/research differences, but there is also a growing sense that much can be gained from strategic focus on both areas, across systems and within institutions and even individual programs. One can argue, though, that there is a real (and very complex) "identity problem" around teaching and research that higher education in most quarters has not yet solved. In practical terms, policy initiatives that seek to designate universities as either research or teaching institutions, with funds directed accordingly, require careful consideration of the broad range of both short- and long-term implications of such strategies.

In some contexts, although research still remains highly prestigious, teaching is now perceived as the major public purpose and activity of universities. To compete in a global knowledge market, universities have had to prioritize teaching and student learning across the whole university. The pressure to improve teaching fortunately comes at a time when research about teaching and learning—the scholarship of teaching and learning—is able to provide a framework for guiding institutionwide policies and the decisions of individual teachers. Universities—particularly in Europe, North America, and parts of Australasia—are now better positioned to leverage educational theory as a reflective tool for implementing procedures and policies for teaching and assessment on a universitywide basis, rather than departmentally, as has been typical in the past. In some institutions around the world, course design and assessment methods are increasingly based on intended student-learning outcomes, rather than content transmission from teacher to student. A great deal more research remains to be done, however, particularly in terms of understanding teaching and learning dynamics in a wider range of national and institutional settings. Effectively assessing needs, developing culturally appropriate approaches that maximize positive learning outcomes, and finding ways to provide appropriate materials and resources for the least-privileged higher education institutions and systems the world over is a critically important agenda item for the coming years.

10

Information and Communications Technology and Distance Education

Despite massive advancements in enrollment numbers over the last decade (especially in Africa, Latin America and the Caribbean, the Middle East, and eastern and central Europe), the demand for higher education has exceeded supply in many parts of the world, particularly in developing countries where the gross enrollment ratio is still quite low. The demand for higher education has been fueled by numerous factors. First, the number of primary and secondary students has grown considerably in the last decade, creating a large pool of prospective higher education students in the system. Second, the opportunities and demands of the globalized economy are such that lifelong learning has become much more necessary and common in many parts of the world. Third, the competition for existing and growing numbers of jobs requiring training beyond secondary school is escalating the need for more access to higher education.

Countries the world over have been making considerable efforts to expand the provision of higher education to accommodate the regular-age cohorts, as well as to deal with the rising numbers of nontraditional and lifelong learners. However, expansion based on traditional models of educational provision has peaked in many countries, particularly in contexts of limited public funding, and disconnects between supply and demand are expected to persist. This situation has sparked an interest in finding more versatile and cost-effective ways, new and old, of meeting tertiary education needs. Distance education has thus emerged as an extremely important option for higher education expansion and delivery in many quarters, particularly in the period since the 1990s, which has witnessed rapid and groundbreaking advancements in information and communications technologies (ICTs). Distance education represents an area of enormous potential for higher education systems around the world struggling to meet the needs of growing and changing student populations, as well as ambitious national development agendas. At the same time, real risks and challenges must be recognized and addressed.

Meanwhile, the advent of many new and innovative technologies in the past decade has had enormous implications for higher education. This is directly related to any discussion of distance education but also extends well beyond that specific realm. To different degrees around the world, ICTs have had an extraordinary impact on everything from teaching and learning; institutional management, administration, and finance; to external relations; library services; research production and dissemination; and student life (Guri-Rosenblit, 2009). At the same time, the "actual effects" of new technologies in recent decades have not always measured up to the "sweeping expectations" that have characterized their arrival on the scene (Guri-Rosenblit, 2009). The ICT revolution has presented a broad and complex set of costs and benefits for higher education, yet there remains a great deal of uncertainty about how these effects may play out over time and across very diverse regions of the world.

Key Terminology and Definitions

A wide range of (often overlapping) terms and definitions are employed in the discussion of distance education and educational technology, particularly with the advent of many new technologies in recent years. Even for experts deeply involved in this topic, it is extremely difficult to get firm a grasp on the varied terminology. Indeed, it has been noted that there are

> more than 20 terms which describe the employment of the new technologies in education, such as: Internet mediated teaching, technology-enhanced learning, web-based education, online education, computer-mediated communication (CMC), telematics environments, e-learning, virtual classrooms, I-Campus, electronic communication, information and communication technologies (ICT), cyberspace learning environments, computer-driven interactive communication, open and distance learning (ODL), distributed learning, blended courses, electronic course materials, hybrid courses, digital education, mobile learning, and technology enhanced learning. (Guri-Rosenblit, 2009, p. 2)

Meanwhile, the terms *borderless, cross-border, transnational,* and *international* education have become fashionable with the increasingly international reach of distance providers and new educational technologies, which also serves to highlight many interesting complexities that relate to educational delivery across national borders.

One way to simplify this discussion is to focus on what may be the umbrella terms of e-learning and distance education. These terms are often used interchangeably, but their conflation is not always accurate or appropriate, given that many applications of ICT represent more "technologically clever ways of replicating traditional, face-to-face education models" (Butcher, 2008, p. 3) than they do innovative distance models. Guri-Rosenblit (2009) asserts that e-learning and distance education are decidedly "not the same thing" (p. 6). E-learning "refers to any type of learning using electronic means of any kind (TV, radio, CD-ROM, DVD, mobile phone, personal organizer, Internet, etc.)" (Arafeh, 2004, quoted in Guri-Rosenblit, 2009, p. 2). Furthermore, e-learning is interpreted as "a relatively new phenomenon" used "for a variety of learning purposes that range from supplementary functions in conventional classrooms to full substitution of the face-to-face meetings by online encounters" (Guri-Rosenblit, 2009, p. 7). By contrast, distance learning involves any effort that does not require students to assemble in a particular location but instead "reaches out to students wherever they live or wish to study" (Guri-Rosenblit, 2009, p. 7). Distance education can therefore be understood more as a "method of delivery than an educational philosophy," while "distance is not a defining characteristic of e-learning" (Guri-Rosenblit, 2009, p. 9). Meanwhile, the terms "dual" or "mixed-mode" education capture the idea of using face-to-face and ICT instructional tools in conjunction with one another, which is an increasingly common approach taken by many higher education providers.

The speed of innovation and the experimental nature of many applications of technology to the higher education sector add another layer of complexity to the efforts to develop a common language around these activities. This "Tower of Babel Syndrome" (Guri-Rosenblit, 2009) shows no immediate signs of being resolved.

Manifestations of ICTs in Higher Education
A wide range of ICT elements have been deployed in higher education over the last decade. Notable applications include databases, e-mail, Web sites, social networking tools (such as chat rooms, bulletin boards, and discussion boards), blogs (essentially Web sites, such as Wikipedia, featuring ongoing posts of information, ideas, commentaries, and other content), wikis (page or collection of Web pages), Real Simple Syndica-

tion (known commonly by its acronym RSS, for subscriptions to online content from preferred sources), podcasts (typically for audio content), online videos, and instant messaging, among others (Butcher, 2008).

Particularly (but not exclusively) in the world's most developed economies, ICTs are ubiquitous in the higher education sector and constitute a basic part of institutional infrastructure. In the last decade, the presence of these technologies within tertiary education has expanded exponentially and touched virtually all dimensions of the higher education enterprise. Electronic databases house student, staff, and administrative records, as well as course and library materials. University Web sites situate institutions both globally and locally, providing a public image that can be accessed from anywhere in the world, at any time, and serving as an informational crossroads for all members of the community interested in engaging with the institution. ICT resources—like e-mail, instant messaging, and online social networking spaces—provide avenues for academic collaboration, joint research, and personal and professional networking. Computer laboratories give students and staff access to hardware and software for coursework and research. Continuously available wireless networks and remote-access library databases have altered the notions of time and place for work and study on campuses. Networked classrooms, equipped with a range of audio and visual equipment, have expanded the range of materials that may be introduced to students and the methods by which information and ideas can be shared. The open educational resources (OER) movement (a term adopted at a UNESCO meeting in 2002 [D'Antoni, 2008]) was famously initiated in 2001 by the Massachusetts Institute of Technology in the United States with its Open Courseware initiative (S. M. Johnstone, 2005). Since that time, development and use of OER has picked up significant momentum (S. M. Johnstone, 2005), making notable inroads onto the agendas of the higher education sectors in less-developed countries (D'Antoni, 2008). OER provide free access to courses, curricula, and pedagogical approaches not available locally. And finally, various combinations of online and virtual resources in the last decade have laid a most important foundation for the expansion of the distance-education sector.

The extent to which new technologies and digital applications are implemented, however, differs across national and institutional contexts (Guri-Rosenblit, 2009). Unfortunately, in the face of a real "digital divide" between richer and poorer countries and institutions, the capacity for implementation often appears to be inversely proportional to the perceived need and strong desire for access to these resources. At the institutional level, for example, elite, resource-rich research universities with ample means to access and support state-of-the-art technologies may choose not to employ technology in ways that dramatically expand access, given their missions to serve small numbers of carefully selected, high-performing students and scholars. At the other end of the spectrum, large distance-teaching institutions around the world are eager to employ ICT to expand access but are hampered by resource-infrastructure deficiencies (Guri-Rosenblit, 2009).

This analysis plays out at the national level, as well. In many developing countries, new technologies are often considered the key to realizing successful cost-effective strategies for increased access to higher education. Yet, there are enormous costs and difficulties embedded in the reliance on ICT. Hardware, software, technical support, training, and continual upgrades are all expensive. And the effective deployment of new technologies in countries where even reliable access to electricity is uncertain complicates matters even further. For many of the world's developing countries, some people argue that the more traditional "industrial model of distance education still provides a much cheaper and more feasible possibility [for expanding access to higher education] than trying to adopt the new digital technologies" (Guri-Rosenblit, 2009, p. 71). The reliance on "older broadcast technologies such as radio and television" is perceived as less attractive and innovative by many but may provide better and more effective penetration into relevant communities (Guri-Rosenblit, 2009, p. 71). The fact that the regions of Africa, the Middle East, and Latin America and the Caribbean constitute just 17.2 percent of the world's Internet users (Miniwatts Marketing Group) highlights the key underlying issue of technology infrastructure and access in the developing world.

ICT Promises and Pitfalls

One of the most notable aspects of the ICT revolution over the last decade is the degree to which excitement about innovations has failed, in many respects, to meet optimistic expectations. The realities on the ground across the globe have been much more complex and that higher education has been less open to penetration by ICTs than previously imagined—particularly as concerns teaching and learning (Guri-Rosenblit, 2009). Another significant factor explaining uneven degrees of ICT acceptance and usage has to do with "cultural and political differences" between countries. The failures of the University of Phoenix (transplanted from the United States to the United Kingdom) and the Open University (which attempted to bring a British distance-learning option to the United States), provide interesting examples of such challenges (Guri-Rosenblit, 2009).

Still, the innovative technologies that have emerged in recent years have impacted tertiary education across the globe, presenting the sector with an enormous range of opportunities along with some significant challenges. The ICT explosion does hold the promise of breaking down barriers of time, space, and privilege; lowering costs; and enabling collaboration and creativity in teaching, learning, and research. Particularly the world's wealthier countries have encountered great progress in these areas. In other parts of the world, however, the penetration of ICT into higher education has exacerbated the gap between knowledge-producing "centers" and knowledge-consuming "peripheries" (Altbach, 1998). The world's poorest countries are increasingly left behind as they have limited or no access to the technological pathways that lead to information production and dissemination. Everywhere enormous financial strains have been placed on institutions and systems trying to equip themselves for the Information Age and sustain subsequent innovation. It is extremely costly, for example, to train and compensate skilled staff using new technologies; provide access to expensive online journals and databases; and assure the security of electronically stored data. Real financial and moral/ethical challenges have been embedded in the process of dealing appropriately with the dangerous waste generated by obsolete computer hardware and other components used in e-learning (Guri-Rosenblit, 2009).

Perhaps most fundamental to higher education, most parts of the world have faced a disconnect between employing new ICTs and leveraging them to enhance quality, particularly in terms of teaching and learning. The Information Age requires the strenuous reinforcement of certain basic skills, including reading and writing, along with more advanced skills like problem identification, problem solving, and the ability to engage in effective "complex communication" with others (F. Levy and Murnane, 2006). In a "brave new world" of limitless choice and vast amounts of data circulating freely in cyberspace, tertiary-level educators have new kinds of responsibilities. Among these are the need to foster disciplined thinking, "navigate . . . ethical dilemmas effectively and positively," cope with a sometimes overwhelming array of choices, and encourage creativity and initiative in the learning process (F. Levy and Murnane, 2006).

Meanwhile, research indicates that, even in the face of incredibly powerful and innovative technologies, teachers in both developed and developing countries "remain central to the learning process" (Guri-Rosenblit, 2009, p. 36). To effectively harness the potential of new technologies, however, teaching staff require support, training, and guidance to learn new skills and determine how best to incorporate technology in teaching strategies for individual teaching styles and student learning needs.

Distance-Education Providers and Approaches

Distance learning has been in existence for generations, but the sector has been transformed significantly over time with the advancement and application of new technologies. Beginning with mail correspondence in the early 20th century, distance education then benefited from the emergence of radio and TV platforms, followed by CD-ROM technology some two decades ago. The distance-learning landscape was then dramatically expanded and transformed by the introduction of the Internet, along with such key applications as e-mail and electronic messaging. ICTs have exponentially boosted the potential of distance education to reach enormous new pools of students. It has also allowed for real growth in numbers and types of providers, curriculum developers, and modes of delivery, as well as innovations in both pedagogical approaches and content.

Today, print and electronic options are both used around the world, and the delivery of open and distance education is typically understood to fall into two distinct categories—synchronous and asynchronous. Synchronous delivery involves all participants at the same time, while asynchronous delivery implies engagement by the various parties involved at different times (UNESCO, 2005b).

The typology of institutions providing distance education includes single-mode institutions, dual-mode institutions, consortia, and nontraditional providers. Single-mode institutions focus exclusively on providing distance education, while dual-mode institutions offer a combination of distance education and more traditional face-to-face course and/or program options. Consortia are comprised of two or more institutions working collaboratively to provide distance learning. Finally, nontraditional providers may include entities such as multinational corporations, nongovernmental organizations and development partners, as well as governments. Profit-making affiliates of traditional not-for-profit educational institutions may also be considered a part of this group (UNESCO, 2005b). The scope of actors involved in distance-education provision was especially extensive at the height of the information-technology bubble in the late 1990s and 2000, when many new actors jumped into the arena. Examples run the gamut from Harvard University (an elite private institutions and arguably the world's most prestigious university) to third-tier institutions such as technical and community colleges; from initiatives sanctioned by regional bodies with very targeted areas of focus, such as access expansion for small states of the Commonwealth, to the UN-sanctioned Global Virtual University, and government-supported entities such as the Syrian Virtual University.

For several decades, the sector has been dominated to a certain extent by large-scale "open" universities. The Indira Gandhi National Open University (IGNOU) in India, for example, describes itself as the largest university in the world, with

> nearly 2 million students in India and 33 other countries through . . . twenty-one Schools of Study and a network of 59 regional centers, more than 2300 Learner Support Centers and around 52 overseas centres. The University offers 175 . . . Certificate, Diploma, Degree and Doctoral programs, comprising around 1500 courses. . . . (IGNOU, 2009, p. 7)

In Africa, the University of South Africa claims to be the continent's premier distance-learning institution, with a total student body "in excess of 265,000," as well as "excellent infrastructure, cutting-edge technology, innovative learner support systems and a significant regional presence in South and southern Africa" (*Higher Education in Africa: What Does the Future Hold?* 2008, p. 5). Another example in Africa is the African Virtual University (AVU). Initially launched in Washington, DC in 1997 as a World Bank project, it is now an independent intergovernmental organization, headquartered since 2002 in Kenya. Over the last 10 years, the African Virtual University has acquired the largest network of open, distance, and e-learning institutions in Africa. It works across borders and language groups in Anglophone, Francophone, and Lusophone Africa, present in over 27 countries with more than 50 partner institutions (AVU).

Meanwhile, the University of Phoenix in the United States claims to be the largest private university in North America, with more than 100 degree programs at the associate's, bachelor's, master's, and doctoral levels. It boasts nearly 200 locations, largely in the United States, Canada, and Puerto Rico. Founded in 1976, the University of Phoenix is a for-profit corporate entity owned by the Apollo Group with enrollments of more than 250,000 students who may choose from exclusively online or campus-based learning options or a "FlexNext" approach that combines both formats (University of Phoenix). Megauniversities— "with over 100,000 students and using largely distance learning methods" (McIntosh and Varoglu, 2005, p. 6)—are found in a wide variety of countries. China was home to three such institutions as of 2003, including the Shanghai TV University. The Korea National University, the Open University in the United Kingdom, Spain's National

Distance Education University, and Turkey's Anadolu University also belong to the megauniversities "club" around the world (McIntosh and Varoglu, 2005).

The rationales for engagement in distance-education activities are as varied as the actors themselves. Motivations include revenue generation, broadening and expanding access, improving educational quality, and raising institutional profiles. It is extremely difficult to calculate the numbers of students engaged in distance education worldwide. However, the existence (as of 2005) of nearly two-dozen megauniversities (UNESCO, 2005a), a number of which boast having over one million students, speaks to a quantitatively significant phenomenon.

Distance-Education Opportunities and Benefits

Distance education presents important opportunities for the higher education sector globally and has already provided a range of benefits in different parts of the world over the last decade. The advantages of this nontraditional form of higher education delivery may be most immediate and apparent to those systems that have struggled to meet high demands for access—a common phenomenon across much of the developing world, in particular. In Africa, for example, despite considerable growth in enrollment numbers in the last decade, the gross enrollment ratio there hovers around 5 percent, with considerable disparity by country and subregion. Some countries have been expanding access quite aggressively. In Ethiopia, for example, more than a dozen universities were established within a short period of time, and the country recently unveiled a plan to build 10 more. However, even with this kind of commitment to expansion, the economic state of many developing countries keeps them unable to expand the traditional higher education system quickly enough to satisfy the rising demand. Thus, in the absence of sufficient local and/or traditional providers—and against a backdrop of increasing demand for higher education, owing to the knowledge-driven global economy—alternative approaches to higher education provision are extremely attractive and in some cases the only viable option. Expanding access to tertiary education through distance education has therefore never been more crucial or of interest. Indeed, a good number of flagship universities and newly established private institutions are already actively involved in the delivery of distance education in a number of countries. For instance, the University of Ghana, considered a flagship university in Africa, started a distance-education program in 2007, while in Ethiopia a number of newly established colleges are also distance-education providers.

Distance education is also of particular interest to small and more isolated countries, which can be severely limited in their abilities to expand traditional brick-and-mortar institutions. Even if they have sufficient resources, it may not be sufficiently cost effective for such systems to invest heavily in this area, particularly in light of the constant need to upgrade facilities and technology. In addition, the ephemeral nature of knowledge in today's fast-paced global information society means that many developments in key fields—such as economics, finance, the sciences, and technology—are extremely fast paced, while the life span of innovative products is quite short. The demands inherent in building and retooling new programs to keep up with these developments may make it more desirable to access programming via distance-education methods. Of course, this state of affairs does not mean that well-resourced small countries cannot themselves become major providers of distance education. In 2000, the government of the Indian Ocean island nation of Mauritius proposed a plan for developing the country into a "knowledge hub," with building its capacity to provide distance learning as one of its eight strategic initiatives (Mohamedbhai, 2008).

In many countries around the world, the need for continuous learning and ongoing skill upgrades has become increasingly apparent. In countries where nations struggle to cater to the traditional-age cohort of 18-to-24-year-olds, the challenge is daunting of providing lifelong-learning opportunities for broad swathes of the adult population via traditional delivery modes of delivery. In many places around the world, distance education can and has already played a growing role in filling this gap. Much of the appeal of distance education today is attributed to its ability to accommodate the needs of a wide variety of learners. By allowing many different kinds of individuals to access information, materials, and coursework remotely, distance education provides great flexibility and versatility and can draw in an enormous range of individuals who might otherwise be unable to physically attend classes—ranging from students who are fully employed, those located far from educational centers, women who are attempting to balance family and school commitments, and even the incarcerated. ICTs have made learning possible virtually anytime and anywhere in the world, taking flexibility in higher education program delivery to the highest level.

Risks and Challenges of Distance Education
Despite the wide range of benefits that can be derived from distance education, a number of very real risks and challenges can accompany this mode of educational delivery. One of the most difficult challenges facing distance education currently relates to quality assurance. As dis-

tance education markets expand and the importance and acceptance of the sector in higher education circles rises, the emergence of questionable, even fraudulent, providers is cause for growing concern.

The liberalization of the global economy, which is eliminating business and commercial barriers around the world, has made it increasingly possible—and lucrative—for educational providers to operate across borders. These providers are often not answerable to the jurisdictions of the national regulatory systems of users, nor are they fully controlled in the countries where they operate or from which they hail. Even in systems where quality-assurance and accreditations agencies function well, they often lack clear mandates on matters of program delivery beyond regional or national borders. In addition, most countries have limited resources and regulatory backing to cope with the emerging issues related to distance education, track fraudulent entities and diploma mills, and take appropriate measures to curb unscrupulous practices and providers (Kimani, 2008). The widely reported case of fraud and diploma-mill activity by the now defunct Saint Regis University is a prime example of how a bogus operation can leverage the relatively thin oversight of distance education—even in a country like the United States, which boasts a fairly robust tradition of quality assurance and accreditation compliance. The expansion and growth of private distance-education providers has also brought with it new kinds of accrediting institutions, often driven by financial gain. This makes the task of identifying legitimate institutions, programs, and providers even more difficult.

Increasingly, distance-education delivery depends on the newest innovations in ICTs. The fundamental challenge here is that access to ICTs and the Internet varies widely around the world. Teledensity—"a term commonly used to describe the number of telephone lines per some unit of the population" (Harvard University Center for International Development), which can also shed light on the degree to which a community or nation has access to computers, the Internet, and e-gadgets—is not uniform around the world and is an indicator of the immense divide between "haves" and "have-nots" across the globe. Even in contexts with relevant technologies and infrastructure, barriers still exist, given that the cost of access for those with fewer resources is considerably higher than for those with the necessary financial means.

The disparity in ICT quality and access is seen not only across regions and national borders, but also across rural and urban settings within the same country. Phone and Internet access, power supply (and reliability), and requisite infrastructure are often more available in the main urban areas. Not coincidentally, the largest student populations in distance education still reside in major cities, creating a notable imbalance in distance- (and higher) education access within countries. The availability of ICTs does not necessarily translate into access to technology resources for education. Numerous regulatory, administrative, technical, and logistical challenges hamper the use and deployment of such technologies. For instance, many developing countries experience a shortage of technical expertise—and/or resources to support it—that is much needed in such areas as end-user support and in the prevention of e-malfeasance, such as virus attacks, hacking, and phishing. Furthermore, managing available resources, such as bandwidth, has also become more of a challenge. As distance education becomes increasingly dependent on the Internet such issues will continue to hamper the field.

Another challenge for distance education, particularly in terms of its international dimensions, relates to language. English has emerged as the dominant language of scholarship, research, business, and diplomacy. As a consequence, English-speaking countries (such as the United States, United Kingdom, Canada, and Australia) have been well positioned to operate in the distance-education arena far beyond their national borders. Tertiary programming, using English-language materials and/or instruction, has effectively infiltrated many parts of the world that have traditionally delivered higher education in languages other than English. This trend of breaking down old patterns of higher education delivery that were long driven by colonial language ties has been rapidly accelerated by the advent of high-tech ICTs.

It is also important to recognize that distance education thrives when it can operate in an economy of scale. Distance education curricula and programs are often designed in standard formats for use by a large and diverse set of learners. To a great extent, these products are developed in and marketed by providers situated in the more developed countries of the North. Curricula, program design, methodological approaches, and content are all affected in this process, and developing countries—which are home to a large and growing percentage of end users of distance-education programs and materials—have little choice but to accept educational products that often do not adequately address local needs, interests, or values.

Key Considerations for the Future

The ongoing introduction of innovations in educational technologies and the evolving nature of the distance-education enterprise around the world make it difficult to predict future developments. However, several issues bear thoughtful consideration, especially in terms of the way that institutions will look and behave. For example, some observers suggest that traditional campuses will see a degree of qualitative transformation by existing more "on a digital platform of shared information, materials, and experience" that will allow for improved access and quality (Vest, 2007, p. 109). A greater reliance on cooperative arrangements, such as consortia, to leverage resources and share costs inherent in implementing ICTs in higher education, may occur. And more and different kinds of dual-mode universities—employing both ICTs and traditional program delivery methods—may emerge (Guri-Rosenblit, 2009).

It has to date been quite difficult to consolidate findings related to the use and effectiveness of ICTs in teaching and learning, but a critical mass of scholars, practitioners, and policymakers seems ready to push for progress in this area. Extracting meaningful research findings on the effects of technology on teaching and learning has been hampered by the speed of innovation, which often renders study results obsolete as new technologies replace old ones. However, there is an especially important need in the current environment—with the growing focus on lifelong learning and ongoing professional education and (re) training—to provide real flexibility in teaching and learning within higher education, and research is needed to guide these efforts. And although ICTs have clearly been an incredibly important tool for academics in their research activities, their effects on teaching have been less clear. Furthermore, it appears quite important for teaching staff to receive support and guidance in terms of implementing technology in their teaching activities. Finding ways to do this that are both contextually appropriate and cost effective, looms large on the horizon (Guri-Rosenblit, 2009).

Additionally, making sense of emerging technologies and the ways that these will effect both distance education and other aspects of the academic enterprise are extremely important agenda items for the future. One key example here is the role that m-learning—that is, applications that can be run on mobile phones and other mobile platforms—may play in the coming years. There are exciting possibilities for the ways in which m-learning may open up access in some of the world's poorest countries, where Internet access is most limited and unreliable. Research out of the Philippines (Ramos, Trinona, and Lambert, 2006), Japan (Thornton and Houser, 2004), and South Africa (Visser and West, 2005), is laying the groundwork for more exploration in this area. Meanwhile, so-called "immersive education" offers one window on the next generation of educational technologies, focused on virtual and simulation technologies, 3-D graphics and interactive applications, and gaming approaches. Although immersive education applications are potentially exciting, special attention will need to be paid to how these expensive cutting-edge tools can be made accessible to underresourced countries and institutions.

Finally, strengthening capacity in regard to technology issues and open and distance learning is an extremely important objective in a global context characterized by profound inequity. Notable here are such resources as UNESCO's Open and Distance Learning Knowledge Base (UNESCO, n.d.-b), and the 19 UNESCO chairs and four University Twinning and Networking initiatives around the world, all focused on open and distance learning topics (UNESCO, n.d.-a). These multilateral efforts hold the promise of not only moving the international discourse forward in this area but also sustaining quality research and sound policymaking practices.

Conclusion

ICTs and distance education are different but tightly interconnected aspects of higher education that have come to play an increasingly important role in postsecondary policymaking and practice over the last decade. The need to serve larger and more diverse populations of students, in different ways and over a much longer period of their lives, is exerting tremendous pressures on higher education systems and institutions the world over. Distance education has long been a cost-effective and flexible method for drawing in underserved students. ICTs and related technologies have vastly expanded the potential to deliver postsecondary education at a distance but have also exacerbated inequalities within and across countries. Meanwhile, quite apart from distance education, innovative educational technologies have transformed many institutions around the world—academically and administratively— while creating new linkages and new chasms between rich and poor countries and higher education systems. Many of the enthusiastic promises held out by early adopters of ICTs—particularly those that touted the democratizing effects of the new technologies at a global level—have either failed to materialize over the last decade or have only been realized in limited and piecemeal ways. There has been an uneven adoption of (and extraction of benefits from) ICTs in higher education around the world, due in large part to the same kinds of resource inequities that vex many other aspects of the higher education enterprise. Contextually based needs assessment, significant capacity building (in human, material, and economic terms), relevant research, and ongoing review and support from key stakeholders will be critically important in most parts of the world if ICTs are to deliver on many of the promises they hold and distance education is to enable the access and flexibility so critically needed in many quarters.

11

Research

Research and innovation (the production of new knowledge) are closely linked with the teaching function within the modern university. Both research and innovation, valuable in their own right, have achieved greater legitimacy in society through the use of new knowledge for economic and social development and the employment of university graduates in strategic positions in the private and public sectors. Research has been and continues to be an extremely important contribution of the university to the larger society.

The three missions of the modern university—teaching, research, and public service—live in constant tension with each other at different levels. Governments have tended to set priorities for different kinds of higher education institutions, often designating "teaching only" and "research only" institutional types. Universities, to the extent that they enjoy autonomy to develop their own plans and programs, must often make hard choices in setting priorities and allocating resources, in cases where they retain multiple missions.

Teaching and research do not necessarily live happily together within the same organization. In many universities professors conduct research while actively teaching classes, although these functions are often dispersed and tend to be poorly integrated. Some units (i.e., disciplinary departments) organize teaching, while others (i.e., laboratories, centers, and institutes) manage research infrastructure, research staff, and projects. Other offices deal with knowledge transfer and relations with the community. Research and research training are an intrinsic part of the education process of graduate students—in particular at the doctoral level—but are seldom incorporated into undergraduate programs. Meanwhile, professional and vocational programs traditionally have made better use of accumulated knowledge and tend to emphasize practical applications of knowledge over research training, although this is changing in both new and old professional fields.

The academic profession, whose ranks are largely nurtured by research-trained professionals, is facing an increasingly differentiated labor market. There is now a tendency toward separate "teaching-only" and "research-only" positions compared with the traditional "teaching and research" position. "Public service" is often included in academic job descriptions and sometimes influences the way professors allocate their time.

A vast literature deals with these changes all over the world. Most recently, mass demand for higher education has driven the expansion of "teaching-only" institutions and programs since they require less investment. The trend is toward more differentiation between institutions. Teaching-only private institutions, increasingly with distance-education facilities, have expanded access in many countries. In Europe and North America, first-cycle (or short-cycle) instructional programs offered by smaller institutions have absorbed much of the demand at lower cost.

Teaching-only institutions attend to the needs of a highly heterogeneous student body and nurture capacity for specialized functions but also help contain public spending on higher education. With new goals in mind, governments often attempt to reorganize, merge, or tinker in a variety of ways with preexisting institutions, assigning specific functions to each of them. The underlying assumption is that the costs of research, teaching, and service activities can be planned and managed more efficiently at higher levels. This assumption usually meets with considerable resistance from institutions and the academic communities.

At the same time that countries are accommodating mass enrollment at the postsecondary level, demand for graduate degrees is increasing as well. Graduate education, however, traditionally involves at least some research training and tends to be taught by professors engaged in research. This is particularly true in disciplinary master's and doctoral degrees where the next generation of professors and researchers is prepared. But this is also increasingly the case with the growing number of professional master's programs and doctoral programs.

Mass systems cannot ignore the importance of the teaching/research link, but many challenges are emerging. The first issue is finding the correct balance of public/private investment to ensure that basic research continues, that research is supported in new fields of study, and that research continues in applied fields. The second issue is to find appropriate strategies for the rational allocation of limited resources.

Yet another challenge is to integrate the research function more broadly across the university. Cultivating more research capacity in the developing world is also critically important. Finally, the dramatic expansion of teaching-only institutions (whether de facto or by design) distances more and more students from exposure to research.

The Knowledge Economy

An important trend has been the spectacular growth of scientific and technological research that forms the underpinning of the knowledge economy. "Big science" has not always favored university-based research. In the past, governments and industry in many countries have steered research funding to dedicated government institutions. In recent decades, however, basic and applied research have prospered in university laboratories as well as in industry, with isolated research institutes losing ground. New fields of study being developed at universities, such as biotechnology, genomics, nanotechnology, optical technology, and information science promise new research that will offer practical applications for industry. Government support to university-based research has increased in recent years to encourage these projects.

Governments worldwide are the largest supporters of academic science, which increasingly takes place within higher education, but private funding of university-based research has also increased. However, large-scale public investment in laboratories, equipment, and expensive research programs requires an appropriate institutional base and tends to be made selectively. Despite the exponential increase in university-based research in recent years, funding for scientific research has tended to be concentrated in a relatively small number of institutions. Additionally, the shift from block-grant funding of public universities that covers teaching *and* research to competitive funding for project-specific awards, which also provide funds for equipment, laboratories, or libraries, has contributed to the emergence of the modern research university. In the new knowledge economy, the boundaries between academic and applied research have become more blurred, leading university researchers to develop closer and more interdependent relations with industry.

The so-called "triple helix" of university/government/industry linkages has resulted in important organizational changes within the university. In some countries and universities, special offices and positions have materialized and prospered to encourage new "entrepreneurial" thinking and to generate new income streams for the university. Thus, the strengthening of the research function is clearly contributing to organizational changes that go with increased research capacity.

Although these changes have supported a stronger research role for the modern university, they have also encouraged further differentiation between institutions— research-intensive versus teaching and research or teaching-only universities—and within them.

Systemwide Policy and the Research University

The notion of systemwide design—with individual institutions becoming embedded in national frameworks and regulated through system rather than local institutional planning—has become a major policy trend worldwide during the last few decades (Teichler, 2006; Guri-Rosenblit, Sebkova, and Teichler, 2007). A top-down approach translates into differentiated funding for teaching and research, varying degrees of autonomy to develop research and teaching programs and to award degrees, and changed rules for faculty recruitment, assessment, and promotion.

A recent examination of the relationship between teaching and research in European university systems found three different patterns (Schimank and Winnes, 2000). The first type includes situational relations, with different segments of the university devoted to teaching and/or research. Still declaring the unity of teaching and research as a guiding principle, faculty are assumed to do both and paid accordingly from government block grants that provide basic funding. Within this system, the pressures of enrollment growth and restricted government funding have inclined faculty to dedicate more time to teaching, with a negative impact upon research. Germany and Italy were primary examples of this situation, but things are starting to change in both countries, which may improve their research profile.

A second pattern reflects differentiation of roles, funding, and institutional focus. Early examples of this dynamic were found in Sweden, the United Kingdom, and Norway, and (more recently) in the Netherlands. In these countries, undergraduate teaching is entrusted to lecturers, while professors and research staff are allowed to concentrate on research, which (by policy or de facto) is primarily conducted among a reduced number of institutions.

Finally, the third type is characterized by a strict differentiation between research and teaching institutions—funded and organized independently of each other. This pattern is evident in France but also in many other parts of the world, particularly the countries of the former Soviet bloc. Traditionally, research played a secondary role in universities in these countries and was mainly related to graduate training of young scientists and scholars.

Latin America reflects slightly different patterns. Research is either conducted at separate institutions, as in the third pattern above, or (more often) is concentrated in a few elite (almost always public) universities. Research activity is often further concentrated within the universities in separate centers remote from the instructional activity that supports first-cycle university and professional degree programs.

At the National Autonomous University of Mexico (UNAM)—the largest producer of PhDs in that country—graduate teaching and research are located within so-called research institutes, physically and administratively separated from the *facultades* where undergraduate and professional training takes place. The Center of Research and Advanced Studies, the second-largest producer of research in Mexico is a separate research and graduate training branch of the National Polytechnic Institute.

The concentration of research at a few institutions, often of the "multiversity" type, is reflected in the large numbers of publications that originate from this small group. For example, one public university is responsible for 37 percent of all research papers in Chile; similarly, one university produces 30 percent of the papers in Mexico; a single university produces 25 percent in Brazil; and just one institution is responsible for 18 percent in Argentina. In Chile, for instance, universities are the main actor in science production, with the five oldest institutions responsible for almost 80 percent of the research carried out in the country (Bernasconi, 2008).

Allocation Strategies and Hierarchies

Research universities worldwide sit at the top of the higher education hierarchy. They are able to concentrate resources and power and often have an influential role within the education system, thanks to the prestige and influence of their faculty and graduates. Government-funding patterns contribute to the status of these institutions. Governments typically reward, with additional funding, those institutions with a proven record of research output and research management. Most governments concentrate their research investment in relatively few institutions. In many countries—including Germany and France, but also China, the Russian Federation, some eastern European countries—these institutions have historically played a leading role in international scientific research.

Most European countries, as well as Japan and Canada, have funded academic research through general-fund block grants, with these funds accounting for 50 percent or more of total government R&D support to the universities (National Science Board, 2008). The current trend is to allocate research funding to universities on a competitive basis to make more efficient use of research funds and target problem-oriented or industry-oriented research programs. Between 1981 and 2003, the percentage of research funding through general university funds dropped from 78 percent to 65 percent in the 16 OECD countries for which information is available. Governments have balanced the decrease in research support by encouraging research centers to embark on collaborations with private companies.

The United Kingdom has led the funding reform movement in Europe since the 1980s, linking research assessment with further research funding to concentrate efforts in the most productive departments. Germany, one of the more state-dependent higher education and research systems, is currently attempting to restructure its universities—a largely homogenous segment of public research and teaching institutions—through a much more focused research-funding policy (Pritchard, 2006). For the European Union as a whole, the share of higher education expenditure on R&D as a percent of the total R&D spending has increased consistently over the last few years and is currently larger than in the United States or Japan (European Commission, 2003, p. 78).

Among the new scientific powerhouses, China's policy since the late 1990s has also focused research support on a small number of universities. Specifically, China has provided special funding packages to build world-class universities. The funding packages from the central government—often with additional subsidies from municipal funds—are administered by the central university administration. Thus, it is a vertically managed, noncompetitive allocation based on high-level decisions about which institutions have the capacity to become research-intensive universities. In the words of Qiang Zha,

> Chinese higher education institutions are being structured in a hierarchical way according to their functions and goals. On the top are the national elite universities that focus on research . . . They educate the majority of doctoral students, in addition to master's and bachelor students. They are designated as the "national team" to move China's innovation capacity to a higher level and play a leading role in performing research activities that are of great importance to national development and security as well as collaborating in international research efforts. The universities at the second rank are oriented to both research and teaching, mainly educating master's and bachelor students, with doctoral students only in a few specific disciplines. The universities at the third rank are those that are

fundamentally teaching oriented, training mainly undergradu-ates. Finally, down at bottom of the hierarchy is a new tier of institutions, the higher vocational college, providing only 2–3 year programs . . . The last two categories constitute the major-ity of China's higher education institutions, taking on most of the expansion and increasing their enrolment dramatically, while the enrolment expansion in the elitist universities has only been symbolic. (Qiang Zha, forthcoming)

Many governments have found it difficult to rank institutions in terms of their research capacity as a basis for concentrating support. Block funding for research and teaching, usually justified on the grounds of the indissoluble link between these functions, is strenuously defended by the university professoriate in Europe, Latin America, and elsewhere. Retaining a research mission gives universities special status and privi-leges, not afforded to teaching-only and vocational schools (such as teacher-training institutions). Still, academic research production and government support remain largely concentrated among a handful of institutions although the "research-university model" is becoming the standard that most universities aspire to (Bernasconi, 2007).

Trends for Hosting Basic Research and R&D
The strengthening of academic research worldwide has been a rather striking feature of the overall growth trend in scientific research during the last few decades. Among the rich countries (i.e., members of the OECD) the share of R&D carried out by higher education has increased at the expense of government institutes and has grown even faster than R&D performed by industry.

Basic research has been identified as a special feature of academic research:

In 2003, it accounted for about 18% of the gross domestic expenditures on R&D in the OECD area, up from 15% in 1981. The higher education sector represents less than one fifth of all R&D expenditures in the OECD area, but it carries out the bulk of basic research in most OECD countries. In 2003, on average, 54% of an OECD country's basic research was carried out in the higher education sector. And the government and higher education sectors accounted together for 82% of all basic research. (Vincent-Lancrin, 2006, p. 174)

Among OECD countries, the early model of science and technology policy in support of fundamental research included both dedicated institutions with government support—such as the CNRS in France, the Max Planck institutes in Germany, the Consiglio Nazionale delle Richerche in Italy, the Consejo Superior de Investigaciones Científicas in Spain, and Riken in Japan—and university research. More recently, however, branches of former research-only institutes have moved to universities and over time have developed closer links to them.

In the developing world, scientific and technological research after World War II was largely a state-supported enterprise concentrated in separate government research institutes. "Big Science," whether in India, Brazil, or Argentina, or in the socialist countries following the example of the Soviet Union, was typically housed outside of the university, as was most applied research in fields such as agriculture and food production, public health, and industrial technology. This has changed quite radically since the 1990s with the downfall of the Soviet Union and of the Soviet-dominated Eastern European Bloc, although with sharp differences between countries.

> The shares of higher education and non-university academic research in Hungary and Estonia in the 80s and still in the early 1990s reflect the typical "socialist" science system with smaller university sectors and relatively large shares of nonuniversity academic research. In Estonia, the situation was extreme—the share of the governmental sectors exceeded that of the university sector. The situation dramatically changed in the course of the following ten years. The relation between the two sectors in Estonia very much resembled that of Finland in 2003. The industry sector was already present in 1993, but remained constant until 2003. The development in Hungary was slow, and reflects minor and less pronounced changes. Nonetheless, the data reflect a trend in the direction of the western model. (Glanzel and Schlemmer, 2007, p. 270)

China straddles both models—continuing to support and develop independent research institutes while simultaneously investing heavily in university-based research. Public research institutes make (in absolute numbers) the second-largest contribution to international science. Enterprise research contributes only marginally to international publications, but it provides 6 percent of the content found in national publications. Hospitals are important producers of publications domestically, but not internationally (Zhou and Leydesdorff, 2006).

In Brazil, independent research institutes are still important in terms of research production in applied fields such as public health and agriculture, but disciplinary research production is concentrated primarily in seven public universities. These universities were responsible for 60 percent of the internationally indexed research production coming out of Brazil. A similar pattern is found in Argentina, where the government was reluctant to fund university-based groups before the 1980s but has changed its policy quite dramatically since then.

The growth in university research capacity and output has been well documented. In the 1980s and 1990s, the number of university-based researchers increased about 7 percent a year within the OECD countries, and they produced about 82 percent of the world's scientific articles. The higher education sector devotes 64 percent of its R&D activities to basic research and is the only sector that is mainly devoted to it. Yet, the most distinctive feature of the modern university throughout the world during the last decade is the growing ties to industry for the production of new knowledge.

Since the 1970s the knowledge-production function of universities has become a source of both formal and informal collaboration with industry through contract research, cooperative research, consulting, networking, and increasingly through the mobility of research personnel between academia and industry. In the past, support for science was provided by governments in pursuit of national interests and identified with public enterprise and research institutes. There has been a clear shift, however, with university research more closely linked to private industry in many countries. The notion of a "third stream" of activities, or "third mission" of the university, is actually aligned with research capacity (Laredo, 2007).

University-Industry Linkages

The issue of industry linkages will be covered more fully in the following chapter, but new emerging patterns will be introduced here.

In 1980, only 20 universities in the United States housed their own office for patenting and licensing, but 112 more created them in the following two decades, with university research parks growing rapidly (Geiger, 2006). Between 1980 and 2004, the number of patents issued to US universities increased from about 350 to about 3,300 (Popp Berman, 2008). Research universities, both private and public, now have large permanent bureaucracies to commercialize intellectual property and to turn research into profit centers. Universities in the United States—but not yet in most European countries—have consolidated these functions under high-level authorities within the university, with a technology-transfer office typically at the center of operations. More recently, these offices have been transformed into technology-transfer complexes that include offices for industrial research, intellectual property, marketing and monitoring technology licensing, commercial development of start-up companies, research parks, business incubators, and venture capital funds. Start-up costs, however, are quite high, thus limiting the number of universities that can bear them. The top 100 research universities, performing some 80 percent of the total research carried out by US higher education, belong to this group. As in much of the world, the concentration of research funds among the top US research universities has remained steady over the last two decades, with only 5 of the top 20 institutions in 1986 not in the top 20 in 2006.

In Europe, government-funding patterns for university research have changed in recent years with a shift toward competitive problem-oriented or industry-oriented public programs. University researchers and research centers are encouraged to embark on collaborations with private companies including incentives to complement their research activities with technology-transfer activities. Still, very little reliable data are available on the phenomenon of university patenting, since most European public universities have lacked the necessary autonomy and administrative skill now routine at many US universities, and have (until recently) tended to resist rather than encourage faculty engagement in patenting activities or linking with industry.

Historically, continental European universities have left intellectual property rights in the hands of faculty and their industry research partners without university involvement on the order of US and British patterns. In countries such as France and Italy large public laboratories and governmental agencies still dominate the public research system and retain control over intellectual property rights to results of publicly funded research. A recent comparative analysis shows that while in the United States universities and other nonprofit organizations retain almost 70 percent of academic patents filed by domestic inventors, in France and Italy fewer than 10 percent are retained (Lissoni, Llerena, and McKelvey, 2008). The "entrepreneurial university" with professional administrators to manage research funding, activity, and output may not be viable in many parts of the world, even when there is a strong research orientation.

Reform and Expansion of Graduate Education

The European model of doctoral training—which has influenced many other countries around the world—was, until recently, based mainly on independent research undertaken by the doctoral candidate with the advice and guidance of one supervisor, closely following the model of a master/apprentice relationship. Historically, only a select number of academically oriented students would pursue this option. The reform and expansion of graduate education, in particular at the doctoral level, has challenged this model. In a growing number of universities and countries the research activity of doctoral candidates is complemented by other forms of training.

A mix of different program designs and structures seems to be common practice in most countries, reflecting the need to increase the number of doctoral candidates and the disciplinary differences to be taken into consideration. Graduate schools modeled after those of US universities are becoming common in many developing countries, although they normally adapt to local institutional cultures and the persistence of long-cycle, professional degree programs in many cases.

Brazil adapted the US university model of a graduate school following the 1968 reforms there. Graduate programs have multiplied since the 1970s and are regularly evaluated, ranked, and financed by CAPES, a government agency in charge of enhancing the quality of the professoriate. The Brazilian system currently awards some 10,000 doctorates and 30,000 master's degrees each year, a 300 percent increase in 10 years. Graduate programs are ranked on the basis of their research productivity and then financed accordingly. Thus, those ranked in the higher categories receive the most fellowship support. The CAPES evaluation system has led to extraordinary results in terms of the incorporation of research into the university in conjunction with developing graduate-level education. Some limitations apparent in the Brazilian context, however, most likely affect other systems as well. It has been difficult to apply the same basic evaluation criteria for research in science to the social sciences and humanities or applied fields. This highlights the difficulty of dealing with new interdisciplinary areas and taking into account the diversification of the graduate education system (Schwartzman, et al., 2008).

In the Republic of Korea, the Brain Korea 21 plan of 1998 promoted the concentration of research efforts within the traditional elite universities responsible for doctoral education. Top universities integrate research and graduate education and are measured by their research activity and production of doctorates; most of these top-tier universities have strong undergraduate programs as well.

Through the development of research-based doctoral programs, universities are increasingly involved in cooperation at the doctoral level with other sectors such as industry, independent research organizations, and government. Building strong links between universities with other sectors ultimately supports efforts to increase the transmission of knowledge as an impetus to innovation while retaining the important link between teaching and research. In the new code, the third mission feeds back into a more solid association between teaching and research within doctoral programs.

Research and the Academic Profession

The various changes in the world of academic research in recent years have resulted in markedly different kinds of academic careers. A study of academics affiliated with US university research centers clearly shows major changes in careers paths and productivity within the last couple of decades. "There is now a revolving door between industry and university research jobs" (Dietz and Bozeman, 2005, p. 365). About half of the respondents had held one or more jobs in industry, and almost that many began their careers in nonacademic jobs, either in industry or government, including a number who took their first academic job five or more years into their career. Researchers who spend more time in industry and receive more industry funding produce the largest number of patents but tend to have lower numbers of publications.

In 2006, more than half of recent doctoral holders in science and engineering were employed in academia, but a substantial proportion of them had contract, research-only jobs, with limited terms. "Non-faculty ranks (i.e., full- and part-time adjunct faculty, lecturers, research associates, administrators, and postdocs) increased . . . 85% [from 1993 to 2006], in sharp contrast to the 15% rise in the number of full-time faculty" (National Science Board, 2008, Table 5-12). Research-only temporary appointments are heavily staffed in the United States by international researchers holding temporary visa permits. A recent study of contracted postdoctoral researchers in Australia highlights the insecurity associated with the research-only career and the scarcity of teaching/research positions available upon completion of short-term research fellowships (Äkerlind, 2005).

Since the 1980s there has been a significant increase has occurred in the proportion of positions in UK universities offered on a temporary or fixed-term basis, the largest number in research positions (Ackers and Oliver, 2007). The European Union directives are pursuing the goal of maximizing both flexibility and security in employment. In practice, however, according to some observers security remains a rhetorical gesture:

> Many, but not all, of the positions from which an "early career" researcher may access an academic career will involve at least a period of time on a fixed or temporary contract. In an increasing number of situations, researchers will find themselves negotiating various forms of teaching-intense contracts as graduate teaching assistants, hourly paid lecturers, techni-

cians, or demonstrators, or will negotiate fixed-term teaching fellowships and lectureships. In other situations, particularly, but not exclusively in the sciences, the post will take the form of a fixed-term research-intensive position including doctoral scholarships, contract research positions, and research fellowships. (Ackers and Oliver, 2007, p. 56)

Conclusion

The research function within higher education has evolved in significant ways over the last decade. With a few notable exceptions, research activities traditionally took place outside of the university, but this is changing rapidly. Today, research is recognized as an important social role of the university, not just in the traditional disciplines and scientific fields, but also in interdisciplinary areas and emerging fields. A worldwide expansion of graduate programs and graduate enrollment has necessitated broader emphasis on research activities.

Research funding and activity are sources of international status and prestige. But research funding tends to be concentrated in elite institutions within countries but further concentrated in wealthier nations. However, a number of developing countries are pushing forward ambitious agendas to improve the amount and quality of their research activities. This is particularly evident in the cases of China, the Republic of Korea, Mexico, Brazil, and Chile.

Research is, to a large extent, dependent on public funding. At the same time, university-industry linkages are becoming more common and more important. These arrangements hold important potential for expanding the possibilities for research funding and capacity development; however, they also introduce dilemmas, particularly in terms of intellectual property rights and the revenue streams that commercialized technologies may generate. University-industry linkages also provide important career-development options for researchers, who are moving more frequently than ever back and forth between academia and industry. Still, employment opportunities for researchers are not equally promising everywhere. In some contexts, the rapid expansion of the number of researchers has forced many graduates into short-term contract positions with limited career potential.

The increasing importance of and widespread desire to focus more heavily on research in many university settings has also highlighted significant variations and tensions relating to the balance of teaching and research responsibilities within institutions. Indeed, the evolving role of research in higher education has brought to the fore fundamental questions about mission, quality, and relevance as these pertain to the multiple stakeholders who look to tertiary education to meet key social and economic needs. In the coming years, a wider variety of institutions as well as national and regional systems of higher education will confront the challenge of finding an appropriate balance between the research imperative and the other critically important functions of tertiary education.

12

University-Industry Linkages

During the past several decades a significant change has been seen in the way policymakers regard higher education. In contrast to the past—when higher education was a part of social policy—today it is increasingly regarded as a critical component of national and regional economic policy. The 1980s saw the first wave of change, particularly in the United States, where the Bayh-Dole Act was enacted to facilitate the role of universities in patent-based technology transfer, and various programs were instituted to strengthen university-industry relationships at the federal as well as state levels. Today, many countries have explicit metrics about university engagement with the economy; some, such as England and Scotland, have gone further and established dedicated government-funding streams based on such metrics. Interestingly, the meaning of "desirable engagement" continues to undergo change.

First, the notion of engagement is becoming broader—well beyond the initial focus on intellectual-property licensing or startups. A recent OECD review concluded that universities could serve a broad range of functions for regional economic development through education, research, as well as culturally related activities (OECD, 2007). The key policy question no longer consists of a narrow issue on how to make universities work better with industry but of a broader one on what they can perform in innovation and economic development, particularly at a local level.

Second, different universities now have varying functions, based on their capabilities and industrial contexts (Lester, 2005; Hatakenaka, 2008). Research-intensive universities differ from teaching-focused institutions, and regions and nations recognize the relevance of both types. Universities in developing countries differ considerably from universities in industrialized contexts.

Third, universities are no longer expected to work in isolation; rather, they are perceived to be interactive players who work closely not only with industry but with community and government. They represent an integral part of the national or regional innovation systems (Mowery and Sampat, 2005) and a critical component of the evolving triple helix in which universities, government, and industry change their roles through interaction (Etzkowitz and Leydesdorff, 1997).

What caused this paradigm transformation? Changing global contexts provided powerful impetus. Ongoing globalization has made countries and regions even more aware of their competitiveness. National and regional governments rely more on universities to become an anchor in their national and regional innovation systems, which is critical for their survival as knowledge economies. The paradigm change was in part prompted by the new understanding that scientific discoveries entail significant tacit knowledge. This means that not all scientific information can flow freely out of universities through publications; a certain high value is associated with direct contact with scientists. Geographical proximity matters, as well as face-to-face interactions. Technological innovation is advanced by having a two-way flow of information—not only of science from universities to industry but of technological know-how from industry to universities.

Developments in Research-Related Roles
Intellectual-Property Licensing
When they first began to engage in these activities, many universities and governments had inflated expectations about licensing outcomes, particularly concerning revenues. Today a greater realism reveals that not all universities can expect successful licensing, unless they have significant research capacity in areas such as biomedical science, with a critical mass of professionals working in technology transfer offices, a large enough portfolio of patents, and a certain amount of luck at developing a few "blockbuster" patents which make a significant difference in revenue (Geiger, 2004a; Thursby and Thursby, 2007).

In the United States, many universities started licensing activities in the 1980s and 1990s, and the number of new entrants is no longer large. Recent years have also seen mixed signals in terms of performance. The net royalties rose from US$1 billion in 2000 to nearly US$1.6 billion in 2005 (National Science Board, 2008), while the US patents granted increased from 1,550 in 1995 to 3,450 in 2003 but declined to 2,944 in 2005 (though "pipeline" indicators such as numbers of disclosures and patent applications show upward trends). The Europeans, on the other hand, report healthy annual increases in the number of patents granted (24 percent) as well as license income (12 percent) between 2004 and 2007 (Arundel, Kanerva, and Bordoy, 2008). In Japan, the number of patents owned by universities increased from 2,313 in 2003 to 4,225 in 2007, with licensing revenues rising by over 40 percent during the same period (Ministry of Education, Culture, Sports, Science and Technology, Japan, 2008).

There remains significant diversity in the ownership of intellectual property. In the United States, the norm has been for universities to own rights; in Europe, one survey found that a quarter of institutions reported either individual or company ownership of university inventions (Arundel, Kanerva, and Bordoy, 2008). In Japan, the situation has been changing rapidly in favor of institutional ownership, and yet a large majority (on the order of 90 percent) of "university-related inventions" were still owned by companies or individual academics (Kodama and Suzuki, 2007; Kanama and Okuwada, 2008).

At universities in developing countries, patenting and licensing have been much less prominent generally, given fewer technologically mature companies and the underdeveloped legal environment to protect intellectual-property rights. However, there are some signs of change, particularly in emerging economies. China has already become one of the major players in patenting with its patent system introduced in 1985 and World Trade Organization membership since 2000. Patenting activities are also increasing rapidly in other emerging economies such as Brazil, Mexico, and India (World Intellectual Property Organization, 2008).

Indeed, Chinese universities have engaged in patenting from the beginning. In 1985, over half of all domestic patent applications came from public research institutions and universities (with 50 percent of that share belonging to universities). The proportion dipped in the mid-1990s during the general surge of patent applications in China, but it rose to nearly 40 percent in 2005 (with more than two-thirds belonging to universities) (Motohashi, 2008).

Start-ups/Spin-offs
The creation of start-ups/spin-offs was another activity that has been emphasized in many OECD countries since the early days, motivated by the images of successful academic innovations that commercialized key scientific discoveries (particularly in biotechnology) from a handful

of US research universities. According to the Association of University Technology Managers (AUTM), 555 start-up companies were created in the United States in 2007, up from 454 in 2000, with a cumulative total of 3,388 companies still operating (AUTM, 2008). In Europe, one survey reported that the number of start-ups increased by 10 percent annually between 2004 and 2007 and that European universities have been more efficiently generating these operations based on funds invested in research than US universities (Arundel, Kanerva, and Bordoy, 2008). In Japan, the total number of university start-ups reached 1,773, tripling in six years (Ministry of Economy, Trade and Industry, Japan, 2008). However, the simple numbers may not indicate much in terms of true success, as many countries are discovering. As a result, efforts are being undertaken to measure the performance of these companies (e.g., the number of jobs created).

Fewer reports have focused on start-ups in developing countries. Now, emerging accounts on China's experience provide valuable insights. Chinese universities have become active in creating enterprises since the late 1980s, even when they possessed little research capability. Though they are sometimes described as "spin-offs," these entities are significantly different from those in other countries, in that they are owned and managed by universities. Some of these companies have been spectacularly successful, with about 40 university enterprises already listed on stock markets in China and Hong Kong (Eun, Keun, and Wu, 2006).

However, in contrast to start-ups in OECD countries, these Chinese companies do not tend to entail significant scientific discoveries; rather, the companies function as mechanisms, through which skilled personnel move from universities to the commercial sector (Chen and Kenney, 2007). Given very limited technological capabilities of existing firms, creating enterprises was one of the few ways in which universities could contribute to the development of industrial capabilities (Eun, Keun, and Wu, 2006).

It is not clear how long this practice of university enterprise will continue in China. Both the government and universities appear to be going through a rethinking process, as many enterprises have not been successful, and managerial responsibilities are increasingly demanding, especially given more mature market conditions (Ma, 2007; Kroll and Liefner, 2008). While Chinese universities may transform the way they deal with their enterprises, particularly with respect to their management relations, without question their universities have been critical in the context of underdeveloped industry by injecting talent through new companies. In that sense, they are similar to that of Japanese universities, in the early phase of Japanese industrial development (Odagiri and Goto, 1996), where academics were crucial in the adaptation of Western technology.

Industry-Funded Research

The increasingly dominant norm of "open innovation" has led research-oriented companies to work closely with universities. This aspect, together with continued efforts of universities to work with industry, is reflected in the continued upward trend in industry-funded academic research in OECD countries; this share rose from 3 percent around 1980 to 6 percent in the 2000s. Although in individual countries, such as the United States and the United Kingdom, the share has declined since 2000; this was a result of recent increases in government research funding.

Countries with less-well-established research capabilities in universities, such as the Republic of Korea and China, have higher proportions of industry funding, mainly because the government funding of university research stands significantly lower. However, some developing countries, with a very limited industrial base, will be unable to pay for technical advice and research work meant to be conducted by universities.

Consulting

Consulting is a common activity undertaken by many academics worldwide. The operation is usually not visible or easy to monitor, given that many academics undertake such work privately. However, the overall significance has been increasingly acknowledged. For instance, in one survey of R&D managers, 32 percent rated consulting as very important for industrial R&D, as compared with 21 percent for contract research, 18 percent for patents, and 10 percent for licenses (Cohen, Nelson, and Walsh, 2002). In one survey of Massachusetts Institute of Technology professors, consulting was perceived as the major channel of knowledge transfer, followed by publications, graduates, and collaborative research; patents and licenses were deemed one of the least-important channels (Agrawal and Henderson, 2002).

The United Kingdom represents an unusual case in which efforts have been made to track the volume of academic consultancy, based on a strong move among universities to "formalize" private consultancy into institutional contracts. University records indicate that the consultancy volume has more than doubled even in real terms in the last six years (though some of this growth is likely attributable to the encouraging effects of the effort to institutionalize contracts), and today its size is significant at 37 percent of contract-based research incomes (Higher Education Funding Council of England, 2008).

Education-Related Roles
Role of Graduates
Highly skilled graduates are increasingly recognized as key inputs for successful industrial development in a given locality (Puuka and Marmolejo, 2008). In some cases, such as India and China, the large number of inexpensively trained graduates, particularly in science and engineering, has been crucial to meet the growing industrial demand (Athreye, 2005). In Ireland and Finland, professional institutions were created as an alternative to conventional university education, which was seen to be unresponsive to industrial requirements. The institutional responsiveness was particularly essential when new disciplines such as computer science emerged and appeared to give countries a competitive edge, as was clear in the case of Ireland (Sands, 2005).

The development of the software industry appears greatly facilitated by the early establishment of computer science as a new discipline in US universities. Universities, thus, not only contributed to key knowledge formation but also organized and delivered education programs to supply updated skills. Indeed, the American universities' ability to create and legitimate computer science as a new field was unparalleled by European or Japanese universities (Mowery 1999).

Responsive education also matters at advanced degree levels, such as master's and PhDs. In retelling the story of Silicon Valley in the United States, one of its founding fathers, Gordon Moore, cautioned against a simplistic overemphasis of Stanford University's role, yet acknowledged liberally the critical function the university played in responsively providing advanced-degree engineers and scientists in relevant fields (Moore and Davis, 2004).

Cooperative Education and Student Projects
An emerging literature describes specific student participation in work-study programs. The co-op education program at the University of Waterloo in Canada is regarded as innovative in three different ways (Bramwell and Wolfe, 2008). First, it helps firms identify appropriate graduates for recruitment. Second, students help firms acquire new skills and knowledge from the university. Third, the cooperative students and programs help "circulate" knowledge across local firms and the university. In problem-based learning activities at Aalborg University, in Denmark, student groups work on specific problems identified in local firms and community and government organizations; the program is reported to have similar benefits to the locality and the university as in the case of the University of Waterloo (Puuka and Marmolejo, 2008).

Similar examples exist in developing countries as well. In Bolivia, a majority of academic staff rated student internships as one of the most-relevant contributions to industry (Vega-Jurado, Fernández-de-Lucio, and Huanca, 2008).

Entrepreneurship Education

Much emphasis has been placed on entrepreneurship education in OECD countries. Today, a wide range of programs, from isolated courses on entrepreneurship to comprehensive practical programs, support the development of entrepreneurs, though the full programs are more difficult for universities to offer given the needed expertise and novelty of entrepreneurship as a field of research (Klofsten, 2000). While not much data exist on the prevalence of different types of entrepreneurship education in universities, one Web-based review of 66 universities in sub-Saharan Africa found that over 80 percent offered some course in entrepreneurship, while four universities had specialized entrepreneurship centers (Kabongo, 2008).

The Global Entrepreneurship Monitor, an international group of researchers, has been conducting an annual global survey of entrepreneurship since 1999. As an indication of the growing prominence of entrepreneurship education the agency has introduced entrepreneurship training as a special topic in its 2008 survey (Bosma, et al., 2009). This preliminary analysis indicates generally positive relationships between entrepreneurship training and entrepreneurial attitude, aspirations, and activities. The findings showed a wide variation in the proportion of 18-to-64-year-olds who received training in colleges and universities, from 1 percent in Turkey or 4 percent in the Republic of Korea, 13 percent in Chile and Peru, 16 percent in Finland, to 20 percent in Colombia. Fuller analysis as well as future survey results will no doubt provide a far better global picture of entrepreneurship education going forward.

Executive Education and Professional Development

In many business schools in North America (and increasingly elsewhere) executive education is a critical activity, and many universities also offer short-term, often tailored education programs for working adults. However, this, like consultancy, is another category of activity that is not usually monitored. Again, the United Kingdom provides an unusual example of surveying this activity annually; surveys find that university incomes from this type of contracted activities are also significant—at about 62 percent of contract research incomes.

Culture-Related Developments

Universities can help to set the social, cultural, and intellectual tone of a locality, as highlighted by a recent OECD review (OECD, 2007; Puuka and Marmolejo, 2008). Cultural events surrounding universities can make the locality more appealing to educated professionals and their employers, which is important given that a creative class of professionals is drawn to cultural and creative contexts (Florida, 2002). To this end, universities in the northeast of England worked actively to create a cultural quarter in Newcastle city center (Duke, et al., 2006; Cross and Pickering, 2008).

Some universities have also taken their responsibility for community development more seriously. The University of Pennsylvania in the United States embraced community development as part of its strategic mission (Maurrasse, 2001). This was an unusual move for a globally competitive research university that happened to be located in an economically depressed urban neighborhood. This university is today engaged in a wide array of community initiatives, ranging from economic development plans in collaboration with local communities, extensive support to local schools, and a variety of "service" programs including student projects and volunteering. In Finland, the Jyvaskyla University of Applied Science works with local stakeholders to bring the long-term unemployed back into working life (Goddard, et al., 2006).

Institutional Development for Boundary Spanning

To develop these capabilities significant institutional development has been initiated to strengthen "boundary-spanning" capacity. These changes include establishing appropriate policies and processes, administrative support units, internal organizational structure, and external intermediary organizations such as science parks.

Establishing Policies and Processes

In many countries, setting up appropriate institutional policies and processes has been the first step toward encouraging boundary-spanning activities by individual academics. Many institutions clarified their rules about external engagement. For instance one of the early steps taken by many UK universities was to introduce a "one-day-a-week" rule for consulting/external activities. In Japan, policies to address conflicts of interest and conflicts of commitment have been considered critical. Streamlining processes for external contracts, with clarification of monetary and other rewards that academic staff can expect, have also been undertaken. Some universities explicitly changed promotion criteria to enhance the prospects for promotion through "third stream activities."

For ensuring the general "responsiveness" of education programs, it may not be enough to have externally active academic staff. While boundary-spanning academics are more likely to be aware of external needs and may even reflect such knowledge in their individual courses, it is essential to have processes in place to ensure timeliness and relevance of program offerings.

Administrative Support

Three types of boundary-spanning roles in research, education, and culture require three different types of administrative support units. For instance, many universities in OECD countries have established technology transfer offices since the 1980s to support research-related functions such as patenting/licensing, contract research, and consulting. These perform important boundary-spanning functions. Even in the United States, where technology transfer offices have a longer history, staff to support these offices is still increasing, growing from 929 in 1998 to 1,926 in 2007, with about half of the staff working on nonlicensing activities (AUTM, 2008).

For education-related functions, administrative support units are less visible, but most universities with special programs, such as cooperative education or student projects, have specific administrative support staff and sometimes even units for arranging such activities.

Similarly, for cultural and community-related functions, specific administrative support is also likely to be essential. Again, at the University of Pennsylvania, a unit to support community-service activities was developed, first within a department, but moved to become part of the central administration to provide universitywide support (Maurrasse, 2001).

Internal Organizational Structure

The traditional academic disciplinary structures are often inappropriate for engagement with the external world, as practical issues are usually interdisciplinary. In the United States, external engagements with government as well as industry were greatly enhanced by the development of "organizational research units"—some of which developed as organizational structures to bring together academics from different disciplines to cope with external research needs (Geiger 2004a, 2004b). Various experiments have been introduced to colocate university units with businesses and other stakeholders. Examples of this include the North Carolina Centenary Campus (Geiger 2004b) or the Science City Initiative in Newcastle, in the United Kingdom.

External Intermediaries—Such as Science Parks
The interest in science parks and incubation facilities has been growing steadily since the 1980s, first in the United States and Europe but more recently in developing countries as well. Since Stanford Industrial Park was created in 1951, the number of science parks in the United States has gradually increased, with a more rapid growth in the 1980s and the past decade, leading to over 170 science parks today. The United Kingdom's science parks also evolved in close conjunction with universities, starting with Cambridge and Herriot Watt in the early 1970s. The trend expanded in the 1980s and 1990s, with about 100 existing today. Their record of performance has been mixed at best (Castells and Hall, 1994; Mowery and Sampat, 2005); however, they continue to be regarded as key instruments for regional economic development. One recent study in the United States shows a significant change in their orientation. Science parks are moving away from recruitment of external R&D organizations toward company incubation and new enterprise development. This includes a greater commitment from universities to promote interactivity, in the form of living and work space that is increasingly used to accommodate both academics and industrialists (Battelle Technology Partnership Practice, 2007).

In Asia, different types of science and technology parks emerged, often without formal ties with universities. In China, science parks emerged in the late 1980s as part of national policy to establish special technology zones. Today, China has 53 national and nearly 200 state-level science parks, along with 63 university-owned science parks developed since 1990. In India, the government initiative to establish simplified administrative processes, particularly to promote information technology businesses led to the creation of 39 science and technology parks in existence today. These areas are more like industrial parks, however, and are particularly focused on facilitating export-oriented businesses. Nonetheless, the most "successful" examples—such as Zhongguancun in China or Bangalore in India—tend to be characterized by proximity to elite higher education institutions.

Conclusion
There has been a global rise in expectations about the responsibilities of higher education institutions in innovation and economic development. Policymakers define higher education institutions as crucial not only for education but also for scientific research, innovation, and regional economic development. The ongoing global economic crisis is unlikely to change such expectations and indeed may even encourage stronger expectations in this area.

13

Future Trends

This report has demonstrated that higher education continues to be defined, as it has always been, by who enrolls, who teaches, how knowledge is produced and disseminated, and by the sector's societal role. What has changed quite dramatically is the context of higher education—the rapid pace of globalization, the increasing mobility of students and scholars, the movement of academic programs and institutions across borders, the extraordinary impact of technology, and above all massification. Higher education now sits at the crossroad of tradition and new possibilities.

Change is as inevitable as the passage of time, but line of movement in the modern world seems to be accelerating and presenting higher education more complex challenges with each passing decade. It is safe to predict that the trends addressed in this report will continue, for these are difficult issues that cannot easily be solved. But it is important to keep in mind that, as these old and new challenges are addressed, the worldwide changes around us will continue. Shifting demographics, technological breakthroughs, and the volatility of international political and economic conditions make it unlikely that patterns of the past will easily or reliably predict the future (Le Bras, 2008).

Changing Patterns of Enrollment

This report has argued that the main force shaping higher education during the past half century, and certainly since the last UNESCO world conference in 1998, has been the continuing massification of systems—the expansion of enrollments worldwide. The expansion has continued at a staggering rate—from an estimated enrollment of 51,160,000 tertiary-level students in 1980 to 139,395,000 in 2006 (Teichler and Bürger 2008). Demand for higher education will continue to grow but will come from separate sectors in different countries. Globally, post-secondary education will continue to expand, but in sharp contrast from the past several decades, much of that growth will be in developing countries, especially in China and India.

On the surface it would appear that the developed countries have, in large part, achieved universal access to higher education. But major variations have turned up in some countries and significant access problems for underserved population sectors. Countries such as Japan, the Republic of Korea, and Finland have achieved universal enrollment ratios approaching 80 percent (Yonezawa and Kim 2008). (See enroll-ment ratio tables in the Appendix). In a growing number of countries, mainly in Europe and East Asia, demographic trends reflect a decline in the number of young people who comprise the traditional age cohort enrolling in higher education, but the demand has grown among non-traditional populations. Systems and institutions will need to adjust to these new and, in many ways, unprecedented realities.

Although efforts to address demand have successfully expanded access in many countries, expansion has not resolved persistent social inequities. Furthermore, socioeconomic background and parental edu-cation all too often influence the level of education an individual will achieve. The underlying causes of inequalities are pernicious and not easily resolved (Vincent-Lancrin, 2008b). Underserved students from lower socioeconomic classes; underrepresented racial, ethnic, and reli-gious minority groups; older students; and the disabled will require new services and infrastructure to participate successfully (Ebersold 2008). Modern societies are increasingly concerned with greater access for these population groups.

From Access to Completion

The theme throughout this report has been that the challenges confront-ing higher education during the past decade are the same ones of the previous decade. The change consists of our appreciation for the com-plexity of the issues and the difficult choices that need to be made as we try to address them. Access—improving possibilities for entry to postsec-ondary education—is one of the most complicated of these issues.

Mass enrollment has opened access to previously excluded popula-tion groups. In most countries, gender inequality has been eliminated, and the student population largely resembles the gender percentages in the general population. Inequality of access, however, continues to affect other population groups such as lower-socioeconomic classes, ethnic and religious minorities, rural populations (particularly in developing countries), and others traditionally underrepresented in postsecondary education. We have shown that these groups have made progress, but they are clustered in specific sectors within higher education and less likely to be present in the higher-prestige institutions and programs of study.

By the time of the last UNESCO report, access was measured with enrollment totals and gross enrollment ratios. We have come to recognize that enrollment growth must also be considered against completion rates. We have not succeeded in making higher education more inclusive or accessible if high percentages of these new students fail. Policymakers and the general public are beginning to take on this broader view of access. In the age of growing accountability, institutions will be measured by their success at supporting students through to completion, not by simply getting more students through the door. This new perspective implies changes—not only in how academic institutions measure success—but will undoubtedly affect reputations and budgetary allocations as well.

The meaning of "completion" has changed, as well. Traditionally, students collected credits, sat for examinations, and were then awarded degrees and certificates. These were the measures used universally to document academic achievement. Increasingly, universities are being asked to be more accountable for what and how their students learn. Greater emphasis is placed on measuring the "value added" as a result of academic study. What does a student learn and how do you measure it? Answering these questions is not easy, and little consensus exists about how this is best addressed. Concern will rise with the nexus of issues surrounding achievement and learning. Initiatives like the Bologna process will test new measures that will undoubtedly have significant influence on future trends.

Diversification

Mass enrollment has created the need for diversified academic systems—hierarchies of institutions serving different needs and constituencies. Diversified systems—necessary for financial, academic, and vocational reasons—will continue to be central to higher education worldwide. In general, governments will manage the diversification with "steering" mechanisms that will control the scope and nature of academic systems.

The private sector will be an important aspect of diversification. It has been the fastest-growing segment of postsecondary education worldwide and will continue to expand in many countries, simply because public institutions will not be able to keep pace with student demand. In academic systems that are no longer growing, the recently emerged private sector is likely to stabilize and become both a permanent and central option amid the diverse array of postsecondary institutions. While most private institutions will serve a mass clientele, some may emerge as semielite or even as elite research universities. Quality will continue to be a major preoccupation for higher education, in general, but special care will need to be taken to ensure that private higher education—and the for-profit institutions, in particular—maintain appropriate standards and serve society in much the same way that public institutions do.

New technologies and new providers have only just begun to diversify opportunities. This trend will most certainly continue.

Privatization and Funding
Public higher education has begun, and will continue, to take on practices and characteristics of private institutions. A combination of influences—neoliberal attitudes, limited public financing, increasing costs, the need to address expanded social expectations, and build better management systems, etc.—will oblige public postsecondary institutions to look for additional sources of income. This will be done through increased sharing of costs with students (tuition and fees) and through income generation from other sources—including research, consulting, and university-industry partnerships. The increased privatization of public institutions will continue to have significant impacts on the nature of these institutions.

Tuition and other fees charged to students will increase and become more ubiquitous worldwide. Countries where public institutions currently charge little or no tuition are likely to increase what students must pay to study. Where tuition is already significant, increases are also likely. The amounts assigned to students will vary according to the economic and political circumstances of each environment and probably will reflect differing social philosophies and ideologies, as well. One of the many challenges ahead will be to ascertain that cost does not become a barrier to access when students have the intellectual capacity to study but not the private financial means.

New Technologies
Information and communications technology has already profoundly affected higher education worldwide. The impact can be seen in the communication of knowledge through e-mail, blogs, wikis, and podcasts; the rapid expansion of distance education, electronic publication

of scientific journals and books, and to some extent academic management. The new technologies will continue to affect all aspects of higher education. The next stage of this aspect of the revolution will undoubtedly transform our approach to teaching and learning through distance-education programs and within the walls of traditional universities. However, it will not, as some have predicted, replace either traditional universities or traditional modes of teaching and learning.

Information and communications technology will probably not have the dramatic impact on access for the immediate future that some analysts predicted. Individuals with limited resources in developing nations are as likely to be distant from the necessary infrastructure and equipment as they are from bricks-and-mortar institutions. Initiatives to close the "digital divide" are in the early stages, and this action may no longer be as serious a problem by the next trend report. For the present, the extent to which different countries can integrate new technology varies tremendously.

The Concern for Quality

Quality will continue to be a high priority for higher education. During the last decade quality-assurance schemes for higher education have been implemented almost everywhere. At this next stage, the trend is toward standards that can be referenced internationally. In other words, there is a need to move toward mutual recognition and trust so that national programs for quality assurance will provide international validity. Regional conferences and summits have taken place throughout the world to address this challenge. The Bologna process is guiding Europe toward shared benchmarks and standards that will make it possible to compare qualifications awarded in all participating countries.

The growing international mobility of students and scholars is helping to drive the need for a way to evaluate and compare qualifications earned in different parts of the world. This effort will depend on finding a mechanism for certifying and integrating national quality-assurance schemes on an international level. A number of international organizations are engaged in discussions of how best to achieve this process.

Despite more than a decade of formalizing quality-assurance programs, many elements of measuring and monitoring quality remain problematic. The idea of exactly where quality resides in higher education remains somewhat elusive.

The Struggle for the Soul of Higher Education

The traditional societal mission of higher education has been under pressure for the last half century. Universities, traditionally seen as key cultural institutions to be responsible for public enlightenment, are increasingly obliged to respond to the many new pressures described in this report. The "commercialization" of higher education has placed considerable strain on its social mission. The debate concerning the primary mission and priorities of higher education will continue in many parts of the world, with a possible hindering of protecting activities that serve the public good in the face of growing financial constraints and market influence.

Individual countries will be challenged to balance local needs and priorities with standards, practices, and expectations articulated at the international level. Will research focus on local needs or be more inclined to pursue issues more attractive to international journals and funders? How will countries ensure that foreign providers and partners will address local educational needs and priorities?

The Professionalization of Higher Education Management and Leadership

As higher education institutions and systems have become larger and more central to society and individuals, there is a growing need for professional management and leadership. Training programs are slowly emerging, as are "think tanks" and policy forums. Academic institutions and systems are beginning to collect data about themselves for use in policymaking and improvement. There is a growing need for complete and accurate regional and international data for analysis as well. The higher education enterprise is simply too large, complex, and central to be managed without data and professionalism.

Conclusion

The unstoppable progress of globalization will oblige higher education institutions of all kinds to prepare an increasingly diverse cohort of students with skills and knowledge that will support their insertion into an increasingly borderless economy. Even the current global financial crisis, which will create problems for higher education in many countries, will not fundamentally alter the landscape. This challenge requires policymakers, administrators, and professors to reconsider the structure of traditional degree programs as well as the pedagogy of the past. "Talk and chalk" (Butcher, 2008) is far from adequate as we move further into the 21st century.

What has become ever more apparent is that all of the trends described in this report are interrelated. Trying to examine these trends separately is similar to trying to pull an individual string from a knotted mass—tugging one brings along several others. Mass enrollment has created a demand for expanded facilities for higher education. Larger enrollments result in more diverse student expectations and needs. Expansion and diversification create a need for new providers. System growth requires additional revenue and new channels for obtaining it. All of this (expansion, diversity, and funding shortages) generates concern for quality. This knotted ball of string will roll forward, with each trend adjusting to the endless tugs at higher education as a global system.

The enormous challenge ahead is the uneven distribution of human capital and funds that will allow some nations to take full advantage of new opportunities while other nations drift further and further behind.

REFERENCES

Ackers, L., and Oliver, L. 2007. From flexicurity to flexsecquality? The impact of the fixed-term contract provisions on employment in science research. *International Studies of Management and Organization* 37 (1): 53–79.

Adelman, C. 2009. *The Bologna process for U.S. eyes: Re-learning higher education in the Age of Convergence.* Washington, DC: Institute for Higher Education Policy.

African Virtual University. http://www.avu.org/ (accessed January 15, 2009).

Agarwal, P., M. E. Said, M. Sehoole, M. Sirozi, and H. de Wit. 2008. Summary, conclusions, and recommendations. In *The Dynamics of international student circulation in a global context,* ed. H. de Wit, P. Agarwal, M. E. Said, M. T. Sehoole, and M Sirozi, 233–61. Rotterdam: Sense.

Agrawal, A., and R. Henderson. 2002. Putting patents in context: Exploring knowledge transfer from MIT. *Management Science* 48: 44–60.

Äkerlind, G. S. 2005. Postdoctoral researchers: Roles, functions and career prospects. *Higher Education Research and Development* 24 (1): 21–40.

Altbach, P. G. 1998. *Comparative higher education: Knowledge, the university, and development.* Hong Kong: Comparative Education Research Centre, University of Hong Kong.

———. 1999. Comparative perspectives on private higher education. In *Private Prometheus: Private higher education and development in the 21st century,* ed. P. G. Altbach, 1–14. Westport, CT: Greenwood.

———, ed. 2003. *The decline of the guru: The academic profession in developing and middle-income countries.* New York: Palgrave Macmillan.

———. 2004. Globalization and the university: Realities in an unequal world. *Tertiary Education and Management* 10:32–33.

———. 2005. The private higher education revolution: An introduction. In *Private higher education: A global revolution,* ed. P. G. Altbach and D. C. Levy, 1–12. Rotterdam: Sense.

———. 2006. Globalization and the university: Realities in an unequal world. In vol. 1 of *International handbook of higher education,* ed. J. J. F. Forest and P. G. Altbach, 121–40. Dordrecht, Netherlands: Springer.

———. 2007. *Tradition and transition: The international imperative in higher education.* Rotterdam, Netherlands: Sense.

———. 2009. The giants awake: The present and future of higher education systems in China and India. *Economic and Political Weekly* 44, no. 23 (June 6): 39–51.

Altbach, P. G., and J. Balán. 2007. *World class worldwide: Transforming research universities in Asia and Latin America.* Baltimore: Johns Hopkins University Press.

Altbach, P. G., and J. Knight. 2007. The internationalization of higher education: Motivations and realities. *Journal of Studies in International Education* 11, nos. 3–4: 274–90.

Altbach, P. G., and D. C. Levy, eds. 2005. *Private higher education: A global revolution,* Rotterdam, Netherlands: Sense.

Amaral, A., V. L. Meek, and I. M. Larsen. 2003. *The higher education managerial revolution?* Dordrecht, Netherlands: Kluwer Academic.

Arafeh, S. 2004. *The implications of information and communications technologies for distance education: Looking toward the future.* Arlington, VA: SRI International.

Arundel, A., M. Kanerva, and C. Bordoy. 2008. Summary report for respondents: The ASTP survey for fiscal year 2007. Association of European Science and Technology Transfer Professionals. http://www.astp.net/Survey%202008/Summary_2008_ASTP_report.pdf (accessed May 12, 2009).

Association of University Technology Managers. 2008. U.S. Licensing Activity Survey, FY2007 Survey. http://www.autm.net/AM/Template.cfm?Section=FY_2007_Licensing_Activity_Survey (accessed April 22, 2009).

Athreye, S. S. 2005. The Indian software industry. In *From underdogs to tigers: The rise and growth of the software industry in Brazil, China, India, Ireland, and Israel,* ed. A. Arora and A. Gambardella, 7–40. Oxford and New York: Oxford University Press.

AUQA. *See* Australian Universities Quality Agency.

Australian Universities Quality Agency. AUQA audit reports: Self-accrediting institutions. http://www.auqa.edu.au/qualityaudit/qa/ (accessed December 14, 2008).

AUTM. *See* Association of University Technology Managers.

AVU. *See* African Virtual University.

Azam, M., and A. Blom. 2008. *Progress in participation in tertiary education in India from 1983 to 2004.* Washington, DC: World Bank.

Barrow, C. 2008. Globalization, trade liberalization, and the transnationalization of higher education. Presentation at Boston College, November 18.

Battelle Technology Partnership Practice and Association of University Research Parks. 2007. *Characteristics and trends in North American research parks: 21st century directions.* Columbus, OH: Battelle Memorial Institute.

Ben-David, J., and A. Zloczower. 1962. Universities and academic systems in modern societies. *European Journal of Sociology* 3 (5): 45–84.

Bernasconi, A. 2007. Are there research universities in Chile? In *World class worldwide: Transforming research universities in Asia and Latin America,* ed. P. G. Altbach and J. Balán, 234–59. Baltimore: Johns Hopkins University Press.

———. 2008. Is there a Latin American model of the university? *Comparative Education Review* 52 (1): 27–52.

Biggs, J. B. 1993. From theory to practice: A cognitive systems approach. *Higher Education Research and Development* 12 (1): 73–85.

———. 1996. Enhancing teaching through constructive alignment. *Higher Education* 32 (3): 347–64.

———. 2001. The reflective institution: Assuring and enhancing the quality of teaching and learning. *Higher Education* 41 (3): 221–38.

Biggs, J. B., and C. Tang. 2007. *Teaching for quality learning at university.* Maidenhead, UK: Open University Press/McGraw Hill Education.

Bloom, D., D. Canning, and K. Chan. 2005. *Higher education and economic development in Africa.* Washington, DC: World Bank.

Böhm, A., D. Davis, D. Meares, and D. Peace. 2002. *Global student mobility 2025: Forecasts of the global demand for international higher education.* Sidney: IDP Education Australia.

Bologna Declaration. 1999. http://www.bologna-berlin2003.de/pdf/bologna_declaration.pdf (accessed March 1, 2009).

Bosma, N., Z. J. Acs, E. Autio, A. Coduras, and J. Levie. 2009. *Global entrepreneurship monitor: 2008 executive report.* London: Global Entrepreneurship Research Association.

Boyer, E. L. 1990. *Scholarship reconsidered: Priorities of the professoriate.* Princeton, NJ: Carnegie Foundation for the Advancement of Teaching.

Brainard, J. 2008. Race and ethnicity of students at 1,400 colleges and universities. *Chronicle of Higher Education* 55 (5): B26.

Bramwell, A., and D. A. Wolfe. 2008. Universities and regional economic development: The entrepreneurial University of Waterloo. *Research Policy* 37 (8): 1175–87.

Brunner, J. J., P. Santiago, C. García Gaudilla, J. Gerlach, and L. Velho. 2006. *Thematic review of tertiary education.* Paris: OECD.

Butcher, N. 2008. ICT and higher education: A summary of key issues for consideration. Paper presented for the first meeting of the conference committee for the UNESCO 2009 World Conference on the New Dynamics of Higher Education.

Campbell, S. 2008. Assessment reform as a stimulus for quality improvement in university learning and teaching: an Australian case study. Paper presented at the OECD conference on Outcomes of Higher Education: Quality Relevance and Impact, September, 8–10, Paris.

Canton, E., and A. Blom. 2004. *Can student loans improve accessibility to higher education and student performance: An impact study of the case of SOFES, Mexico.* Washington DC: World Bank.

Cao, Y. 2007. Chinese private colleges and the labor market. PhD diss., University at Albany, State University of New York.

Castells, M., and P. G. Hall. 1994. *Technopoles of the world: The making of twenty-first-century industrial complexes.* London and New York: Routledge.

Catania Declaration: Euro-Mediterranean Area of Higher Education and Research. 2006. http//www.miur.it/UserFiles/2209.pdf (accessed April 7, 2009).

Centre for Educational Research and Innovation (CERI) and Organization for Economic Cooperation and Development (OECD). 2004. *Quality and recognition in higher education: The cross-border challenge.* Paris: OECD.

CHEA. *See* Council for Higher Education Accreditation.

Chen, K., and M. Kenney. 2007. Universities/research institutes and regional innovation systems: The cases of Beijing and Shenzhen. *World Development* 35 (6): 1056–74.

Clark, B. R. 1987. *The academic life: Small worlds, different worlds.* Princeton, NJ: Carnegie Foundation for the Advancement of Teaching.

Cohen, W. M., R. R. Nelson, and J. P. Walsh. 2002. Links and impacts: The influence of public research on industrial R&D. *Management Science* 48:1–23.

Council for Higher Education Accreditation. 2009. Degree mills: An old problem and a new threat. http://www.chea.org/degreemills/frmPaper.htm (accessed March 31, 2009).

Cross, E., and H. Pickering. 2008. The contribution of higher education to regional cultural development in the north east of England. *Higher Education Management and Policy* 20 (2): 125–38.

Crozier, F., B. Curvale, R. Dearlove, E. Helle, and F. Hénard. 2006. Terminology of quality assurance: Towards shared European values? *ENQA Occasional Papers,* no. 40.

D'Andrea, V., and D. Gosling. 2005. *Improving teaching and learning in higher education: A whole institution approach.* Maidenhead, UK: Society for Research into Higher Education and Open University Press.

D'Antoni, S. 2008. *Open educational resources: The way forward.* Paris: UNESCO, International Institute for Educational Planning.

David, M. E. 2009. Access and Equity. Paper for the trend report for the UNESCO 2009 World Conference: The New Dynamics of Higher Education.

Declaration of the regional conference on higher Education in Latin America and the Caribbean – CRES 2008. http://www.cres2008. org/en/index.php (accessed February 1, 2009).

Dietz, J. S., and B. Bozeman. 2005. Academic careers, patents, and productivity: Industry experience as scientific and technical human capital. *Research Policy* 34, (3): 349–67.

Dougherty, K. J., and G. S. Kienzl. 2006. It's not enough to get through the open door: Inequalities by social background in transfer from community to four-year colleges. *Teachers College Record* 108 (3): 452–87.

Douglass, J. A. 2004. The dynamics of massification and differentiation: A comparative look at higher education systems in the United Kingdom and California. *Higher Education Management and Policy* 16 (3): 9–34.

Duke, C., R. Hassink, J. Powell, and J. Puukka. 2006. *Supporting the contribution of higher education institutions to regional development. Peer review report: North east of England.* http://www.oecd.org/ dataoecd/16/54/35889695.pdf (accessed March 1, 2009).

Eaton, J. S. 2004. Accreditation and recognition of qualifications in higher education: The United States. In *Quality and recognition in higher education: The cross-border challenge,* ed. Centre for Educational Research and Innovation, 63–74. Paris: OECD Centre for Educational Research and Innovation.

Ebersold, S. 2008. Adapting higher education to the needs of disabled students: Developments, challenges and prospects. In *Higher education to 2030.* Vol. 1, *Demography,* ed. S. Vincent-Lancrin, 221–40. Paris: OECD.

ENQA. *See* European Network for Quality Assurance.

Etzkowitz, H., and L. A. Leydesdorff. 1997. *Universities and the global knowledge economy: A triple helix of university-industry-government relations.* London and New York: Pinter.

Eun, J.-H., L. Keun, and G. Wu. 2006. Explaining the "university-run enterprises" in China: A theoretical framework for university-industry relationship in developing countries and its application to China. *Research Policy* 35 (9): 1329–46.

European Commission. 2003. *Third European Report on Science & Technology Indicators, 2003*, Brussels, European Commission.

———. 2008a. *The impact of ERASMUS on European higher education: Quality, openness, and internationalisation*. Enschede, Netherlands: European Commission.

———. 2008b. Lifelong learning programme—A single umbrella for education and training programmes. http://ec.europa.eu/education/lifelong-learning-programme/doc78_en.htm (accessed May 6, 2009).

European Network for Quality Assurance. 2007. *Report of standards and guidelines for quality assurance in the European higher education area*. 2nd ed. Helsinki: ENQA.

Ezell, A. 2007. *Accreditation mills*. Washington, DC: American Association of Collegiate Registrars and Admissions Officers.

Fallis, G. 2007. *Multiversities, ideas and democracy*. Toronto: University of Toronto Press.

Florida, R. L. 2002. *The rise of the creative class: And how it's transforming work, leisure, community and everyday life*. New York: Basic Books.

Gaillard, J., M. Hassan, and R. Waast. 2005. Africa. *World Science Report*. Paris: UNESCO, 177–201.

Geiger, R. L. 2004a. *Knowledge and money: Research universities and the paradox of the marketplace*. Stanford, CA: Stanford University Press.

———. 2004b. *Research & relevant knowledge: American research universities since World War II*. New Brunswick, NJ and London: Transaction.

———. 2006. The quest for "economic relevance" by US research universities. *Higher Education Policy* 19 (4): 411–31.

Glänzel, W., and B. Schlemmer. 2007. National research profiles in a changing Europe (1983–2003): An exploratory study of sectoral characteristics in the triple helix. *Scientometrics* 70 (2): 267–75.

Global student statement to the UNESCO World Conference on Higher Education +10. 2009. http://www.esib.org/documents/statements/0901_WCHE_Global_Student_Statement.pdf (accessed May 6, 2009).

Goddard, J., H. Etzkowitz, J. Puukka, and I. Virtanen. 2006. Supporting the contribution of higher education institutions to regional development. Peer review report: Jyvaskyla Region of Finland. http://www.oecd.org/dataoecd/27/24/368091119.pdf (accessed March 1, 2009).

Gorard, S., E. Smith, H. May, L. Thomas, N. Adnett, and K. Slack. 2006.

Review of widening participation research: Addressing the barriers to participation in higher education. http://www.hefce.ac.uk/pubs/RDreports/2006/rd13_06/ (accessed May 1, 2009).

Grubb, N. W., R. Sweet, M. Gallagher, and O. Tuomi. 2006. *Korea: Country note*. Paris: Organization for Economic Cooperation and Development.

Gupta, A. 2006. *Affirmative action in higher education in India and the US: A study in contrasts*. Berkeley: Center for Studies in Higher Education, University of California, Berkeley.

Gupta, A., D. C. Levy, and K. B. Powar. 2008. *Private higher education: Global trends and Indian perspectives*. New Delhi: Shipra.

Guri-Rosenblit, S. 2009. *Digital technologies in higher education: Sweeping expectations and actual effects*. New York: Nova Science.

Guri-Rosenblit, S., H. Sebkova, and U. Teichler. 2007. Massification and diversity of higher education systems: Interplay of complex dimensions. *Higher Education Policy* 20 (4): 373–89.

Gürüz, K. 2008. *Higher education and international student mobility in the global knowledge economy*. Albany: State University of New York Press.

Harvard University Center for International Development. Readiness for the networked world: A guide for developing countries—glossary of terms. http://cyber.law.harvard.edu/readinessguide/glossary.html (accessed April 28, 2009).

Hatakenaka, S. 2008. The role of higher education institutions in high tech industry: What does international experience tell us? Paper presented at the World Bank ABCDE Conference, Cape Town, South Africa, June 9–11.

Herbst, M. 2007. *Financing public universities: The case of performance funding*. Dordrecht, Netherlands: Springer.

Higher Education Funding Council of England. 2008. *Higher education-business and community interaction survey 2006–7*. Bristol, UK: HEFCE.

Higher education in Africa: What does the future hold? 2008. *Unisawise* (Spring): 3.

Hockings, C., S. Cooke, H. Yamashita, S. McGinty, and M. Bowl. 2008. Switched off? A study of disengagement among computing students at two universities. *Research Papers in Education* 23, (2): 191–203.

IGNOU. *See* Indira Gandhi National Open University.

Indira Gandhi National Open University. 2009. *IGNOU profile 2009*. New Delhi: IGNOU.

International Network for Quality Assurance Agencies in Higher Education. 2007. Networks of quality agencies: Working

together. http://www.inqaahe.org/admin/files/assets/subsites/1/
documenten/1233592273_working-together.pdf (accessed April 1,
2009).

INQAAHE. *See* International Network for Quality Assurance Agencies
in Higher Education.

Insee, P. G. , and D. G. Dares. 2007. France: Mass and class—Persisting
inequalities in postsecondary education in France. In *Stratification
in higher education: A comparative study,* ed. Y. Shavit, 220–39. Palo
Alto, CA: Stanford University Press.

ISO. *See* International Organization for Standardization.

Johnstone, D. B. 1986. *Sharing the costs of higher education: Student
financial assistance in the United Kingdom, the Federal Republic of
Germany, France, Sweden, and the United States.* New York: College
Entrance Examination Board.

———. 2004. The economics and politics of cost sharing in higher
education: Comparative perspectives. *Economics of Education
Review* 23 (4): 403–10.

———. 2006. *Financing higher education: Cost-sharing in international
perspective.* Rotterdam: Sense.

Johnstone, S. M. 2005. Open educational resources serve the world.
EduCause Quarterly 28 (3): 15.

Kabongo, J. D. 2008. The status of entrepreneurship education in
colleges and universities in sub-Saharan Africa. Proceedings of
the 39th annual meeting of the Decision Sciences Institute. http://
www.decisionsciences.org/Proceedings/DSI2008/docs/545-2365.
pdf (accessed May 1, 2009).

Kanama, D., and K. Okuwada, K. 2008. *A study on university patent
portfolios: Portfolio of patent application from Tohoku University.*
Tokyo: Science and Technology Foresight Center, National Institute
of Science and Technology Policy, Ministry of Education, Culture,
Sports, Science and Technology.

Kerr, C. 2001. *The uses of the university.* Cambridge, MA: Harvard
University Press.

Kimani, M. 2008. Red alert: Accreditation scam unearthed. *Business
Daily.* http://www.bdafrica.com/index.php?option=com_content&t
ask=view&id=6333&Itemid=5822 (accessed January 15, 2009).

Kinser, K., and D. C. Levy. 2006. For-profit higher education: United
States tendencies, international echoes. In *International handbook
of higher education,* ed. J. J. F. Forest and P. G. Altbach, 107–20.
Dordrecht, Netherlands: Springer.

Klofsten, M. 2000. Training entrepreneurship at universities: A Swedish
case. *Journal of European Industrial Training* 24 (6): 337–44.

Knight, J. 2003. Updating the definition of internationalization. *International Higher Education* no. 33:2–3.

———. 2004a. Internationalization remodeled: Definition, approaches, and rationales. *Journal of Studies in International Education* 8 (1): 5–31.

———. 2004b. Quality assurance and recognition of qualifications in post-secondary education in Canada. In *Quality and recognition in higher education: The cross-border challenge*, ed. Centre for Educational Research and Innovation and Organisation for Economic Co-operation and Development, 43–62. Paris: Organization for Economic Cooperation and Development.

———. 2006a. *Higher education crossing Borders: A guide to the implications of the General Agreement on Trade in Services (GATS) for cross-border education.* Vancouver, BC: Commonwealth of Learning.

———. 2006b. *Internationalization of higher education: New directions, new challenges. 2005 IAU global survey report.* Paris: International Association of Universities.

Kodama, F., and J. Suzuki. 2007. How Japanese companies have used scientific advances to restructure their businesses: The receiver-active national system of innovation. *World Development* 35, (6,): 976–90.

Kroll, H. and Liefner, I. 2008. Spin-off enterprises as a means of technology commercialisation in a transforming economy: Evidence from three universities in China. *Technovation* 28 (5): 298–313.

Laredo, P. 2007. Revisiting the third mission of universities: Toward a renewed categorization of university activities? *Higher Education Policy* 20 (4,): 441–56.

Larraín, C., and S. Zurita. 2007. The new student loan system in Chile's higher education. *Higher Education* 55 (6): 683–702.

Lavelle, L., and Rutledge, S. 2006. China's B-school boom: Meet the new managerial class in the making. http://www.businessweek.com/magazine/content/06_02/b3966074.htm (accessed April 1, 2009).

Le Bras, H. 2008. Are long-term demographic forecasts possible? Turning points and trends. *Higher education to 2030: Demography*, vol. 1, 19–39. Paris: OECD.

Lester, R. 2005. *Universities, innovation and the competitiveness of local economies: A summary report from the local innovation systems project—Phase I.* Cambridge: Massachusetts Institute of Technology.

Levy, D. C. 1986. *Higher education and the state in Latin America: Private challenges to public dominance.* Chicago: University of Chicago Press.

———. 2006. The private fit in the higher education landscape. In *International handbook of higher education,* ed. J. J. F. Forest and P. G. Altbach, 281–92. Dordrecht, Netherlands: Springer.

Levy, D. C., and W. Zumeta. Forthcoming. Private higher education and public policy around the world: Influences and implications. *Journal of Comparative Policy Analysis.*

Levy, F., and Murnane, R. 2006. How computerized work and globalization shape human skill demands. http://web.mit.edu/flevy/www/ (accessed May 20, 2009).

Lissoni, F., P. Llerena, M. McKelvey, and B. Sanditov. 2008. Academic patenting in Europe: New evidence from the KEINS database. *Research Evaluation* 17 (2): 87–102.

Liston, C. 1999. *Managing quality and standards.* Buckingham, UK: Open University Press.

Lloyd, M. 2006. Slowly enabling the disabled. *Chronicle of Higher Education* 52 (49): 35.

Ma, W. 2007. The flagship university and China's economic reform. In *World class worldwide: Transforming research universities in Asia and Latin America,* ed. P. G. Altbach and J. Balán, 31–53. Baltimore: Johns Hopkins University Press.

Maassen, P. A. M. 1987. Quality control in Dutch higher education: Internal versus external evaluation. *European Journal of Education* 22 (2): 161–70.

Mabizela, M. 2007. Private surge amid public dominance in provision of higher education in Africa. *Journal of Higher Education in Africa* 5 (2 and 3): 15–38.

Mabizela, M., D. C. Levy, and W. Otieno, eds. Forthcoming. *Private surge amid public dominance: Dynamics in the private provision of higher education in africa. Journal of Higher Education in Africa.*

Maldonado-Maldonado, A. 2002. The national autonomous university of Mexico: A continuing struggle. *International Higher Education,* no. 26:18–19.

Marton, F., D. Hounsell, and N. J. Entwistle. 1997. *The experience of learning.* Edinburgh: Scottish Academic Press.

Maurrasse, D. J. 2001. *Beyond the campus: How colleges and universities form partnerships with their communities.* New York: Routledge.

McIntosh, C., and Z. Varoglu. 2005. *Perspectives on distance education: Lifelong learning & distance higher education.* Paris: UNESCO and Commonwealth of Learning.

Miller, M. A., and P. Ewell. 2005. *Measuring up on college-level learning.* San Jose, CA: National Center for Public Policy and Higher Education.

Ministry of Economy, Trade and Industry (Japan). 2008.「平成19年度大学発ベンチャーに関する基礎調査」について（METI/経済産業省 [Heisei 19 nendo daigakuhatsu venture ni kansuru kiso chosa]. http://www.meti.go.jp/press/20080818001/20080818001.html (accessed May 20, 2009).

Ministry of Education, Culture, Sports, Science and Technology (Japan). 2008.　「平成19年度大学発ベンチャーに関する基礎調査」について（METI/経済産業省）[Heisei 19 nendo daigakuto ni okeru sangakurenkei jisshi jokyonituite]. http://www.mext.go.jp/a_menu/shinkou/sangaku/sangakub/08080708.htm (accessed May 12, 2009).

Miniwatts Marketing Group. Internet usage statistics. http://www.internetworldstats.com/stats.htm (accessed April 12, 2009).

Mohamedbhai, G. 2008. Mauritius. In Teferra and Knight, 262–302.

Moore, G., and K. Davis. 2004. Learning the Silicon Valley way. In Building high-tech clusters: Silicon Valley and beyond, ed. T. F. Bresnahan and A. Gambardella, 7–39. Cambridge and New York: Cambridge University Press.

Morley, L., and R. Lugg. 2009. Mapping meritocracy: Intersecting gender, poverty and higher educational opportunity structures. Higher Education Policy 22:37–60.

Motohashi, K. 2008. Assessment of technological capability in science industry linkage in China by patent database. World Patent Information 30 (3): 225–32.

Mowery, D. C. 1999. The computer software industry. In Sources of industrial leadership: Studies of seven industries, ed. D. C. Mowery and R. R. Nelson, 133–68. Cambridge and New York: Cambridge University Press.

Mowery, D. C., and B. N. Sampat. 2005. Universities in national innovation systems. In The Oxford handbook of innovation, ed. J. Fagerberg, D. C. Mowery, and R. R. Nelson, 209–39. Oxford: Oxford University Press.

Mulumba, M. B., A. Obaje, K. Kobedi, and R. Kishun. 2008. International student mobility in and out of Africa: Challenges and opportunities. In Teferra and Knight, 2008, 490–514.

Murakami, Y., and A. Blom. 2008. Accessibility and affordability of tertiary education in Brazil, Colombia, Mexico and Peru within a global context. Washington, DC: World Bank.

NAFSA: Association of International Educators. 2008. The economic benefits of international education to the United States for the 2007-2008 academic year: A statistical analysis. www.nafsa.org/_/File/_/eis08/Guam.pdf (accessed March 1, 2009).

National Committee of Inquiry into Higher Education. 1997. *Higher education in the learning society: Report of the National Committee (Dearing report)*. London: HMSO.

National Science Board. 2008. *S&E indicators 2008*. National Science Foundation. http://www.nsf.gov/statistics/seind08/start.htm (accessed April 27, 2009).

Neave, G. 1994. The politics of quality: Developments in higher education in western Europe 1992–1994. *European Journal of Education* 29 (2): 115–34.

Obasi, I. N. 2006. New private universities in Nigeria. *International Higher Education*, no. 45:14.

Odagiri, H., and A. Goto. 1996. *Technology and industrial development in Japan: Building capabilities by learning, innovation, and public policy*. Oxford: Clarendon Press; Oxford and New York: Oxford University Press.

OECD. *See* Organization for Economic Cooperation and Development

Organization for Economic Cooperation and Development. 2004. *Quality and recognition in higher education: The cross-border challenge*. Paris: OECD.

———. 2007. *Higher education and regions: Globally competitive, locally engaged*. Paris: OECD.

———. 2008. *Higher education to 2030*. Vol. 1, *Demography*. Ed. S. Vincent-Lancrin. Paris: OECD.

———. The assessment of higher education learning outcomes. http://www.oecd.org/document/51/0,3343,en_2649_35961291_40119475_1_1_1_1,00.html (accessed May 20, 2009).

Otieno, W., and D. C. Levy. 2007. *Public disorder, private boons? Intersectoral dynamics Illustrated by the Kenyan case*. Albany: University at Albany, State University of New York.

Piquet, M. 2006. Australian multicultural equity and fair go. In *Race and inequality: World perspectives on affirmative action*, ed. E. Kennedy-Dubourdie, 127–52. Surrey, UK: Ashgate.

Popp Berman, E. 2008. Why did universities start patenting? Institution-building and the road to the Bayh-Dole act. *Social Studies of Science* 38 (6): 835–71.

Pritchard, R. 2006. Trends in the restructuring of German universities. *Comparative Education Review* 50 (1): 90–112.

Program for Research on Private Higher Education. 2008. PROPHE 92 country data summary: 2000–2007. http://www.albany.edu/dept/eaps/prophe/data/International_Data/PROPHEDataSummaryJAN08.doc (accessed May 11, 2009).

———. National data on private higher education. http://www.albany.edu/dept/eaps/prophe/data/national.html (accessed May 11, 2009).

PROPHE. *See* Program for Research on Private Higher Education.

Prosser, M., and K. Trigwell. 1999. *Understanding learning and teaching: The experience in higher education.* Buckingham, UK: Open University Press; Philadelphia, PA: Society for Research into Higher Education.

Purcell, F. B., R. Matross Helms, and L. E. Rumbley. 2005. *Women's colleges and universities in international perspective: An overview.* Rotterdam: Sense.

Puukka, J., and F. Marmolejo. 2008. Higher education institutions and regional mission: Lessons learnt from the OECD Review Project. *Higher Education Policy* 21 (2): 217–44.

Ramos, A., J. Trinona, and D. Lambert. 2006. Viability of SMS technologies for non-formal distance education. In *Information and communication technology for social development,* ed. J. Baggaley, 69–80. Jakarta: ASEAN Foundation.

Riesman, D. 1958. *Constraint and variety in American education.* Garden City, NY: Doubleday Anchor.

Rinne, R. 2008. The growing supranational impacts of the OECD and the EU on national education policies, and the case of Finland. *Policy Futures in Education* 6 (6): 665–85.

Rumbley, L. E. 2007. Interview with Jane Knight: IAU Global survey report on internationalization of higher education. The CIHE podcast initiative. http://www.bc.edu/cihe/podcast/ (accessed February 1, 2009).

———. 2008. Interview with Kai-ming Cheng: Humanities and social science education in Hong Kong and East Asia. The CIHE podcast initiative. http://www.bc.edu/cihe/podcast/ (accessed February 1, 2009).

Rumbley, L. E., I. F. Pacheco, and P. G. Altbach. 2008. *International comparison of academic salaries. An exploratory study.* Chestnut Hill, MA: Boston College Center for International Higher Education.

Sadlak, J., and N. C. Liu. 2007. *The world-class university and ranking: Aiming beyond status.* Bucharest: UNESCO-CEPES.

Salmi, J. 2009. *The challenge of establishing world-class universities.* Washington, DC: World Bank.

Sands, A. 2005. The Irish software industry. In *From underdogs to tigers: The rise and growth of the software industry in Brazil, China, India, Ireland, and Israel,* ed. A. Arora and A. Gambardella, 41–71. Oxford: Oxford University Press.

Schimank, U., and M. Winnes. 2000. Beyond Humboldt? The relationship between teaching and research in European university systems. *Science and Public Policy* 27 (6): 397–408.

Schwartzman, S., A. Junqueira Botelho, A. da Silva, and M. Cristophe. 2008. Brazil. In *University and development in Latin America: Successful experiences of research centers,* ed. S. Schwartzman, 145–200. Rotterdam: Sense.

Schwarz, S., and D. F. Westerheijden. 2004. Preface. In *Accreditation and evaluation in the European higher education area,* ed. S. Schwarz and D. F. Westerheijden, ix–xiii. Dordrecht, Netherlands: Kluwer Academic.

Semela, T., and E. Ayalew. 2008. Ethiopia. In Teferra and Knight, 159–207.

Shavit, Y., R. Arum, and A. Gamoran, eds. 2007. *Stratification in higher education: A comparative study.* Palo Alto, CA: Stanford University Press.

Shuell, T. J. 1986. Cognitive conceptions of learning. *Review of Educational Research* 56 (4): 411–36.

Slancheva, S. and D. C. Levy. 2007. *Private higher education in post-communist Europe: In search of legitimacy.* New York: Palgrave Macmillan.

Task Force on Higher Education and Society. 2000. *Higher education in developing countries: Peril and promise.* Washington, DC: World Bank.

Teferra, D. 2007. *Building research capacity in Ethiopian universities: The realities and the challenges.* http://www2.bc.edu/~teferra/Building_Research_Capacity_in_Ethiopia.html (accessed May 6, 2009).

———. 2008. The international dimension of higher education in Africa: Status, challenges, and prospects. In Teferra and Knight, 44–79.

Teferra, D., and J. Knight, J. 2008. *Higher education in Africa: The international dimension.* Chestnut Hill, MA: Boston College Center for International Higher Education; Accra, Ghana: Association of African Universities.

Teichler, U. 2006. Changing structures of the higher education systems: The increasing complexity of underlying forces. *Higher Education Policy* 19 (4): 447–61.

Teichler, U., and S. Bürger. 2008. Student enrolments and graduation trends in the OECD area: What can we learn from international statistics. In *Higher education to 2030.* Vol. 1, *Demography,* ed. S. Vincent-Lancrin, 151–72. Paris: OECD.

Thompson, L. 2008. Breaking ranks: Assessing quality in higher education. Organization for Economic Cooperation and

Development (OECD). http://www.oecd.org/document/47/0,33 43,en_21571361_38973579_41707887_1_1_1_1,00.html (accessed May 12, 2009).

Thornton, P., and C. Houser. 2004. Using mobile phones in education. Paper presented at the 2nd IEEE International Workshop on Wireless and Mobile Technologies in Education, IEEE Computer Society, Washington, DC.

Thursby, J. G., and M. C. Thursby. 2007. University licensing. *Oxford Review of Economic Policy*, 23 (4): 620–39.

Trow, M. 2006. Reflections on the transition from elite to mass to universal access: Forms and phases of higher education in modern societies since WWII. In *International handbook of higher education*, ed. J. J. F. Forest and P. G. Altbach, 243–80. Dordrecht, Netherlands: Springer.

Tyler, R. W. 1949. *Basic principles of curriculum and instruction*. Chicago: University of Chicago Press.

US Bureau of the Census. 1998. *World population profile: 1998*. Washington, DC: US Bureau of the Census.

———. 2008 World population information. httpp://www.census.gov/ipc/www/idb/worldpopinfo.html (accessed April 4, 2009).

UNESCO. 2004. Higher education in a globalized society: UNESCO education position paper. Paris: UNESCO.

———. 2005a. Mega universities. http://portal.unesco.org/education/en/ev.php-URL_ID=42857&URL_DO=DO_TOPIC&URL_SECTION=201.html (accessed April 12, 2009).

———. 2005b. Open and distance learning. http://portal.unesco.org/education/en/ev.php-URL_ID=48440&URL_DO=DO_TOPIC&URL_SECTION=201.html (accessed April 12, 2009).

———. 2008. World population information. http://www.census.gov/ipc/www/idb/worldpopinfo.html (accessed April 21, 2009).

———. n.d.-a. Distance education. http://portal.unesco.org/education/en/ev.php-URL_ID=6940&URL_DO=DO_TOPIC&URL_SECTION=201.html (accessed April 12, 2009).

———. n.d.-b. Higher education open and distance learning knowledge base. http://portal.unesco.org/education/en/ev.php-URL_ID=42843&URL_DO=DO_TOPIC&URL_SECTION=201.html (accessed April 12, 2009).

———. n.d.-c. UNESCO portal on higher education institutions. http://portal.unesco.org/education/en/ev.php-URL_ID=49864&URL_DO=DO_TOPIC&URL_SECTION=201.html (accessed April 1, 2009).

UNESCO-IESALC. 2008. Espacio de encuentro latinoamericano y

caribeño de educación superior. http://www.iesalc.unesco.org.ve/
index.php?option=com_content&view=article&id=186&catid=3&I
temid=14&lang=es (accessed April 7, 2009).

United Nations Population Fund. 2007. *Framework for action on
adolescents and youth.* New York: UN Population Fund.

University of Phoenix. Campus and online formats. http://www.
phoenix.edu/online_and_campus_programs/learning_formats.
html (accessed April 12, 2009).

Usher, A. 2006. *Grants for students: What they do, why they work.* Toronto:
Educational Policy Institute.

———. 2009. Ten years back and ten years forward: Developments and
trends in higher education in the Europe region. Paper presented
at the UNESCO Forum on higher education in the Europe
region: Access, values, quality and competitiveness, May 21–24,
Bucharest.

Van Damme, D., P. Van der Hijden, and C. Campbell. 2004. Quality
and recognition in higher education: The cross-border challenge.
In *Quality and recognition in higher education: The cross-border
challenge,* ed. K. Larsen and K. Momii, 75–106. Paris, OECD.

van Ginkel, H. J. A., and M. A. Rodrigues Dias. 2007. Institutional and
political challenges of accreditation at the international level. In
Higher education in the world 2007, ed. J. Tres, 37–57. New York:
Palgrave Macmillan.

Vega-Jurado J., I. Fernández-de-Lucio, and R. Huanca. 2008.
University-industry relations in Bolivia: Implications for university
transformations in Latin America. *Higher Education* 56 (2):
205–20.

Verbik, L,. and V. Lasanowski. 2007. *International student mobility:
Patterns and trends.* London: Observatory on Borderless Education.

Vest, C. M. 2007. *The American research university from World War II to
World Wide Web.* Berkeley: University of California Press.

Vincent-Lancrin, S. 2006. What is changing in academic research?
Trends and futures scenarios. *European Journal of Education* 41 (2):
169–202.

———. 2008a. The reversal of gender inequalities in higher education:
An on-going trend. In *Higher education to 2030.* Vol. 1, *Demography,*
ed. S. Vincent-Lancrin, 265–98. Paris: OECD.

_____. 2008b. What is the impact of demography on higher education
systems? A forward-looking approach for OECD countries. In
Higher education to 2030. Vol. 1, *Demography,* ed. S. Vincent-Lancrin,
41–93. Paris, OECD.

Visser, L., and P. West. 2005. The promise of M-learning for distance education in South Africa and other developing nations. In *Trends and issues in distance education: International perspectives*, ed. Y. Visser, et al., 131–36. Greenwich, CT: Information Age Publishing.

Vlasceanu, L., L. Grünberg, and D. Pârlea. 2007. *Quality assurance and accreditation: A glossary of basic terms and definitions.* Bucharest: UNESCO-CEPES.

Washburn, J. 2005. *University, Inc.: The corporate corruption of American higher education.* New York: Basic Books.

Weisskopf, T. 2004. *Affirmative action in the United States and India: A comparative perspective.* New York: Routledge.

Wells, P. J., J. Sadlak, and L. Vlasceanu. 2007. *The rising role and relevance of private higher education in Europe.* Bucharest: UNESCO-CEPES.

World Bank. 2008. G20: Global financial crisis: Responding today, securing tomorrow. http://web.worldbank.org/WBSITE/EXTERNAL/NEWS /0,,contentMDK:21972885~pagePK:64257043~piPK:437376~theSit ePK:4607,00.html. (accessed April 13, 2009).

———. 2009. Global initiative on quality assurance capacity. http:// web.worldbank.org/WBSITE/EXTERNAL/TOPICS/EXTEDUCA TION/0,,contentMDK:21723791~isCURL:Y~menuPK:617592~pa gePK:148956~piPK:216618~theSitePK:282386,00.html (accessed April 17, 2009).

World Intellectual Property Organization. 2008. World patent report: A statistical review. http://www.wipo.int/ipstats/en/statistics/ patents/wipo_pub_931.html (accessed April 28, 2009).

Yonezawa, A., and T. Kim. 2008. The future of higher education in the context of a shrinking student population: Policy challenges for Japan and Korea. In *Higher education to 2030.* Vol. 1, *Demography*, ed. S. Vincent-Lancrin, 199–220. Paris: OECD.

Zha, Q. Forthcoming. Diversification or homogenization: How governments and markets have combined to (re)shape Chinese higher education in its recent massification process. *Higher Education.*

Zhou, P., and L. Leydesdorff. 2006. The emergence of China as a leading nation in science. *Research Policy* 35 (1): 83–104.

ABOUT THE AUTHORS

PHILIP G. ALTBACH is J. Donald Monan, S.J. University Professor and director of the Center for International Higher Education in the Lynch School of Education at Boston College. He was the 2004–2006 Distinguished Scholar Leader for the New Century Scholars initiative of the Fulbright program. He has been a senior associate of the Carnegie Foundation for the Advancement of Teaching and served as editor of the *Review of Higher Education, Comparative Education Review,* and as an editor of *Educational Policy.* He is author of *Turmoil and Transition: The International Imperative in Higher Education, Comparative Higher Education, Student Politics in America,* and other books. Dr. Altbach coedited the *International Handbook of Higher Education.* His most recent book is *World Class Worldwide: Transforming Research Universities in Asia and Latin America.* Dr. Altbach has taught at the University of Wisconsin-Madison and the State University of New York at Buffalo, and was a postdoctoral fellow and lecturer on education at Harvard University. He is chairperson of the International Advisory Council of the Graduate School of Education at Shanghai Jiao Tong University.

LIZ REISBERG is a Research Associate at the Boston College Center for International Higher Education, where she manages the Center's online International Higher Education Clearinghouse (IHEC), conducts research, and contributes to Center publications. She also teaches in the graduate program in higher education administration. Dr. Reisberg is the founder and former executive director of The MBA Tour, a company that organizes professional recruitment tours throughout the world to help business schools meet talented candidates for their MBA programs. Dr. Reisberg has more than two decades of experience working in international recruitment and admissions as well as training admissions professionals. She has also provided consulting support and guidance to countries developing quality-assurance mechanisms for the improvement of university education. Dr. Reisberg has held national positions in NAFSA: Association of International Educators. She earned her PhD at Boston College, focusing her dissertation research on new strategies for quality assurance for higher education in Argentina. Dr. Reisberg authored a book on the education system of Argentina and has written several articles in Spanish and English about education reform in Latin America and quality-assurance schemes.

LAURA E. RUMBLEY is a Research Associate at the Boston College Center for International Higher Education. She leads the Center's Podcast Initiative, is Managing Director of the International Network for Higher Education in Africa (INHEA), and serves as an adjunct faculty member at the Lynch School of Education at Boston College. Dr. Rumbley holds a PhD in higher education administration; her doctoral dissertation focused on internationalization in the universities of Spain. She has over a decade of experience in the administration of international education programs in the United States. Dr. Rumbley is a former US Foreign Service Officer, a former Rotary Foundation Ambassadorial Scholar, and a Salzburg Seminar alumna. She has authored and coauthored several publications on topics ranging from trends in US study abroad, internationalization in Spanish higher education, and academic salaries in comparative perspective.

ABOUT THE CONTRIBUTORS

JORGE BALÁN was a senior program officer at the Ford Foundation from 1998 until 2007, where he managed both domestic and international portfolios with a focus on higher education research and policy. He currently serves as a senior researcher at the Center for the Study of State and Society (CEDES) in Buenos Aires, Argentina, and is a visiting scholar at the Ontario Institute for Studies in Education at the University of Toronto. He has taught at the School of Education at New York University, held a chair at the University of Buenos Aires between 1986 and 1997, and has been a visiting professor at the University of Oxford, the University of Chicago, and the University of Texas at Austin. Dr. Balán is coeditor of a 2007 book entitled *World Class Worldwide: Transforming Research Universities in Asia and Latin America* (Johns Hopkins University Press).

JOHN BIGGS has held Chairs in Education in Canada, Australia, and Hong Kong. He has published extensively on student learning and the implications of his research for teaching. His concept of constructive alignment, a form of outcomes-based education, is outlined in *Teaching for Quality Learning in University* (McGraw-Hill/Open University Press). The third edition, coauthored with Catherine Tang, is based on their experience in implementing constructive alignment in several universities in Hong Kong.

MIRIAM E. DAVID is Professor of Sociology of Education and Associate Director (Higher Education) of the ESRC's Teaching & Learning Research Programme at the Institute of Education University of London. She has been a professor for over 20 years (formerly at London South Bank and Keele Universities), and is recognized internationally for her research on social diversity, gender, and inequalities in education, including lifelong learning and higher education. She is coeditor (with Philip Davies) of *21st Century Society*, the journal of the Academy of Social Sciences; an executive editor of the *British Journal of Sociology of Education*; and a former editor of the *Journal of Social Policy* (1992–1999).

SACHI HATAKENAKA is an independent consultant and researcher specializing in organizational and policy issues in higher education and innovation systems. For the past decade, the focus of her work has been the economic roles of higher education and research institutions both in OECD and developing countries. She has worked at the World Bank on science and technology policies and human resource development and has conducted research at Massachusetts Institute of Technology as well as Oxford University. She currently advises governments, international organizations, and universities worldwide.

D. BRUCE JOHNSTONE is Distinguished Service Professor of Higher and Comparative Education, emeritus, at the State University of New York at Buffalo. He was director of the Center for Comparative and Global Studies in Education, and of the International Comparative Higher Education Finance and Accessibility Project. Dr. Johnstone also served as the Distinguished Scholar Leader for the 2007–2008 New Century Scholars project of the Fulbright Program. In a 25-year administrative career, Dr. Johnstone has held posts of vice president for administration at the University of Pennsylvania, president of the State University College of Buffalo, and chancellor of the State University of New York system, the latter from 1988 through 1994.

DANIEL C. LEVY is Distinguished Professor in the School of Education at the University at Albany, State University of New York. He also holds a joint appointment in Latin American Studies and affiliations with Political Science and the Public Policy Program. Levy is the founder and director of PROPHE (Program for Research on Private Higher Education), a global scholarly network funded by the Ford Foundation. Levy's seven books and over one hundred articles concentrate on higher education policy globally, related nonprofit sectors, or Latin American politics.

CATHERINE TANG is the former Head of Educational Development in the Hong Kong Institute of Education and in the Hong Kong Polytechnic University. Her main interest is in enhancing student learning, with a particular focus on the role of assessment, and the implications for staff development. She has been involved in large-scale teaching development projects in teaching and assessment. She coauthored with John Biggs the third edition of *Teaching for Quality Learning in University* (McGraw-Hill/Open University Press). She now consults with universities on implementing outcomes-based education.

DAMTEW TEFERRA is Director for Africa and the Middle East for the Ford Foundation International Fellows Program (IFP). In this capacity, he is responsible for administration of the IFP program in Africa and the Middle East, including Fellow selection, placement, monitoring and other related program activities. Prior to joining IFP, he served as Research Associate Professor of Higher Education at the Center for International Higher Education, Boston College. He is also the Director and Founder of the International Network for Higher Education in Africa (INHEA) and former founding editor-in-chief of the *Journal of Higher Education in Africa*. He holds a PhD in Higher Education Administration from Boston College. One of his books (coedited with Philip G. Altbach), *African Higher Education—An International Reference Handbook*, received the 2006 Porter-Conover Award of the African Studies Association.

APPENDIX

Gross Enrolment Ratio (GER)

This table provides comparison data, by country, on primary, secondary, and tertiary education enrolment, in both 2000 and 2007. UNESCO defines the Gross Enrolment Ratios or (GER) as the total enrolment in a specific level of education, regardless of age, expressed as a percentage of the eligible official school-age population corresponding to the same level of education in a given school year.

The purpose of the statistic is to show the general level of participation in a given level of education. It indicates the capacity of the education system to enroll students of a particular age group. It can also be a complementary indicator to net enrolment rate (NER) data by indicating the extent of over-aged and under-aged enrolment.

A high GER generally indicates a high degree of participation, whether the pupils belong to the official age group or not. A GER value approaching or exceeding 100% indicates that a country is, in principle, able to accommodate all of its school-age population, but it does not indicate the proportion already enrolled. The achievement of a GER of 100% is therefore a necessary but not sufficient condition for enrolling all eligible children in school. When the GER exceeds 90% for a particular level of education, the aggregate number of places for pupils is approaching the number required for universal access of the official age group. However, this is a meaningful interpretation only if one can expect the under-aged and over-aged enrolments to decline in the future to free places for pupils from the expected age group.

GER at each level of education should be based on total enrolment in all types of schools and education institutions, including public, private and all other institutions that provide organized educational programmes. In terms of limitations, it is important to note that GER can exceed 100% due to the inclusion of over-aged and under-aged pupils/students because of early or late entrants, and grade repetition. In this case, a rigorous interpretation of GER needs additional information to assess the extent of repetition, late entrants, etc. (UNESCO Institute for Statistics Glossary, http://www.uis.unesco.org/glossary/)

Table 1: Gross Enrolment Ratios (GER)

Country or region	Primary		Secondary		Tertiary	
	2000	2007	2000	2007	2000	2007
Afghanistan	22	103	13 [+1]	28	...	...
Albania	102	...	70	...	15	...
Algeria	108	110	...	83 [**,-2]	16 [**,+1]	24
Andorra	...	88 [*]	...	82 [*]	...	10 [*,-1]
Angola	...	...	15	...	1 [-1]	3 [-1]
Anguilla	111 [**]	93 [**,-1]	107 [**]	83 [**,-1]	. [**]	5 [**,-1]
Antigua and Barbuda	...	102 [*]	...	105 [*]	.	...
Argentina	114	114 [-1]	86	84 [-1]	53 [**]	67 [-1]
Armenia	99	110	90	89	24	34
Aruba	115	114	98	105	29	33

Table 1: Gross Enrolment Ratios (GER) cont.

Country or region	Primary		Secondary		Tertiary	
	2000	2007	2000	2007	2000	2007
Australia	101	107	162	149	66	75
Austria	104	101	99	102	56	51
Azerbaijan	99 *	116 *	78 *	89 *	16 *	15 *
Bahamas	93 **	103	80 **	94	...	...
Bahrain	107	120 -1	97	102 -1	22 -1	32 -1
Bangladesh	...	91	46	43	5	7
Barbados	99	105	96	103	38	53
Belarus	112	97	87	95	53	69
Belgium	106	103	146	110	58	62
Belize	117	123 +1	68	79	...	...
Benin	77	96 -1	20	32 **,-2	4	5 -1
Bermuda	103 *,+1	100 *,-1	87 *,+1	84 *,-1	61 *,+1	19 *,-2
Bhutan	78	111 +1	42	56 +1	3 **	5
Bolivia	115	108	80 **	82	36	...
Bosnia and Herzegovina	...	98	...	85	...	37
Botswana	105	107 -2	75 **	76 -2	3	5 -2
Brazil	150	130	104	100	16	30
British Virgin Islands	110 *	108 **	98 **	101 **	52 **	75 **,-2
Brunei Darussalam	111	106	85	97	13	15
Bulgaria	106	101	92	106	44	50
Burkina Faso	44	71 +1	10	18 +1	1 **	3 +1
Burundi	60 *	114	...	15	1	2
Cambodia	102	119	18	40	2	5
Cameroon	86	110	27	25 *	4 **	7
Canada	99	99 -1	107	102 -1	59	...
Cape Verde	118	101	63 +1	79	2	9
Cayman Islands	108 *	90 **,-2	96 *	102 **,-2	19 **	...
Central African Republic	73 *,+1	74 +1	12 **,+1	...	2	1 -1
Chad	66	74	11	19	1	1 **,-2
Chile	100	106	83	91	37	52
China	117 +1	112	63	77	8	23
Colombia	115	116	69	85	23	32
Comoros	84	85 **,-2	24 **	35 **,-2	1	...
Congo	83	106	34	...	5	...
Cook Islands	88 *	73 **	66 *	73 **	. *	**
Costa Rica	108	110	61	87	16	25 **,-2
Côte d'Ivoire	69	72	22 **	...	7 **	8
Croatia	93	99	85	92	31	46
Cuba	111	102 +1	79	93	22	109
Cyprus	97 *	102 *	92 *	98 *	20 *	36 *
Czech Republic	103	101	88	96	29	55
Democratic People's Republic of Korea	...	...	...	...	...	...
Democratic Republic of the Congo	48 -1	85	18 -1	33	1 **,-1	4
Denmark	101	99	127	119	58	80
Djibouti	32	56 +1	14	29 +1	-	3

Table 1: Gross Enrolment Ratios (GER) cont.

Country or region	Primary		Secondary		Tertiary	
	2000	2007	2000	2007	2000	2007
Dominica	103 *	86 *,-1	95 *	106 *,-1	. *	. *,-2
Dominican Republic	116	102 +1	61	79	...	...
Ecuador	115	118	57	70	...	35
Egypt	101 **	105	85 **	...	37 **,-1	35 **,-2
El Salvador	111	118	54	64	17	22
Equatorial Guinea	135	124	33 **	...	3	...
Eritrea	57	55	25	29	1	...
Estonia	103	99	92	100	56	65
Ethiopia	52	91	13	30	1	3
Fiji	107	94	80	82	...	15 **,-2
Finland	100	98	124	111	83	94
France	107	110	110	113	53	56
Gabon	146 **	...	49 **	...	7 -1	...
Gambia	87	83 +1	33	49 +1	1 **	...
Georgia	100	99	79	90	38	37
Germany	105	104	98	100	...	...
Ghana	80	104 +1	38	53 +1	3	6
Gibraltar	...	...	...	...	.	. -1
Greece	96	101	89	102	51	91
Grenada	96 *	81	...	99	. *	. *,-2
Guatemala	104	113	38	56	...	18
Guinea	61	91	16 **	38 **	...	5 -1
Guinea-Bissau	70	...	18	...	-	...
Guyana	125	112	90 **	107	...	12
Haiti	...	...	...	...	...	...
Holy See	.	.	.	.	...	...
Honduras	107	119	...	64	15	...
Hong Kong SAR of China	103	98 -2	81 +1	86	...	34
Hungary	101	96	96	96	37	69
Iceland	101	97	108	111	46	73
India	94	112 -1	46	55 -1	10	12 -1
Indonesia	109 **	117	55 **	73	14 +1	17
Iran (Islamic Republic of)	94	121	79	81 -2	19	31
Iraq	91	99 **,-2	36	45 **,-2	12	16 **,-2
Ireland	104	104	108	113	49	61
Israel	113	111	92	92	50	60
Italy	101	105	93	101	49	68
Jamaica	95	91	86	90	15	...
Japan	101	100	102	101	47	58
Jordan	99	96	89	89	29	40
Kazakhstan	97	109 +1	93	92 +1	28	47 +1
Kenya	97	113	39	53	3	3
Kiribati	109 *	113 *,-2	99 *	88 *,-2	. *	. *,-1
Kuwait	96	98	94	91	22 **,+1	18 -1
Kyrgyzstan	97	95	84	86	35	43

Table 1: Gross Enrolment Ratios (GER) cont.

Country or region	Primary 2000	Primary 2007	Secondary 2000	Secondary 2007	Tertiary 2000	Tertiary 2007
Lao People's Democratic Republic	109	118	35	44	3	12
Latvia	102	95	90	98 **	56	71
Lebanon	101	95 +1	76	80 +1	34	54 +1
Lesotho	114	114 -1	30	37 -1	2 **	4 -1
Liberia	100	83 +1	32	...	16	...
Libyan Arab Jamahiriya	119 **	110 -1	...	94 -1	46	...
Liechtenstein	...	110 *	...	106 *	...	31 *
Lithuania	104	95	98	98	50	76
Luxembourg	101	102	98	97	10	10 -1
Macao, China	103	108	79	99	27	57
Madagascar	99	141	...	26 **	2	3
Malawi	137	116	31	28	- *	-
Malaysia	97	98 -1	65	69 -2	26	30 -1
Maldives	134	111	55	83 **,-1	.	- **,-1
Mali	61	83	19 **	32	2	4
Malta	107	100 -2	89	99 -2	21	32 -2
Marshall Islands	101 **	93 *	72 **,-1	66 *	17 **,+1	...
Mauritania	89	103	19	25 **	4 +1	4
Mauritius	105	101	78	88 **,-2	7	14 +1
Mexico	110	114	72	89	20	27
Micronesia (Federated States of)	...	110	...	91 **	14 **	...
Monaco	...	...	...	...	.	. -1
Mongolia	99	100	63	92	29	48
Montenegro	...	...	...	...	...	...
Montserrat	...	107 *	...	102 *	...	. *
Morocco	92	107	38	56	9	11
Mozambique	75	111	6	18	1	1 -2
Myanmar	...	...	...	...	...	...
Namibia	106	109	59	59	7 +1	6 -1
Nauru	76 *	79 **	45 *	46 **	. *	. *,-1
Nepal	117	124 +1	35	48 +1	4	11
Netherlands	108	107	123	120	52	60
Netherlands Antilles	130	...	87	...	23	...
New Zealand	99	102	112	121	66	80
Nicaragua	101	116	53	69	17 **,+1	...
Niger	33	53	7 **	11	...	1
Nigeria	92	97 -1	24	32 -1	6 -1	10 -2
Niue	93 *	105 *,2	96 **	99 *,-2	. *	. *,-1
Norway	101	99	116	113	69	76
Oman	91	80	78	90	...	25
Pakistan	69 *	92	...	33	...	5 *
Palau	113 *	99 *	86 *	97 *	41 **	...
Palestinian Autonomous Territorie	108	80	82	92	26	46
Panama	109	113	67	70	44	45 -1
Papua New Guinea	69	55 -1	...	...	2 **,-1	...

Table 1: Gross Enrolment Ratio (GER) cont.

Country or region	Primary 2000	Primary 2007	Secondary 2000	Secondary 2007	Tertiary 2000	Tertiary 2007
Paraguay	120 [**]	111 [-2]	61	66 [-2]	16	26 [**,-2]
Peru	121	117	87	98	32 [**,+1]	35 [**,-1]
Philippines	112 [+1]	109	77 [+1]	83	30 [+1]	28 [-1]
Poland	99	97	100	100	50	67
Portugal	124	115	108	101	48	56
Qatar	101	109	88	103	19 [+1]	16
Republic of Korea	100	107	94	98	78	95
Republic of Moldova	101 [*]	94 [*]	82 [*]	89 [*]	33 [*]	41 [*]
Romania	103	105	81	87	24	58
Russian Federation	107	96	...	84	...	75
Rwanda	96	147	10	18	2 [**]	3 [**,-2]
Saint Kitts and Nevis	120 [*]	94 [**]	93 [**]	105 [**]	. [*]	. [*,-2]
Saint Lucia	109	109	75	93	...	9
Saint Vincent and the Grenadines	102	102	69 [**]	75 [-2]	.	. [-2]
Samoa	99	95	78	81 [**,-2]	7	...
San Marino	...	...	...	...	...	...
Sao Tome and Principe	126 [**,+1]	130 [+1]	...	46 [+1]	.	. [+1]
Saudi Arabia	...	98	...	94	22	30 [-1]
Senegal	67	84	16	26 [**]	3 [-1]	8 [+1]
Serbia	104 [**]	97 [*]	89 [**]	88 [*]	...	...
Seychelles	118 [*]	125 [*]	113 [*]	112 [*]	. [*]	. [*]
Sierra Leone	65	147	26 [+1]	32	2 [+1]	...
Singapore	...	...	...	...	...	...
Slovakia	103	102	87	94	29	51
Slovenia	98	104	101	94	56	86
Solomon Islands	85	101 [-2]	20	30 [-2]	.	. [-1]
Somalia	12 [-1]	...	...	...	...	...
South Africa	108	103	86	97 [**]	14	15 [-1]
Spain	106	106	111	120	59	69
Sri Lanka	105 [+1]	109	...	...	...	...
Sudan	49	66	26	33	6 [**]	...
Suriname	120 [+1]	119	72 [+1]	80	...	...
Swaziland	100	113	43	54	4	4 [-1]
Sweden	109	94	152	104	67	75
Switzerland	103	97	94	93	37	47
Syrian Arab Republic	104	126	41	72	...	...
Tajikistan	98	100	74	84	14	20
Thailand	106	104 [+1]	67 [+1]	83 [+1]	35	48 [**,+1]
The former Yugoslav Rep. of Mace	99	95	84	84	23	36
Timor-Leste	126 [+1]	91	35 [**,+1]	53 [-2]	...	...
Togo	104	97	30	39	...	5
Tokelau	101 [**]	...	95 [**]	...	. [**]	. [*,-1]
Tonga	108	113 [-1]	101	94 [-1]	5	...
Trinidad and Tobago	99	100	75 [**]	86 [**]	6	11 [**,-2]
Tunisia	113	105	75 [**]	88	19	31

Table 1: Gross Enrolment Ratio (GER) cont.

Country or region	Primary 2000	Primary 2007	Secondary 2000	Secondary 2007	Tertiary 2000	Tertiary 2007
Turkey	95 [**]	96 [**]	78 [**,+1]	80 [**]	23 [**]	36
Turkmenistan	...	...	...	...	...	...
Turks and Caicos Islands	...	90 [**,-2]	...	86 [**,-2]	.	. [**,-2]
Tuvalu	109 [*]	106 [*,-1]	84 [*,+1]	...	. [*]	.
Uganda	125	116	16	23 [**]	3	...
Ukraine	109	100	99	94	49	76
United Arab Emirates	89	107	75	92 [**]	18 [**]	23 [+1]
United Kingdom	101	104	102	97	58	59
United Republic of Tanzania	69	112 [+1]	6 [**,-1]	...	1 [+1]	1
United States of America	100	99	94	94	69	82
Uruguay	109	114	98	92	34 [**,-1]	64
Uzbekistan	99	95	88	102	13	10
Vanuatu	114	108	34	...	4	...
Venezuela	102	103 [+1]	59	79	28	52 [*,-1]
Viet Nam	106	...	65	...	9	...
Yemen	74 [**]	87 [-2]	43 [**]	46 [-2]	10 [**]	9 [**,-1]
Zambia	80	119	23	43	2 [**]	...
Zimbabwe	100	101 [-1]	43	40 [-1]	4 [**]	...

Average	2000	2007	2000	2007	2000	2007
World	99 [**]	106 [**]	60	66 [**]	19	26 [**]
Low Income	81	97 [**]	33 [**]	40 [**]	5 [**]	7 [**]
Lower Middle Income	105 [**]	112 [**]	57	66 [**]	12	20 [**]
Upper Middle Income	114	109	87 [**]	90	29	44
High Income	101	102	100	100	57	67
Arab States	91	98	61	65 [**]	20 [**]	22 [**]
Central and Eastern Europe	101	97	88 [**]	88	41 [**]	62
Central Asia	99	100	86	95	20	24
East Asia and the Pacific	113 [**]	110	65	78	15	26
Latin America and the Caribbean	120	117	83	89	23	34 [**]
North America and Western Europe	102	102	100	100	60	70
South and West Asia	90	108 [**]	46	...	9	11 [**]
Sub-Saharan Africa	81	99 [**]	25	34 [**]	4 [**]	6 [**]

Source: UNESCO Institute for Statistics

Notes:

...	No data available
*	National estimation
**	UIS estimation
_	Magnitude nil or negligible
.	Not applicable
(p)	Provisional data
X (y)	Data are included in another category/column (y) of the table
+n	Data refer to the school or financial year (or period) n years or periods after the reference year or period
-n	Data refer to the school or financial year (or period) n years or periods prior to the reference year or period

Figure 1a: Tertiary gross enrolment ratio by income level, 2000 and 2007

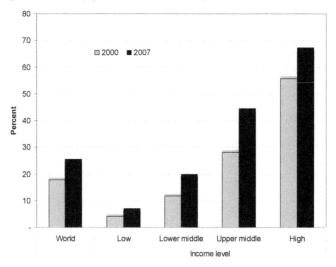

Figure 1b: Tertiary gross enrolment ratio by geographical region, 2000 and 2007

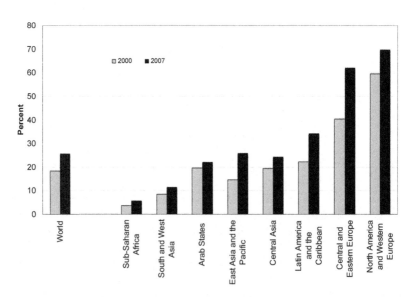

Tertiary Enrolment

This table provides comparison of data for the years 2000 and 2007, for the total number of tertiary students enrolled in each country. Where possible, the percentage of this total that is enrolled in private higher education is also provided. UNESCO defines tertiary education as:

> Programmes with an educational content more advanced than what is offered at ISCED levels 3 and 4. The first stage of tertiary education, ISCED level 5, covers level 5A, composed of largely theoretically based programmes intended to provide sufficient qualifications for gaining entry to advanced research programmes and professions with high skill requirements; and level 5B, where programmes are generally more practical, technical and/or occupationally specific. The second stage of tertiary education, ISCED level 6, comprises programmes devoted to advanced study and original research, and leading to the award of an advanced research qualification (UNESCO, Institute for Statistics Glossary, http://www.uis.unesco.org/glossary)

Table 2: Tertiary Enrolment

| Country or region | Number of Tertiary Students | | | |
| | 2000 | | 2007 | |
	MF	Private (%)	MF	Private (%)
Afghanistan	...	...	...	...
Albania	40,125	...	...	...
Algeria	549,009 ⁻,⁺¹	...	901,562	...
Andorra	...	...	401 ⁻¹	...
Angola	7,845 ⁻¹	...	48,694 ⁻¹	34 ⁻¹
Anguilla	.	.	54	81
Antigua and Barbuda	.	.	...	...
Argentina	1,766,933 ⁻	...	2,202,032 ⁻¹	25 ⁻¹
Armenia	62,794	...	107,398	23
Aruba	1,578	13	2,232	17
Australia	845,132	-	1,083,715	4
Austria	261,229	...	260,975	14
Azerbaijan	117,077	...	135,164	16
Bahamas	...	...	...	...
Bahrain	11,048 ⁻¹	...	18,403 ⁻¹	...
Bangladesh	726,701	63	1,145,401	49
Barbados	8,074	-	11,405	...
Belarus	411,861	9	556,526	13
Belgium	355,748	...	393,687	56
Belize	...	...	...	...

Table 2: Tertiary Enrolment cont.

Country or region	Number of Tertiary Students			
	2000		2007	
	MF	Private (%)	MF	Private (%)
Benin	22,415	...	42,603 [-1]	...
Bermuda	1,942 [+1]	- [+1]	886	-
Bhutan	1,837 **	...	3,998	-
Bolivia	278,763	21	...	...
Bosnia and Herzegovina	...	...	99,414	...
Botswana	6,332	100	10,950 [-2]	100 [-2]
Brazil	2,781,328	...	5,272,877	73
British Virgin Islands	750 **	...	1,200 **, [-2]	...
Brunei Darussalam	3,984	-	5,284	0
Bulgaria	261,321	...	258,692	20
Burkina Faso	11,100 **	...	33,459	17
Burundi	6,132	...	15,623	...
Cambodia	22,108	68	92,340	58
Cameroon	65,697 **	...	132,134	12
Canada	1,212,161	...	...	...
Cape Verde	801	-	5,289	55
Cayman Islands	380 **	...	567 [-1]	...
Central African Republic	6,323	-	4,462 [-1]	- [-1]
Chad	5,901	9	10,468 **, [-2]	...
Chile	452,177	72	753,398	77
China	7,364,111	...	25,346,279	...
Colombia	934,085	64	1,372,674	45
Comoros	714	...	...	...
Congo	15,629	-	...	...
Cook Islands	...	...	...	...
Costa Rica	61,654	...	110,717 **, [-2]	...
Côte d'Ivoire	104,192 **	...	156,772	36
Croatia	96,798	1	139,996	5
Cuba	158,674	-	864,846	-
Cyprus	10,414	56	22,227	68
Czech Republic	253,695	4	363,277	12
Democratic People's Republic of Korea	...	...	...	...
Democratic Republic of the Congo	60,341 **, [-1]	...	237,836	...
Denmark	189,162	-	232,194	2
Djibouti	190	-	2,192	...

Table 2: Tertiary Enrolment cont.

	Number of Tertiary Students			
	2000		2007	
Country or region	MF	Private (%)	MF	Private (%)
Dominica	.	...	.⁻²	...
Dominican Republic	...	...	...	...
Ecuador	...	...	443,509	26
Egypt	2,447,088 **,⁻¹	...	2,594,186 **,⁻²	...
El Salvador	114,675	...	132,246	66
Equatorial Guinea	1,003	...	...	...
Eritrea	4,135	-	...	...
Estonia	53,613	...	68,767	84
Ethiopia	67,732	...	210,456	16
Fiji	...	...	12,717 **,⁻²	...
Finland	270,185	11	309,163	11
France	2,015,344	15	2,179,505	17
Gabon	7,473 ⁻¹	...	...	...
Gambia	1,212 **	...	...	...
Georgia	137,046	54	141,303	21
Germany	...	...	...	...
Ghana	54,658	2	140,017	...
Gibraltar	.	.	.⁻¹	...
Greece	422,317	-	602,858	-
Grenada	.	...	.⁻²	...
Guatemala	...	...	233,885	...
Guinea	...	...	42,711 ⁻¹	6 ⁻¹
Guinea-Bissau	463	...	...	...
Guyana	...	...	7,532	-
Haiti	...	...	...	...
Holy See	9,389 ⁻¹	100 ⁻¹	...	...
Honduras	90,620	21	...	...
Hong Kong SAR of China	...	...	157,858	6
Hungary	307,071	13	431,572	15
Iceland	9,667	9	15,821	21
India	9,404,460	...	12,852,684 ⁻¹	...
Indonesia	3,017,887 ⁺¹	63 ⁺¹	3,755,187	74
Iran (Islamic Republic of)	1,404,880	...	2,828,528	52
Iraq	288,670	12	424,908 **,⁻²	...
Ireland	160,611	5	190,349	9
Israel	255,891	85	327,108	86
Italy	1,770,002	6	2,033,642	8
Jamaica	35,995	...	...	...
Japan	3,982,069	78	4,032,625	80
Jordan	142,190	36	231,657	31

Table 2: Tertiary Enrolment cont.

Country or region	Number of Tertiary Students			
	2000		2007	
	MF	Private (%)	MF	Private (%)
Kazakhstan	370,321	...	772,600	49
Kenya	89,016	...	139,524	15
Kiribati	.	...	. -¹	...
Kuwait	34,779 **,+¹	...	37,521 -¹	26 -¹
Kyrgyzstan	160,684	...	239,380	9
Lao People's Democratic Republic	14,149	23	75,003	24
Latvia	91,237	...	129,497	96
Lebanon	116,014	42	187,055	53
Lesotho	4,470 **	_ **	8,500 -¹	_ -¹
Liberia	44,107	...	...	...
Libyan Arab Jamahiriya	290,060	20	...	...
Liechtenstein	...	...	673	100
Lithuania	121,904	4	199,855	9
Luxembourg	2,437	...	2,692 -¹	_ -¹
Macao, China	7,471	35	23,868	61
Madagascar	32,046	...	58,313	14
Malawi	3,584 *	...	6,458	-
Malaysia	549,205	35	749,165 -¹	33 -¹
Maldives	.	...	_ **,-¹	...
Mali	19,751	...	50,787	...
Malta	6,315	-	9,441 -²	_ -²
Marshall Islands	888 **,+¹	...	...	...
Mauritania	9,033 +¹	...	11,794	...
Mauritius	8,256	...	13,509 +¹	_ +¹
Mexico	1,962,763	30	2,528,664	33
Micronesia (Federated States of)	1,539 **	...	...	...
Monaco	.	...	. -¹	...
Mongolia	74,025	31	142,411	34
Montenegro	...	...	...	...
Montserrat	.	...	.	.
Morocco	276,375	4	369,142	10
Mozambique	11,619	...	28,298 -²	33 -²
Myanmar	553,456 +¹	_ +¹	507,660	-
Namibia	13,339 +¹	100 +¹	13,185 -¹	82 -¹
Nauru	.	...	. -¹	...
Nepal	94,401	26	320,844	42
Netherlands	487,649	...	590,121	...
Netherlands Antilles	2,561	...	...	...
New Zealand	171,962	5	242,651	11
Nicaragua	96,479 **,+¹	...	...	...

Table 2: Tertiary Enrolment cont.

	Number of Tertiary Students			
	2000		2007	
Country or region	MF	Private (%)	MF	Private (%)
Niger	...	...	10,869	29
Nigeria	699,109 -¹	...	1,391,527 -²	...
Niue	.	...	-¹	...
Norway	190,943	12	215,237	14
Oman	...	...	69,018	...
Pakistan	...	...	954,698 *	...
Palau	597 **	...	...	...
Palestinian Autonomous Territories	71,207	60	169,373	55
Panama	118,502	...	130,838 -¹	26 -¹
Papua New Guinea	9,943 **,-¹	...	...	...
Paraguay	83,088	...	156,167 **,-²	57 **,-²
Peru	823,995 **,+¹	...	952,437 **,-¹	54 **,-¹
Philippines	2,432,002 +¹	69 +¹	2,483,988 -¹	66 -¹
Poland	1,579,571	28	2,146,926	32
Portugal	373,745	...	366,729	25
Qatar	7,808 +¹	...	8,881	31
Republic of Korea	3,003,498	81	3,208,591	80
Republic of Moldova	103,944	...	148,449 *	15 *
Romania	452,621	29	928,175	31
Russian Federation	...	...	9,370,428	...
Rwanda	11,628 **	...	26,378 **,-²	...
Saint Kitts and Nevis	.	...	-²	...
Saint Lucia	...	...	1,438	7
Saint Vincent and the Grenadines	.	...	-²	...
Samoa	1,182	...	...	...
San Marino	942	...	929 +¹	...
Sao Tome and Principe	.	.	.	...
Saudi Arabia	404,094	-	636,445 -¹	...
Senegal	29,303 -¹	21 -¹	76,949 **	...
Serbia	...	...	...	...
Seychelles	...	...	.	.
Sierra Leone	8,795 +¹	- +¹	...	...
Singapore	...	...	183,627	61
Slovakia	135,914	-	217,952	7
Slovenia	83,816	97	115,944	10
Solomon Islands	.	...	-¹	...
Somalia	...	...	...	...
South Africa	644,763	...	741,380 -¹	...
Spain	1,828,987	12	1,777,498	14
Sri Lanka	...	...	...	...

Table 2: Tertiary Enrolment cont.

Country or region	Number of Tertiary Students			
	2000		2007	
	MF	Private (%)	MF	Private (%)
Sudan	204,114 **	...	...	...
Suriname	...	...	...	...
Swaziland	4,738	...	5,692 -1	. -1
Sweden	346,878	...	413,710	8
Switzerland	156,879	20	213,112	19
Syrian Arab Republic	...	...	...	...
Tajikistan	79,978	-	147,294	...
Thailand	1,900,272	20	2,503,572	17
The former Yugoslav Rep. of Macedoni	36,922	...	58,199	17
Timor-Leste	...	...	...	...
Togo	...	...	32,502	...
Tokelau	.	...	. -1	...
Tonga	526	...	...	...
Trinidad and Tobago	7,737	-	16,920 **,-2	...
Tunisia	180,044	-	326,185	...
Turkey	1,588,367 **	...	2,453,664	5
Turkmenistan	...	...	...	...
Turks and Caicos Islands	.	.	. -2	...
Tuvalu	.	...	.	...
Uganda	55,767	...	...	...
Ukraine	1,811,538	...	2,819,248	...
United Arab Emirates	43,459 **	...	77,428 *-1	58 *-1
United Kingdom	2,024,138	100	2,362,815	100
United Republic of Tanzania	21,960 *-1	...	55,134	...
United States of America	13,202,880	26	17,758,870	26
Uruguay	91,275 **,-1	...	158,841	11
Uzbekistan	305,409	...	288,550	-
Vanuatu	656	...	...	...
Venezuela	668,109	44	1,381,126 *,-1	45 *,-1
Viet Nam	732,187	13	1,587,609	12
Yemen	173,130 **	...	209,386 **,-1	...
Zambia	24,553 **	...	...	...
Zimbabwe	48,894 **	...	...	...

Table 2: Tertiary Enrolment cont.

Country or region	Number of Tertiary Students			
	2000		2007	
	MF	Private (%)	MF	Private (%)
Average				
World	98,303,539		150,656,459 **	
Arab States	5,545,811 **		7,146,174 **	
Central and Eastern Europe	13,521,198 **		20,749,657	
Central Asia	1,328,239		1,994,408	
East Asia and the Pacific	24,467,390		46,451,377	
Latin America and the Caribbean	11,316,113		17,757,024 **	
North America and Western Europe	27,722,578		34,008,815	
South and West Asia	12,059,852		18,409,207 **	
Sub-Saharan Africa	2,342,358 **		4,139,797 **	

Source: UNESCO Institute for Statistics

Note: In this table, private higher education is defined by funding that does not come directly from government sources. Thus, the data for some countries (such as Israel and the United Kingdom), where public funding is delivered by semi-independent agencies, may give the misleading impression of high percentages of private higher education.

Notes:

...	No data available
*	National estimation
**	UIS estimation
–	Magnitude nil or negligible
.	Not applicable
(p)	Provisional data
X (y)	Data are included in another category/column (y) of the table
+n	Data refer to the school or financial year (or period) n years or periods after the reference year or period
-n	Data refer to the school or financial year (or period) n years or periods prior to the reference year or period

Female Students in Tertiary Education

This table provides comparison data for the years 2000 and 2007 for female students in higher education. Where possible, it presents information on female participation for ISCED levels 5A, 5B, and 6, as well as in the aggregate for all three ISCED levels within the tertiary education sector.

Table 3: Female Students in Tertiary Education

Country or region	Female students by ISCED level (%) 2000			Female students in tertiary education 2000	Female students by ISCED level (%) 2007			Female students in tertiary education 2007
	5A	5B	6	%F	5A	5B	6	%F
Afghanistan								
Albania	60			60				
Algeria		87	-		59	47	46	57
Andorra					59[-1]	49[-1]	[-1]	53[-1]
Angola	39[-1]	[-1]	[-1]	39[-1]				
Anguilla					82	90		83
Antigua and Barbuda								
Argentina	57**	70	58**	60**	57[-1]	69[-1]	57[-1]	60[-1]
Armenia	54		32	54	55		37	55
Aruba	78	55		61	71	53		58
Australia	56	50	47	54	56	53	51	55
Austria	50	65	42	51	53	66	46	54
Azerbaijan	40		30	40	46		28	46
Bahamas								
Bahrain					70[-1]	51[-1]	[-1]	68[-1]
Bangladesh	34**	15**	23**	32	36	25	25	35
Barbados	65	82	60	72	68	68	55	68
Belarus	56	56	46	56	59	54	55	57
Belgium	49	56	35	52	52	58	43	55
Belize								

Table 3: Female Students in Tertiary Education cont.

Country or region	Female students by ISCED level (%) 2000			Female students in tertiary education 2000	Female students by ISCED level (%) 2007			Female students in tertiary education 2007
	5A	5B	6	%F	5A	5B	6	%F
Benin	19 **	24 **	22 **	20 **	…	…	…	…
Bermuda	…	…	…	…	…	71	…	71
Bhutan	32 **	34 **	**	34 **	…	…	…	31
Bolivia	…	…	…	…	…	…	…	…
Bosnia and Herzegovina								
Botswana	49 +1	34 +1	50 +1	47 +1	52 -2	16 -2	-2	50 -2
Brazil	…	55 **	…	56	57	41	51	56
British Virgin Islands	80 **	55 **	**	72 **	75 **-2	56 **-2	**-2	69 **-2
Brunei Darussalam	65	65	.	65	67	60	30	65
Bulgaria	57	65	47	57	54	52	50	54
Burkina Faso	27	27	…	23 **	28	40	26	31
Burundi	25	27	11	27	27	32	.	32
Cambodia	…	.	…	25	35	.	-	35
Cameroon	…	…	…	…	43	49	33	44
Canada	58	52	45	56	58 -2	…	46 -2	54
Cape Verde	51 **	…	**	51 **	55	…	41	55
Cayman Islands	71 **	83 **	.	74 **	90 -1	69 -1	-1	72 -1
Central African Republic	17 **	9 **	**	16	20 -1	30 -1	-1	22 -1
Chad	14	28	20	15	…	…	…	…
Chile	47	46	40	47	53	44	43	49
China	…	…	22	…	…	50	…	48
Colombia	53	47	49	52	52	47	38	51
Comoros	34 **	56 **	**	42 **	…	…	…	…
Congo	25	19	.	24	…	…	…	…
Cook Islands								

Table 3: Female Students in Tertiary Education cont.

Country or region	Female students by ISCED level (%) 2000			Female students in tertiary education 2000	Female students by ISCED level (%) 2007			Female students in tertiary education 2007
	5A	5B	6	%F	5A	5B	6	%F
Costa Rica	53	29	89	53	..	..	..	..
Côte d'Ivoire	24**	32**	24**	28**	..	..	..	..
Croatia	55	46	–	53	30	39	26	33
Cuba	53**	–	53**	53	56	49	45	54
Cyprus	77	50	–	57	64	44	48	64
Czech Republic	48	69	35	50	71	70	39	55
Democratic People's Republic of Korea	..	..	..	..	..	..	..	..
Democratic Republic of the Congo	..	..	..	..	..	..	..	26*
Denmark	51	64	42	57	59	47	46	58
Djibouti	24	57	.	47	37[-1]	46[-1]	.[-1]	40[-1]
Dominica					.[-2]	.[-2]	.[-2]	.[-2]
Dominican Republic	..	..	..	..	..	..	..	..
Ecuador	..	..	..	..	..	..	..	54
Egypt	..	..	..	..	..	..	..	..
El Salvador	58**	38**	17**	54	55	54	14	55
Equatorial Guinea	33	8	.	30	..	..	..	..
Eritrea	14	.	.	14	..	..	..	..
Estonia	56	72	55	58	61	61	55	61
Ethiopia	22	.	.	22	25	2	2	25
Fiji	..	..	..	..	52**[-2]	63**[-2]	43**[-2]	53**[-2]
Finland	54	58	47	54	54	10	52	54
France	55	53	47	54	56	56	46	55
Gabon	34[-1]	42[-1]	37[-1]	36[-1]	..	..	..	..
Gambia	23**	.	.	23**	..	..	..	..
Georgia	49	.	55	49	52	.	63	52

Table 3: Female Students in Tertiary Education cont.

Country or region	Female students by ISCED level (%) 2000			Female students in tertiary education 2000	Female students by ISCED level (%) 2007			Female students in tertiary education 2007
	5A	5B	6	%F	5A	5B	6	%F
Germany	45	64	..	..	48	61	..	..
Ghana	26	24	23	25	35	33	26	34
Gibraltar	-	-	.	.	-¹	-¹	-¹	-¹
Greece	51	49	40	50	54	45	42	50
Grenada					⁻²	⁻²	⁻²	⁻²
Guatemala	..	..	..		45*¹	70*¹	-¹	46*¹
Guinea	..	..	..		..	..	..	..
Guinea-Bissau	-	16	.	16	-¹	..	-¹	..
Guyana	..	..	.		64	80	.	68
Haiti	..	..	..		..	..	..	..
Holy See	34⁻¹	32⁻¹	20⁻¹	30⁻¹	..	..	..	..
Honduras	56	59	41	56	..	..	..	..
Hong Kong SAR of China	..	62	..	54	53	48	42	50
Hungary	54	62	42	54	58	68	49	58
Iceland	64	45	33	62	65	39	57	64
India	38	34	36	38	40⁻¹	-¹	40⁻¹	40⁻¹
Indonesia	42*¹	47*¹	34*¹	43*¹	48	56	39	50
Iran (Islamic Republic of)	46	42	25	45	56	42	33	52
Iraq	..	..	..	34	39**²	22**²	35**²	36**²
Ireland	55	53	45	54	58	50	47	55
Israel	58	55	51	57	56	55	53	56
Italy	56	58	49	56	57	57	52	57
Jamaica	65	65	66	65	..	..	..	..
Japan	37	67	25	45	41	61	30	46
Jordan	47	68	25	51	51	59	30	51

Table 3: Female Students in Tertiary Education cont.

Country or region	Female students by ISCED level (%) 2000			Female students in tertiary education 2000	Female students by ISCED level (%) 2007			Female students in tertiary education 2007
	5A	5B	6	%F	5A	5B	6	%F
Kazakhstan	54	·	51	54	58	·	66	58
Kenya	34	37	33	35	36	38	43	36
Kiribati							·⁻¹	·⁻¹
Kuwait	64**·⁺¹	**·⁺¹	36**	63**·⁺¹	66⁻¹	·	51⁻¹	65⁻¹
Kyrgyzstan	50	·	61	50	56	·	60	56
Lao People's Democratic Republic	34	34		34	41	42		42
Latvia	65	50	52	63	64	63	61	64
Lebanon	53	39	32	52	54	52	43	54
Lesotho	60**	68**	·	62**	51⁻¹	70⁻¹	·⁻¹	55⁻¹
Liberia	43	42	41	43	·	·	·	·
Libyan Arab Jamahiriya	51	45	42	49	·	·	·	·
Liechtenstein	·	·	·	·	32	·	28	32
Lithuania	58	65	55	60	60	60	58	60
Luxembourg	46**	57**	·	52**	·	·	·	·
Macao, China	44	71	39	52	48	61	24	49
Madagascar	46**	48**	48**	46**	48	45	41	47
Malawi	28**	·		28**	34	·	·	34
Malaysia	56	46	42	51	59⁻¹	50⁻¹	48⁻¹	54⁻¹
Maldives	·	·	·	·	·**⁻¹	·**⁻¹	·**⁻¹	·**⁻¹
Mali	·	·	·	32	·	·	·	·

Table 3: Female Students in Tertiary Education cont.

Country or region	Female students by ISCED level (%) 2000			Female students in tertiary education 2000	Female students by ISCED level (%) 2007			Female students in tertiary education 2007
	5A	5B	6	%F	5A	5B	6	%F
Malta	53	57	7	53	56^{-2}	57^{-2}	30^{-2}	56^{-2}
Marshall Islands	$57^{**,+1}$	$56^{**,+1}$	$.^{**}$	$56^{**,+1}$	...	...	...	...
Mauritania	17^{+1}	20^{+1}	$^{+1}$	17^{+1}	26^{-1}	12^{-1}	...	26^{-1}
Mauritius	47	43	44	45	54^{+1}	53^{+1}	39^{+1}	53^{+1}
Mexico	49	40	38	49	51	43	42	50
Micronesia (Federated States of)	...	...	...	...	...	...	...	...
Monaco	...	...	...	...	$.^{-1}$	$.^{-1}$	$.^{-1}$	$.^{-1}$
Mongolia	64	67	54	64	60	70	58	61
Montenegro	...	...	...	...	...	...	...	...
Montserrat	...	...	...	...	...	...	...	...
Morocco	43	33	31	42	49	48	36	48
Mozambique	...	...	...	...	33^{-2}	$.^{-2}$	$.^{-2}$	33^{-2}
Myanmar	...	...	$.$	...	58	74	84	58
Namibia	54^{+1}	35^{+1}	17^{+1}	46^{+1}	43^{-1}	52^{-1}	45^{-1}	47^{-1}
Nauru	...	...	...	...	...	...	...	...
Nepal	...	...	...	28	52	...	42	51
Netherlands	50	54	42	50	...	...	...	...
Netherlands Antilles	59	54	$.$	56	...	...	...	...
New Zealand	58	62	47	59	59	58	51	59
Nicaragua	$52^{**,+1}$	$59^{**,+1}$	$^{+1}$	$52^{**,+1}$	...	47	...	...
Niger	...	...	...	...	21	47	...	29
Nigeria	36^{-1}	52^{-1}	$.^{-1}$	43^{-1}	36^{-2}	46^{-2}	24^{-2}	41^{-2}
Niue	...	...	...	...	$.^{-1}$	$.^{-1}$	$.^{-1}$	$.^{-1}$
Norway	60	43	47	58	61	61	47	60
Oman	...	...	...	...	52	65	26	53

Table 3: Female Students in Tertiary Education cont.

Country or region	Female students by ISCED level (%) 2000			Female students in tertiary education 2000	Female students by ISCED level (%) 2007			Female students in tertiary education 2007
	5A	5B	6	%F	5A	5B	6	%F
Pakistan	..	..	..	..	45*	45*	27*	45*
Palau	69**	..	..	69**	..	..	..	..
Palestinian Autonomous Territories	46	54	-	47	55	47	..	54
Panama	66	42	55	62	61^{-1}	58^{-1}	63^{-1}	61^{-1}
Papua New Guinea	..	..	..	..	..	..	..	..
Paraguay	..	..	..	57	51^{-2}	66^{-2}	..	52**$^{-2}$
Peru	43^{+1}	56^{+1}	..	49**$^{+1}$	47^{-1}	57^{-1}	..	51**$^{-1}$
Philippines	..	..	..	..	55^{-1}	53^{-1}	61^{-1}	54^{-1}
Poland	57	81	44	58	57	80	50	57
Portugal	56	63	52	57	54	62	56	54
Qatar	73^{+1}	..	..$^{+1}$	73^{+1}	74	33	..	64
Republic of Korea	36	36	25	36	37	39	34	38
Republic of Moldova	56	57	53	56	58	56*	50	57*
Romania	51	58	-	52	56	56	46	56
Russian Federation	56	..	43	..	58	53	43	57
Rwanda	34**	34**	..**	34**	41**$^{-2}$	35**$^{-2}$	..$^{-2}$	39**$^{-2}$
Saint Kitts and Nevis					..$^{-2}$	..$^{-2}$	..$^{-2}$	..$^{-2}$
Saint Lucia	..	..	..	..	73	36	..	71
Saint Vincent and the Grenadines					..$^{-2}$	..$^{-2}$	..$^{-2}$	..$^{-2}$
Samoa	40	45	..	44	..	..	..	..

Table 3: Female Students in Tertiary Education cont.

Country or region	Female students by ISCED level (%)			Female students in tertiary education	Female students by ISCED level (%)			Female students in tertiary education
	2000			2000	2007			2007
	5A	5B	6	%F	5A	5B	6	%F
San Marino	59	58	.	58	56[+1]	58[+1]	.[+1]	57[+1]
Sao Tome and Principe								
Saudi Arabia	58	42	38	56	65[-1]	23[-1]	41[-1]	58[-1]
Senegal	..	..	..	..	..	..	..	34**
Serbia	..	..	..	..	..	..	..	..
Seychelles	16[+1]	39[+1]	[+1]	29[+1]	..	..	.[-1]	..
Sierra Leone								
Singapore	50	..	..	..	50	47	36	49
Slovakia	..	78	38	50	60	69	45	59
Slovenia	59	53	-	56	62	53	48	58
Solomon Islands								
Somalia								
South Africa	53	67	38	55	55[-1]	56[-1]	42[-1]	55[-1]
Spain	53	50	51	53	55	52	52	54
Sri Lanka	..	..	..	47**	..	..	..	..
Sudan								
Suriname	49[-1]	43[-1]	.-	..	..	..	..	..
Swaziland	..	..	..	48[-1]	50[-1]	..	50[-1]	50[-1]
Sweden	60	48	43	58	61	52	50	60
Switzerland	44	42	34	43	49	43	41	48
Syrian Arab Republic	25	..	..	25	27	.	30	27
Tajikistan	56	28	..	..	56	.	50	..
Thailand	56	50	50	54	54	47	50	54
The former Yugoslav Rep. of Macedoni	56	44	-	55	54	63	50	55
Timor-Leste	..	..	..	..	..	..	..	..

Table 3: Female Students in Tertiary Education cont.

Country or region	Female students by ISCED level (%) 2000			Female students in tertiary education 2000	Female students by ISCED level (%) 2007			Female students in tertiary education 2007
	5A	5B	6	%F	5A	5B	6	%F
Togo	17	…	…	…	…	…	…	…
Tokelau		…	-		.⁻¹	.⁻¹	-.⁻¹	-.⁻¹
Tonga	31⁻¹	93⁻¹	24⁻¹	55⁻¹	…	…	…	…
Trinidad and Tobago	58	69	46	59				
Tunisia	49**,+¹	40**,⁻¹	49**	48**,+¹	68**,⁻²	26**,⁻²	55**,⁻²	57⁻²
Turkey	40⁺¹	44⁺¹	36⁺¹	41⁺¹	43	41	41	43
Turkmenistan	…	…	…	…	…	…	…	…
Turks and Caicos Islands					.⁻²	.⁻²	.⁻²	.⁻²
Tuvalu								
Uganda	37	31	26	34				
Ukraine	52	54	49	53	55	52	55	54
United Arab Emirates	…	…	…	69**	61⁺¹	57⁺¹	.⁺¹	60⁺¹
United Kingdom	53	58	41	54	55	66	45	57
United Republic of Tanzania	18⁻¹	26⁻¹	24⁻¹	21⁻¹	33⁻²	33⁻²	27**,⁻²	32**,⁻²
United States of America	56	56	42	56	57	60	52	57
Uruguay	60**,⁻¹	73**,⁻¹	…	63**,⁻¹	63	61	42	63
Uzbekistan	37	55	40*	45	41	.	45	41
Vanuatu	…	…	…	…	…	…	…	…
Venezuela	60**	57	…	59	…	…	…	…
Viet Nam	51	17	30	42	60	29	41	49
Yemen	22**	13**	6**	21**	…	…	…	…
Zambia	38**	23**	14**	32**	…	…	…	…
Zimbabwe	29	42	…	37**	…	…	…	…

Table 3: Female Students in Tertiary Education cont.

Country or region	Female students by ISCED level (%) 2000			Female students in tertiary education 2000	Female students by ISCED level (%) 2007			Female students in tertiary education 2007
	5A	5B	6	%F	5A	5B	6	%F
Average								
World	48	49 **	41 **	48 **	51 **	51	44 **	51 **
Low Income	37 **	35 **	32 **	36 **	41 **	37 **	35 **	40 **
Lower Middle Income	41 **	40	39 **	41 **	47 **	50	41 **	48 **
Upper Middle Income	54	56 **	47 **	54	56	52 **	46	55
High Income	52	54	41	52	54	56	47	54
Arab States	42 **	39 **	41	42 **	52 **	40 **	46 **	50 **
Central and Eastern Europe	53	54 **	43	53 **	56	51	45	55
Central Asia	47	55	46	48	52	67 **	51	52
East Asia and the Pacific	42 **	41 **	31	...	48 **	49	36 **	48
Latin America and the Caribbean	52 **	57 **	51 **	53	54 **	54 **	50 **	54 **
North America and Western Europe	54	56	43	54	56	59	49	56
South and West Asia	39	36	34	38	42	39	35 **	42 **
Sub-Saharan Africa	36 **	43 **	32 **	38 **	37 **	45	32 **	40 **

Source: UNESCO Institute for Statistics

Notes:

...	No data available
*	National estimation
**	UIS estimation
_	Magnitude nil or negligible
.	Not applicable
(p)	Provisional data
X (y)	Data are included in another category/column (y) of the table
+n	Data refer to the school or financial year (or period) n years or periods after the reference year or period
-n	Data refer to the school or financial year (or period) n years or periods prior to the reference year or period

School Life Expectancy (SLE)

This table provides SLE data by country, for the years 2000 and 2007. It also provides regional and world averages for this statistic. UNESCO defines school life expectancy as the total number of years of schooling which a child of a certain age can expect to receive in the future, assuming that the probability of his or her being enrolled in school at any particular age is equal to the current enrolment ratio for that age.

The purpose of the statistic is to show the overall level of development of an educational system in terms of the average number of years of schooling that the education system offers to the eligible population, including those who never enter school.

A relatively high SLE indicates greater probability for children to spend more years in education and higher overall retention within the education system. It must be noted that the expected number of years does not necessarily coincide with the expected number of grades of education completed, because of repetition. Since school life expectancy is an average based on participation in different levels of education, the expected number of years of schooling may be pulled down by the magnitude of children who never go to school. Those children who are in school may benefit from many more years of education than the average.

Caution is required when making cross-country comparisons; neither the length of the school year nor the quality of education is necessarily the same in each country. In addition, as this indicator does not directly take into account the effects of repetition, it is not strictly comparable between countries with automatic promotion and those allowing grade repetition. It should also be noted that, depending on countries, the enrolment data do not account for many types of continuing education and training. For these reasons, this indicator should be interpreted in the light of complementary indicators, particularly percentage of repeaters (UNESCO Institute for Statistics Glossary, http://www.uis.unesco.org/glossary).

Table 4: School Life Expectancy (SLE)

Country or region	2000		2007	
	M	F	M	F
Afghanistan	...	...	...	...
Albania	10.3 **	10.5 **	...	...
Algeria	...	...	12.7 **,-2	12.9 **,-2
Andorra	...	...	10.9 *,-1	11.4 *,-1
Angola	...	...	...	...
Anguilla	13.4 **	13.7 **	11.0 **,-1	11.4 **,-1
Antigua and Barbuda	...	...	...	...
Argentina	14.1 **	15.3 **	14.4 -1	16.3 -1
Armenia	10.4 **,+1	11.4 **,+1	11.5	12.5
Aruba	13.2	13.7	13.5	14.1
Australia	20.2	20.6	20.4	20.9
Austria	15.4 **	15.4 **	15.0	15.4
Azerbaijan	11.2 **	11.0 **	12.9 **	12.7 **
Bahamas	...	...	...	...
Bahrain	12.7 **,-1	13.9 **,-1	14.5 **,-1	16.0 **,-1

Table 4: School Life Expectancy (SLE) cont.

Country or region	2000		2007	
	M	F	M	F
Bangladesh	...	...	7.8	8.1
Barbados	12.6 **	14.2 **	13.9 **	16.0 **
Belarus	13.7 **	14.2 **	14.2	15.1
Belgium	17.6 **	18.8 **	15.8	16.3
Belize	...	...	...	...
Benin	8.2 **	5.0 **	...	...
Bermuda	14.9 **,+1	15.6 **,+1	12.5 *,-2	13.7 *,-2
Bhutan	8.5 **	7.1 **	10.6 **,-1	10.0 **,-1
Bolivia	...	...	...	...
Bosnia and Herzegovina	...	...	...	...
Botswana	11.6 **	11.7 **	11.8 **,-2	12.0 **,-2
Brazil	14.2 **	14.8 **	13.5	14.1
British Virgin Islands	14.1 **	16.7 **	15.5 **,-2	19.1 **,-2
Brunei Darussalam	13.1 **	13.7 **	13.6 **	14.2 **
Bulgaria	12.7	13.2	13.6	13.8
Burkina Faso	4.0 **	2.8 **	5.8	4.6
Burundi	...	...	8.7 **	7.7 **
Cambodia	8.3 **	6.6 **	10.4 **	9.2 **
Cameroon	...	...	9.8 **	8.2 **
Canada	15.8 **	16.5 **	...	...
Cape Verde	11.0 **,+1	10.9 **,+1	11.1 **	11.7 **
Cayman Islands	12.8 **	13.6 **	...	...
Central African Republic	...	...	...	...
Chad	6.4 **	3.4 **	7.4 **,-2	4.3 **,-2
Chile	13.0 **	12.8 **	14.6	14.4
China	...	...	11.4 **	11.4 **
Colombia	10.9 **	11.4 **	12.3 **	12.9 **
Comoros	7.6 **	6.3 **	...	...
Congo	9.0 **	7.3 **	...	...
Cook Islands	9.7 **	10.1 **	9.3 **	9.5 **
Costa Rica	10.3	10.5	11.5 **,-2	12.0 **,-2
Côte d'Ivoire	7.3 **	4.8 **	...	...
Croatia	12.0	12.3	13.3	14.0
Cuba	12.5 **	12.8 **	15.6 **	18.8 **
Cyprus	12.1 **	12.6 **	13.7 *	13.9 *
Czech Republic	13.9 **	13.9 **	14.8	15.5
Democratic People's Republic of Korea	...	...	...	...
Democratic Republic of the Congo	...	...	9.1 **	6.4 **
Denmark	15.7 **	16.8 **	16.2	17.5
Djibouti	3.5 **	2.5 **	5.3 **	4.1 **

Table 4: School Life Expectancy (SLE) cont.

Country or region	2000 M	2000 F	2007 M	2007 F
Dominica	12.1 **	12.8 **	12.5 **,-2	13.6 **,-2
Dominican Republic	...	...	...	...
Ecuador	...	...	13.1	13.5
Egypt	...	...	...	...
El Salvador	11.0 **	10.7 **	12.1	12.4
Equatorial Guinea	10.4 **	8.9 **	...	...
Eritrea	5.2 **	3.9 **		
Estonia	14.4	15.6	14.8	16.8
Ethiopia	5.1 **	3.2 **	8.5 **	6.8 **
Fiji	...	...	12.8 **,-2	13.2 **,-2
Finland	17.0 **	18.5 **	16.5	17.7
France	15.4 **	16.0 **	15.9	16.6
Gabon	13.5 **,-1	12.7 **,-1	...	...
Gambia	8.1 **	6.6 **	...	...
Georgia	11.9 **	11.9 **	12.6 **	12.8 **
Germany	...	...	...	...
Ghana	7.9 **	6.9 **	9.6 **	9.0 **
Gibraltar	...	...	...	...
Greece	13.9 **	14.5 **	16.4	16.6
Grenada	...	...	12.0 **,-2	12.2 **,-2
Guatemala	...	...	11.0 **	10.3 **
Guinea	...	...	9.6 -1	6.8 -1
Guinea-Bissau	6.7 **	4.2 **	...	...
Guyana	...	...	12.7 **	12.6 **
Haiti	...	...	...	...
Holy See	...	...	...	...
Honduras	...	...	...	...
Hong Kong SAR of China	...	...	13.9 -2	13.5 -2
Hungary	14.0 **	14.4 **	14.6	15.7
Iceland	16.4 **	17.7 **	17.0	19.7
India	9.4 **	7.3 **	10.6 **,-1	9.4 **,-1
Indonesia	11.0 **,+1	10.6 **,+1	12.5	12.2
Iran (Islamic Republic of)	12.0 **	10.9 **	12.8 **,-2	12.9 **,-2
Iraq	9.6 **	7.0 **	11.1 **,-2	8.3 **,-2
Ireland	16.2	17.2	17.6	18.1
Israel	14.5 **	15.4 **	15.1	16.0
Italy	15.1 **,+1	15.6 **,+1	16.0	16.9
Jamaica	11.3 **	11.7 **	...	...
Japan	14.7 **	14.4 **	15.1 **	14.8 **
Jordan	12.5 **	12.8 **	12.9 **	13.3 **

Table 4: School Life Expectancy (SLE) cont.

Country or region	2000 M	F	2007 M	F
Kazakhstan	12.0	12.6	14.5	15.6
Kenya	8.6 **	8.2 **	10.8 **	10.1 **
Kiribati	11.4 *	14.2 *	11.9 *,-2	12.7 *,-2
Kuwait	11.9 **,+1	13.2 **,+1	11.9 **,-1	13.2 **,-1
Kyrgyzstan	11.7	11.9	12.1	12.9
Lao People's Democratic Republic	9.1 **	7.2 **	10.2 **	8.5 **
Latvia	13.3	15.1	14.5 -1	16.6 -1
Lebanon	12.0 **	12.2 **	12.8 **	13.6 **
Lesotho	9.6 **	10.2 **	10.1 -1	10.5 -1
Liberia	11.2 **	8.2 **	...	...
Libyan Arab Jamahiriya	...	...	...	...
Liechtenstein	...	...	15.7 *	13.5 *
Lithuania	14.1 **	15.1 **	14.9	16.6
Luxembourg	13.4 **	13.7 **	13.4 -1	13.6 -1
Macao, China	12.6 **	12.3 **	15.6	14.6
Madagascar	...	...	9.6 **	9.2 **
Malawi	10.8 **	10.0 **	9.2 **	9.0 **
Malaysia	11.6 **	12.1 **	12.4 -2	13.1 -2
Maldives	12.4 **	12.6 **	12.2 **,-1	12.3 **,-1
Mali	6.0 **	4.0 **	7.7 **,-2	5.4 **,-2
Malta	13.8	13.9	14.8 -2	14.9 -2
Marshall Islands	...	...	...	...
Mauritania	7.3 **,+1	6.7 **,+1	8.1 **,-1	8.0 **,-1
Mauritius	12.5 **	12.1 **	13.7 **,-2	13.4 **,-2
Mexico	12.1 **	11.9 **	13.7	13.5
Micronesia (Federated States of)	...	...	...	...
Monaco	...	...	...	...
Mongolia	8.3	10.1	12.2	13.9
Montenegro	...	...	...	...
Montserrat	...	...	13.8 **	16.9 **
Morocco	9.2 **	7.6 **	11.1 **	9.8 **
Mozambique	...	...	9.1 **,-2	7.4 **,-2
Myanmar	...	...	...	...
Namibia	11.2 **,+1	11.4 **,+1	10.6 **,-1	10.9 **,-1
Nauru	6.7 *	8.1 *	8.2 *,-1	8.8 *,-1

Table 4: School Life Expectancy (SLE) cont.

Country or region	2000 M	2000 F	2007 M	2007 F
Nepal	9.9 **	7.5 **	...	...
Netherlands	16.7 **	16.3 **	16.7	16.6
Netherlands Antilles	14.3	14.6	...	...
New Zealand	16.8 **	18.3 **	19.1	20.6
Nicaragua	9.7 **,+1	10.2 **,+1	...	...
Niger	...	...	4.7 **	3.3 **
Nigeria	8.1 **,-1	6.5 **,-1	...	...
Niue	11.3 **	11.6 **	12.3 *,-2	12.3 *,-2
Norway	16.8 **	18.2 **	16.9	18.2
Oman	...	...	11.5 **	11.5 **
Pakistan	...	...	7.9 **	6.3 **
Palau	13.7 **	15.4 **	...	...
Palestinian Autonomous Territories	12.0 **	12.4 **	12.7	13.7
Panama	12.2 **	13.4 **	12.7 **,-1	14.1 **,-1
Papua New Guinea	...	...	...	...
Paraguay	11.8 **	11.9 **	12.0 **,-2	12.0 **,-2
Peru	14.0 **,+1	13.9 **,+1	13.7 **,-1	14.3 **,-1
Philippines	11.4 **,-1	11.9 **,-1	11.5 **,-1	12.1 **,-1
Poland	14.3 **	15.1 **	14.7	15.8
Portugal	15.6 **	16.3 **	15.1	15.7
Qatar	11.2 **,+1	12.9 **,+1	13.3	14.3
Republic of Korea	16.7 **	14.4 **	18.0	15.7
Republic of Moldova	11.1 **	11.7 **	11.7 *	12.6 *
Romania	11.8 **	12.2 **	13.9	14.8
Russian Federation	...	...	13.2 **	14.3 **
Rwanda	6.8 **	6.5 **	8.5 **,-2	8.6 **,-2
Saint Kitts and Nevis	13.5 **	14.8 **	12.1 **,-2	12.5 **,-2
Saint Lucia	...	...	12.9 **	14.0 **
Saint Vincent and the Grenadines	10.6 **	11.4 **	11.8 **,-2	12.2 **,-2
Samoa	11.8 **	12.4 **	...	...
San Marino	...	...	...	...
Sao Tome and Principe	...	...	10.4	10.5
Saudi Arabia	...	...	13.3 **,-2	13.0 **,-2
Senegal	...	...	7.5 **	6.8 **
Serbia	...	...	...	...

Table 4: School Life Expectancy (SLE) cont.

Country or region	2000		2007	
	M	F	M	F
Seychelles	13.7 *	14.3 *	14.2 *	15.4 *
Sierra Leone	7.9 **,+1	5.8 **,+1	...	...
Singapore	...	...	...	...
Slovakia	13.3 **	13.5 **	14.3	15.4
Slovenia	14.2	15.4	16.1 **	17.6 **
Solomon Islands	7.1	6.3	8.8 -2	8.2 -2
Somalia	...	...	...	...
South Africa	12.7 **	12.9 **	13.0 **,-1	13.2 **,-1
Spain	15.5	16.3	15.8	16.7
Sri Lanka	...	...	...	...
Sudan	...	...	...	...
Suriname	...	...	...	...
Swaziland	9.9 **	9.3 **	10.9 **,-1	10.2 **,-1
Sweden	17.3 **	20.6 **	14.9	16.4
Switzerland	15.2 **	14.5 **	15.1	14.7
Syrian Arab Republic	...	...	...	...
Tajikistan	10.7 **	8.9 **	12.0 **	10.0 **
Thailand	12.2 **,+1	12.3 **,+1	13.4 **	14.5 **
The former Yugoslav Rep. of Macedoni	11.9 **	11.9 **	12.3	12.5
Timor-Leste	...	...	...	...
Togo	...	...	...	...
Tokelau	10.5 **	11.4 **	...	...
Tonga	12.9 **	13.3 **	...	...
Trinidad and Tobago	10.9 **	11.5 **	11.1 **,-2	11.4 **,-2
Tunisia	13.2 **,+1	13.2 **,+1	13.5 **,-1	14.4 **,-1
Turkey	11.9 **,+1	9.8 **,+1	12.4 **	10.8 **
Turkmenistan	...	...	...	...
Turks and Caicos Islands	...	...	10.9 **,-2	11.8 **,-2
Tuvalu	11.1 *,+1	11.4 *,+1	...	...
Uganda	11.0 **	10.0 **	...	...
Ukraine	12.7 **	13.1 **	14.2 *	14.9 *
United Arab Emirates	10.3 **	11.3 **	...	...
United Kingdom	15.8 **	16.4 **	15.4 **	16.5 **
United Republic of Tanzania	5.4 **,-1	5.3 **,-1	...	...
United States of America	14.9	15.8	15.1 **	16.6 **

Table 4: School Life Expectancy (SLE) cont.

Country or region	2000 M	2000 F	2007 M	2007 F
Uruguay	13.5 **	15.2 **	14.9	16.4
Uzbekistan	10.9 **	10.5 **	11.8	11.4
Vanuatu	...	...	...	...
Venezuela	10.0 **	11.0 **	...	...
Viet Nam	10.7	9.9	...	...
Yemen	10.3 **	5.3 **	10.6 **, -2	6.6 **, -2
Zambia	7.4 **	6.6 **	...	...
Zimbabwe	10.1 **	9.4 **	...	...

Average

	2000 M	2000 F	2007 M	2007 F
World	10.2 **	9.4 **	11.2 **	10.7 **
Arab States	10.4 **	9.0 **	...	...
Central and Eastern Europe	12.1 **	12.0 **	13.3	13.4
Central Asia	11.0	10.8	12.2	12.1
East Asia and the Pacific	...	...	11.8	11.8
Latin America and the Caribbean	12.6	12.9	13.2 **	13.6 **
North America and Western Europe	15.4	16.0	15.5	16.5
South and West Asia	8.9	7.1	...	...
Sub-Saharan Africa	7.5 **	6.1 **	9.3 **	7.9 **

Source: UNESCO Institute for Statistics

Notes:

...	No data available
*	National estimation
**	UIS estimation
–	Magnitude nil or negligible
.	Not applicable
(p)	Provisional data
X (y)	Data are included in another category/column (y) of the table
+n	Data refer to the school or financial year (or period) n years or periods after the reference year or period
-n	Data refer to the school or financial year (or period) n years or periods prior to the reference year or period

Internationally Mobile Students by Host Country

This table provides an overview of world student mobility by presenting data on inbound student movement by region, as well as a global total.

Internationally mobile students are those students who have crossed a national or territorial border for the purposes of education and are now enrolled outside their country of origin (UNESCO Institute for Statistics Glossary, http://www.uis.unesco.org/glossary/)

Table 5: Internationally Mobile Students by Host Country

Average	2000	2007
World	1,940,517	2,800,470
Arab States	58,184	80,026
Central and Eastern Europe	138,471	199,955
Central Asia	25,228	52,307
East Asia and the Pacific	262,019	514,290
Latin America and the Caribbean	25,783	53,113
North America and Western Europe	1,362,563	1,816,945
South and West Asia	9,181	10,739
Sub-Saharan Africa	59,087	73,095

Source: UNESCO Institute for Statistics

Figure 5a: Number of internationally mobile students by region of destination, 2000 and 2007

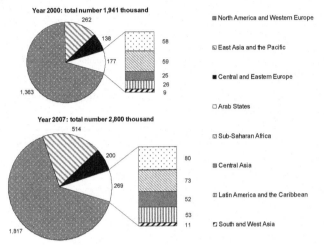

Year 2000: total number 1,941 thousand

Year 2007: total number 2,800 thousand

▦ North America and Western Europe

▧ East Asia and the Pacific

■ Central and Eastern Europe

☐ Arab States

▨ Sub-Saharan Africa

▦ Central Asia

▥ Latin America and the Caribbean

▨ South and West Asia

Public educational expenditure on tertiary education as % of total public education expenditure

This table provides comparison data by country, for the years 2000 and 2007. Data for this table come from annual financial reports prepared by the ministry of finance; national accounts reports by the central statistical office and financial reports from the various government departments engaged in educational activities especially the ministry of education (UNESCO Institute for Statistics Glossary, http://www.uis.unesco.org/glossary)

Table 6: Public educational expenditure on tertiary education as % of total public education expenditure

	2000	2007
Afghanistan	...	...
Albania	...	...
Algeria	...	...
Andorra	...	4.5
Angola	...	8.7 $^{-1}$
Anguilla	**	18.3 $^{-2}$
Antigua and Barbuda	15.1 $^{**,-1}$	...
Argentina	18.4 **	17.8 $^{-1}$
Armenia	...	...
Aruba	10.6	11.5 $^{-2}$
Australia	23.7	24.5 $^{-1}$
Austria	23.6 $^{+1}$	27.3 $^{-2}$
Azerbaijan	6.0	7.0
Bahamas	...	...
Bahrain	...	...
Bangladesh	10.1	11.5
Barbados	27.4	30.2
Belarus	...	20.2
Belgium	22.3 $^{+1}$	22.0 $^{-1}$
Belize	6.5	...
Benin	17.2	20.6 $^{-1}$
Bermuda	...	- $^{-1}$
Bhutan	19.6 **	19.4
Bolivia	28.9	...
Bosnia and Herzegovina	...	...
Botswana	...	27.5
Brazil	22.1	16.7 $^{-1}$
British Virgin Islands	21.8 $^{+1}$	33.1
Brunei Darussalam	...	...
Bulgaria	15.8 $^{+1}$	17.3 $^{-1}$

Table 6: Public Educational Expenditure on Tertiary Education as % of Total Public Education Expenditure cont.

	2000	2007
Burkina Faso	...	11.1 [-1]
Burundi	26.9	15.3 [-2]
Cambodia	5.0 [+1]	3.4
Cameroon	14.2 [**,-1]	23.3
Canada	35.7	...
Cape Verde	...	4.3
Cayman Islands	...	- [-1]
Central African Republic	...	22.8 [-1]
Chad	16.6 [**,-1]	18.7 [-2]
Chile	14.5	15.3
China	24.0 [-1]	...
Colombia	19.9	32.0
Comoros	...	...
Congo	32.6 [+1]	25.9 [**,-2]
Cook Islands	.	...
Costa Rica	19.4	...
Côte d'Ivoire	25.1 [**]	...
Croatia	...	...
Cuba	17.6 [*]	25.1
Cyprus	17.1	23.5 [-1]
Czech Republic	19.0	26.7 [-1]
Democratic People's Republic of Korea	...	...
Democratic Republic of the Congo	...	...
Denmark	30.0	28.7 [-2]
Djibouti	...	...
Dominica	...	.
Dominican Republic	...	14.5
Ecuador	5.2	...
Egypt	...	...
El Salvador	6.7	9.8 [*]
Equatorial Guinea	34.9 [+1]	...
Eritrea	14.0 [**,+1]	19.4 [-1]
Estonia	19.6 [+1]	18.9 [-2]
Ethiopia	...	39.0
Fiji	14.4	...
Finland	34.0	31.7 [-1]
France	17.6	21.4 [-1]
Gabon	...	...
Gambia	...	...
Georgia	...	...
Germany	24.2	25.2 [-1]
Ghana	...	20.8 [-2]
Gibraltar	...	...
Greece	24.0	36.1 [-2]
Grenada	...	...

Table 6: Public Educational Expenditure on Tertiary Education as % of Total Public Education Expenditure cont.

	2000	2007
Guatemala	...	10.9
Guinea	...	30.6 $^{-2}$
Guinea-Bissau	...	...
Guyana	...	5.9
Haiti	...	...
Holy See	. $^{+1}$	...
Honduras	...	...
Hong Kong SAR of China	33.1 $^{+1}$	31.0
Hungary	21.0	19.1 $^{-1}$
Iceland	17.8 **	18.0 $^{-1}$
India	20.3	19.6 $^{-2}$
Indonesia	...	...
Iran (Islamic Republic of)	19.4 $^{+1}$	20.4
Iraq	...	...
Ireland	30.3	23.4 $^{-1}$
Israel	18.3	16.5 $^{-1}$
Italy	18.5 **	17.0 $^{-1}$
Jamaica	21.3 $^{+1}$	20.0
Japan	15.2	17.5 $^{-1}$
Jordan	18.7 $^{-1}$	...
Kazakhstan	...	13.9
Kenya	11.7	15.4 $^{-1}$
Kiribati	...	...
Kuwait	...	32.6 $^{**,-1}$
Kyrgyzstan	14.7	19.0
Lao People's Democratic Republic	12.3	9.2 $^{-2}$
Latvia	16.3	17.9 $^{-1}$
Lebanon	15.5	25.3
Lesotho	16.7	36.8 $^{-1}$
Liberia	...	...
Libyan Arab Jamahiriya	52.7 $^{-1}$	...
Liechtenstein	...	9.1 $^{-1}$
Lithuania	22.7 $^{+1}$	20.6 $^{-1}$
Luxembourg	...	...
Macao, China	28.4	41.0 $^{-1}$
Madagascar	11.9 **	12.7
Malawi	...	...
Malaysia	32.1	37.6 $^{-1}$
Maldives	...	- $^{**,-1}$
Mali	14.6 $^{**,-1}$	11.0 $^{-1}$
Malta	...	...
Marshall Islands	5.6 $^{-1}$	...
Mauritania	14.1 $^{**,-1}$	5.0 $^{**,-2}$
Mauritius	12.7 $^{+1}$	10.3 $^{-1}$
Mexico	14.5 $^{+1}$	17.2 $^{-1}$

Table 6: Public Educational Expenditure on Tertiary Education as % of Total Public Education Expenditure cont.

	2000	2007
Micronesia (Federated States of)	...	...
Monaco	.	...
Mongolia	...	...
Montenegro	...	...
Montserrat	12.3	...
Morocco	18.5	16.9 [-1]
Mozambique	...	12.1 [-1]
Myanmar	26.4 [+1]	...
Namibia	12.0	...
Nauru	...	...
Nepal	18.8 [**]	13.0 [+1]
Netherlands	26.5 [+1]	27.5 [-1]
Netherlands Antilles	...	...
New Zealand	24.7 [+1]	27.0
Nicaragua	...	...
Niger	16.2 [+1]	9.0 [-1]
Nigeria	...	...
Niue	7.4 [-1]	...
Norway	25.4	31.5 [-1]
Oman	9.5 [+1]	7.6 [-2]
Pakistan	...	...
Palau	20.7 [+1]	...
Palestinian Autonomous Territories	...	...
Panama	25.3	...
Papua New Guinea	...	...
Paraguay	17.3	...
Peru	22.6 [+1]	13.6
Philippines	13.8	13.3 [-2]
Poland	14.5	21.8 [-2]
Portugal	18.1	19.0 [-1]
Qatar	...	13.3 [-2]
Republic of Korea	13.5 [-1]	14.0 [-2]
Republic of Moldova	...	19.5
Romania	23.9 [+1]	23.2 [-2]
Russian Federation	16.1	21.9 [-1]
Rwanda	34.7 [**]	25.4
Saint Kitts and Nevis	21.2	...
Saint Lucia	11.1 [**,-1]	- [-1]
Saint Vincent and the Grenadines	...	5.7
Samoa	36.4	...
San Marino	...	...
Sao Tome and Principe	...	...
Saudi Arabia	...	...
Senegal	...	23.5 [-1]
Serbia	...	...

Table 6: Public Educational Expenditure on Tertiary Education as % of Total Public Education Expenditure cont.

	2000	2007
Seychelles	...	17.9 [-1]
Sierra Leone	...	...
Singapore	26.9 [+1]	33.4 [+1]
Slovakia	18.4	21.0 [-2]
Slovenia	21.8 [+1]	21.6 [-1]
Solomon Islands	...	...
Somalia	...	...
South Africa	14.5	12.9
Spain	21.8	22.3 [-1]
Sri Lanka	...	...
Sudan	...	...
Suriname	...	...
Swaziland	36.8	21.3 [-1]
Sweden	27.2	26.8 [-1]
Switzerland	22.3	26.6 [-1]
Syrian Arab Republic	...	...
Tajikistan	...	7.5
Thailand	20.3	17.9
The former Yugoslav Rep. of Macedonia	...	...
Timor-Leste	...	...
Togo	17.4	21.4
Tokelau	...	...
Tonga	...	...
Trinidad and Tobago	13.0 [+1]	...
Tunisia	21.7 [**]	24.3 [-1]
Turkey	30.9	...
Turkmenistan	...	...
Turks and Caicos Islands	9.6	30.7 [-2]
Tuvalu	...	...
Uganda	...	...
Ukraine	32.3	28.8
United Arab Emirates	28.0 [*]	27.6 [**,-2]
United Kingdom	17.5	22.3 [-2]
United Republic of Tanzania	...	...
United States of America	26.3 [+1]	26.3 [-1]
Uruguay	20.5	22.0 [-1]
Uzbekistan	...	...
Vanuatu	7.4	...
Venezuela	...	43.5
Viet Nam	...	...
Yemen	...	...
Zambia	19.4	25.8 [-2]
Zimbabwe	16.6 [**]	...

Notes:

...	No data available
*	National estimation
**	UIS estimation
_	Magnitude nil or negligible
.	Not applicable
(p)	Provisional data
X (y)	Data are included in another category/column (y) of the table
+n	Data refer to the school or financial year (or period) n years or periods after the reference year or period
-n	Data refer to the school or financial year (or period) n years or periods prior to the reference year or period

Full-time and Part-time Tertiary Teaching Staff

This table provides country-by-country numbers for full and part-time tertiary teaching staff for the years 2000 and 2007. UNESCO defines teachers (or teaching staff) as persons employed full time or part time in an official capacity to guide and direct the learning experience of pupils and students, irrespective of their qualifications or the delivery mechanism, i.e. face-to-face and/or at a distance. This definition excludes educational personnel who have no active teaching duties (e.g. headmasters, headmistresses or principals who do not teach) and persons who work occasionally or in a voluntary capacity in educational institutions.

A full-time teacher is defined as a person engaged in teaching for a number of hours of work statutorily regarded as full-time at the particular level of education, while part-time teachers are those whose statutory working hours are less than those required of full-time teachers.

Table 7: Full-time and Part-time Tertiary Teaching Staff

Country or region	2000 Total	2000 Part-time	2007 Total	2007 Part-time
Afghanistan	...	...	...	...
Albania	1,679	...	...	...
Algeria	19,052 *,¹	...	31,683	2,694
Andorra	...	...	81 ⁻¹	63 ⁻¹
Angola	823 **	...	1,286 ⁻¹	...
Anguilla	.	.	14	14
Antigua and Barbuda	.	.		
Argentina	112,721	...	142,296 ⁻¹	115,976 ⁻¹
Armenia	10,235	...	12,521	...
Aruba	164	57	222	46
Australia	...	...	...	...
Austria	26,516 **	...	29,367	598
Azerbaijan	12,459	2,941	16,423	3,563
Bahamas	...	...	...	...
Bahrain	...	...	756 **,⁻²	...
Bangladesh	36,786	-	60,915	-
Barbados	663	340	786	364
Belarus	39,195	...	42,121	8,256
Belgium	22,756	...	26,298	12,659
Belize	...	...	97 ⁻²	...
Benin	763 **	...	...	...
Bermuda	107 *,¹	26 *,¹	88	31
Bhutan	164 **	...	375 ⁻¹	...
Bolivia	12,809	...	...	...
Bosnia and Herzegovina	...	...	...	...
Botswana	477 **,⁻¹	...	529 ⁻²	...
Brazil	183,194	...	367,638	.
British Virgin Islands	60 **	...	110 **,⁻²	...
Brunei Darussalam	483	-	649	.
Bulgaria	24,620	...	21,447	9,316

Table 7: Full-time and Part-time Tertiary Teaching Staff cont.

	Number of teaching staff			
	2000		2007	
Country or region	Total	Part-time	Total	Part-time
Burkina Faso	869 **	...	1,886	...
Burundi	524	212	1,007	...
Cambodia	1,664	...	3,261 -¹	830 -¹
Cameroon	3,011	728	3,040	...
Canada	133,477	...	...	...
Cape Verde	221 **	...	590	...
Cayman Islands	22 **	-	49 -¹	25 -¹
Central African Republic	325	...	...	...
Chad	409	143	1,100 **·-²	...
Chile	...	...	54,649	...
China	523,326	...	1,326,058	303,764
Colombia	85,743	...	88,337 **	...
Comoros	76	...	...	...
Congo	645	387	...	...
Cook Islands	.	...	.	...
Costa Rica	3,874 +¹	...	...	...
Côte d'Ivoire	...	...	...	...
Croatia	...	...	13,075	5,291
Cuba	23,705	...	135,800	94,375
Cyprus	1,082	357	1,824	611
Czech Republic	20,010	...	22,549 -¹	...
Democratic People's Republic of Korea	...	...	...	...
Democratic Republic of the Congo	3,788 -¹	...	16,913	...
Denmark	...	...	...	...
Djibouti	18 **	...	121	...
Dominica	.	...	.-²	...
Dominican Republic	...	...	...	...
Ecuador	15,271 +¹	...	22,714	15,442
Egypt	.	...	...	...
El Salvador	7,501	...	8,370	3,383
Equatorial Guinea	206	...	...	...
Eritrea	250	-	...	...
Estonia	5,707	2,716	6,358 **·-¹	...
Ethiopia	2,497	...	8,355	...
Fiji	.	...	...	...
Finland	17,323 **	...	18,786 **·-¹	...
France	117,740	...	...	...
Gabon	585 -¹	...	...	...
Gambia	88 **	...	...	...
Georgia	26,016	...	15,973	8,947
Germany	274,210	141,474	295,447	165,720
Ghana	2,518	...	4,011	...
Gibraltar	.	.	.-¹	...
Greece	18,824	...	28,998	15,230
Grenada	.	...	.-²	...

Table 7: Full-time and Part-time Tertiary Teaching Staff cont.

Country or region	Number of teaching staff 2000 Total	2000 Part-time	2007 Total	2007 Part-time
Guatemala	...	...	3,843 -1	2,955 -1
Guinea	...	...	1,439 -1	...
Guinea-Bissau	31	...	...	...
Guyana	...	...	583	300
Haiti	...	...	...	...
Holy See	1,152 -1	576 -1	...	...
Honduras	5,549	2,953	...	...
Hong Kong SAR of China	...	...		
Hungary	21,249	...	23,454	6,678
Iceland	1,658 **	...	1,961	1,060
India	399,023	...	...	...
Indonesia	217,403 +1	...	265,527	...
Iran (Islamic Republic of)	64,766	...	133,484	85,502
Iraq	12,068	...	19,231 **,-2	...
Ireland	10,896 **	...	12,396	4,052
Israel	...	...	...	...
Italy	75,081	...	104,421	...
Jamaica	1,751	...	...	...
Japan	472,629	274,569	515,732	301,875
Jordan	4,755	...	9,094	-
Kazakhstan	26,996	10,349	41,207 +1	...
Kenya	...	...	...	...
Kiribati	.	...	.-1	...
Kuwait	2,155 **,-1	...	1,986 **,-1	...
Kyrgyzstan	8,383	...	13,468	579
Lao People's Democratic Republic	1,152	...	3,030	...
Latvia	5,213	2,194	6,867	3,851
Lebanon	8,820	...	23,323 +1	...
Lesotho	342	108	638 -1	253 -1
Liberia	723	...	...	...
Libyan Arab Jamahiriya	12,422	...	...	...
Liechtenstein	...	...	...	...
Lithuania	12,940	5,370	15,802	8,430
Luxembourg	142 **	...	...	...
Macao, China	835	...	1,725	948
Madagascar	1,727	571 *	3,032	1,557
Malawi	605 *	...	861	...
Malaysia	29,915 **	...	39,809 -1	...
Maldives	.	...	- **,-1	...
Mali	963 **	...	976	...
Malta	591	221	712 **,-2	...
Marshall Islands	47 **,+1	...	...	...
Mauritania	301 +1	...	353 -1	...
Mauritius	588 **,-1	...	...	...
Mexico	201,534	...	274,618	198,508

Table 7: Full-time and Part-time Tertiary Teaching Staff cont.

	Number of teaching staff			
	2000		2007	
Country or region	Total	Part-time	Total	Part-time
Micronesia (Federated States of)	90 **	...	...	...
Monaco	.	.	. -1	.
Mongolia	6,642	...	8,754	1,936
Montenegro	...	...	...	...
Montserrat	.	.	.	.
Morocco	18,082	...	18,464	4,777
Mozambique	983 **	...	3,009 -2	1,620 -2
Myanmar	10,470 **	...	10,669	...
Namibia	877 +1	244 +1	763 -1	...
Nauru	.	...	. -1	...
Nepal	4,598 **,+1	...	9,932	126
Netherlands	42,998 **	...	44,632	23,109
Netherlands Antilles	267	...	...	...
New Zealand	11,252	3,676	14,082	5,596
Nicaragua	6,294 **,+1	...	...	...
Niger	463 **	...	1,095 -1	...
Nigeria	52,386 -1	...	...	...
Niue	.	...	. -1	...
Norway	14,612	...	19,182	5,013
Oman	...	...	2,959	17
Pakistan	...	...	52,245 *	.
Palau	55 **	...	...	...
Palestinian Autonomous Territories	3,390	1,104	5,530	2,620
Panama	7,996	...	11,528 -1	...
Papua New Guinea	1,067 **,-1	...	...	...
Paraguay	...	...	...	...
Peru	...	...	...	...
Philippines	93,956 +1	...	112,941 **,-2	...
Poland	85,971	6,663	99,014	1,315
Portugal	...	...	36,069	14,015
Qatar	595 +1	...	1,153	11
Republic of Korea	144,185	87,736	201,851	131,815
Republic of Moldova	7,227	...	8,570 *	...
Romania	26,977	624	30,583	370
Russian Federation	525,200	...	679,229	...
Rwanda	1,190 **	...	1,817 **,-2	...
Saint Kitts and Nevis	.	.	. -2	...
Saint Lucia	...	...	295	167
Saint Vincent and the Grenadines	.	...	. -2	. -2
Samoa	151	...	...	...
San Marino	...	...	...	...
Sao Tome and Principe	.	.	. +1	. +1
Saudi Arabia	20,293	...	27,964 -1	...
Senegal	...	...	...	...
Serbia	...	...	...	...

Table 7: Full-time and Part-time Tertiary Teaching Staff cont.

Country or region	2000 Total	2000 Part-time	2007 Total	2007 Part-time
	Number of teaching staff			
Seychelles	.	...	,	...
Sierra Leone	1,165 *¹	...	...	...
Singapore	...	...	14,209	6,118
Slovakia	12,211	2,287	13,606	2,611
Slovenia	2,491	...	5,609	3,600
Solomon Islands	.	...	, -¹	...
Somalia	...	...	...	...
South Africa	38,642 *¹	...	44,175 -¹	...
Spain	107,032	...	144,091	42,997
Sri Lanka	...	...	...	...
Sudan	4,486 **	...	...	...
Suriname	...	...	...	...
Swaziland	351	...	462 -¹	- -¹
Sweden	29,851	...	36,479	10,190
Switzerland	8,243	...	32,545 -¹	27,708 -¹
Syrian Arab Republic	...	...	...	...
Tajikistan	5,854	...	7,761	...
Thailand	50,639	3,738	75,398 **,+¹	...
The former Yugoslav Rep. of Macedonia	2,774	...	2,774	10
Timor-Leste	...	...	...	...
Togo	388 **	...	470	...
Tokelau	.	...	, -¹	...
Tonga	103 **	...	...	...
Trinidad and Tobago	540	...	1,800 **,-²	...
Tunisia	9,370	...	18,117	
Turkey	65,204	.	89,329	859
Turkmenistan	...	...	...	...
Turks and Caicos Islands	.	...	, -²	...
Tuvalu	,	...	.	
Uganda	3,362	844	...	...
Ukraine	145,890 **	...	196,887	...
United Arab Emirates	2,525 **	...	4,710 *¹	...
United Kingdom	94,360	...	125,585 -¹	...
United Republic of Tanzania	2,064	-	3,003	...
United States of America	1,027,830	436,893	1,310,453	624,343
Uruguay	11,209 -¹	...	15,789	.
Uzbekistan	16,998	...	23,354	3,375
Vanuatu	26 **	...	...	...
Venezuela	53,590	...	108,594 *,-¹	. -¹
Viet Nam	30,309	...	53,518	.
Yemen	5,218 **	...	6,062 **,-²	...
Zambia	...	...	...	...
Zimbabwe	...	...	...	...

Notes:

...	No data available
*	National estimation
**	UIS estimation
_	Magnitude nil or negligible
.	Not applicable
(p)	Provisional data
X (y)	Data are included in another category/column (y) of the table
+n	Data refer to the school or financial year (or period) n years or periods after the reference year or period
-n	Data refer to the school or financial year (or period) n years or periods prior to the reference year or period

Expenditure on Research and Development (R&D)

This table provides information by country on the total gross domestic expenditure on research and development (GERD) in both 2000 and 2007. The data include the total amounts spent (in purchasing power parity, or PPP, dollars), expenditure as a percentage of gross domestic product (GDP), per capita expenditure, and the percentage of GERD allocated to higher education.

Table 8: Expenditure on Research and Development (R&D)

Country or region	000 PPP$		As percentage (%) of GDP		Per capita (PPP$)		GERD performed by higher education sector (%)	
	2000	2007	2000	2007	2000	2007	2000	2007
Afghanistan	⋮	⋮	⋮	⋮	⋮	⋮	⋮	⋮
Albania								
Algeria	395,330 [+1]	157,008 [-2]	0.23% [+1]	0.07% [-2]	12.8 [+1]	4.8 [-2]		
Andorra								
Angola								
Anguilla								
Antigua and Barbuda								
Argentina	1,247,200	4,126,700	0.44%	0.51%	40.1	67.3	33.5%	28.8%
Armenia	11,555	36,289	0.18%	0.21%	3.7	12.1	0.4% [+3]	6.4%
Aruba								
Australia	7,928,616	14,867,501 [-1]	1.61%	2.17% [-1]	414.3	724.2 [-1]	26.8%	25.7% [-1]
Austria	4,469,402 [w]	7,999,924 [w]	1.91% [w]	2.52% [w]	551.0 [w]	956.8 [w]	27.0% [+2]	24.1% [w]
Azerbaijan	59,721	115,259	0.34%	0.18%	7.3	13.6	31.2% [+1]	10.1%
Bahamas								
Bahrain								
Bangladesh								
Barbados								
Belarus	372,283	1,024,087 [p]	0.72%	0.97% [p]	37.0	105.7 [p]	16.9%	11.5%
Belgium	5,564,389	6,997,295 [p]	1.97%	1.91% [p]	545.9	669.1 [p]	20.2%	21.8% [p]
Belize								
Benin								
Bermuda								
Bhutan								
Bolivia	149,261	156,801 [+2]	0.29%	0.28% [+2]	9.1	9.1 [+2]	46.0%	41.0% [+2]
Bosnia and Herzegovina								

APPENDIX 235

Table 8: Expenditure on Research and Development (R&D) cont.

Country or region	000 PPP$		As percentage (%) of GDP		Per capita (PPP$)		GERD performed by higher education sector (%)	
	2000	2007	2000	2007	2000	2007	2000	2007
Botswana	...	84,916 [v,-2]	...	0.38% [v,-2]	...	46.3 [v,-2]	...	5.8% [v,-2]
Brazil	11,507,669	17,336,531 [-1]	0.94%	1.02% [-1]	66.1	91.6 [-1]	24.8%	38.4% [-3]
British Virgin Islands	...	...	...	...	...	...	...	...
Brunei Darussalam	2,490 [x,+2]	6,287 [a,b,-3]	0.02% [x,+2]	0.04% [a,b,-3]	7.1 [x,+2]	17.2 [a,b,-3]	30.9% [a,+2]	8.4% [a,b,-3]
Bulgaria	257,786	417,101	0.52%	0.48%	32.2	54.6	9.9%	9.7%
Burkina Faso	19,659 [x,+1]	18,392 [a,b]	0.19% [x,+1]	0.11% [a,b]	1.6 [x,+1]	1.2 [a,b]	...	...
Burundi	...	...	...	...	...	...	...	...
Cambodia	6,838 [w,+2]	...	0.05% [w,+2]	...	0.5 [w,+2]	...	11.8% [w,+2]	...
Cameroon	...	...	...	...	...	...	...	...
Canada	16,687,599	23,970,003 [p]	1.91%	2.03% [p]	543.8	729.1 [p]	28.1%	36.0% [p]
Cape Verde	...	...	...	...	...	...	...	...
Cayman Islands	...	...	...	...	...	...	...	...
Central African Republic	...	...	...	...	...	...	...	...
Chad	...	...	...	...	...	...	...	...
Chile	751,890	1,229,077 [-3]	0.53%	0.67% [-3]	48.8	76.2 [-3]	43.8%	32.0% [-3]
China	27,029,326 [b]	104,901,417	0.90% [b]	1.49%	21.3 [b]	79.0	8.6% [b]	8.5%
Colombia	275,570	532,093 [-1]	0.14%	0.18% [-1]	6.6	11.7 [-1]	56.0% [b]	52.8% [b]
Comoros	...	...	...	...	...	...	...	...
Congo	...	...	...	...	...	...	...	...
Cook Islands	...	...	...	...	...	...	...	...
Costa Rica	109,534	133,332 [-3]	0.39%	0.37% [-3]	27.9	31.3 [-3]	36.2% [u]	34.0% [-3]
Côte d'Ivoire	...	...	...	...	...	...	...	...
Croatia	509,326	639,224	1.23%	0.93%	113.0	140.3	33.4%	33.7%
Cuba			0.45%	0.51% [u,-2]				
Cyprus	34,226	95,886 [p]	0.24%	0.45% [p]	49.1	123.1 [p]	24.8%	43.1% [p]
Czech Republic	1,861,306	3,802,680	1.21%	1.59%	182.1	373.3	14.2%	16.9%
Democratic People's Republic of Korea	...	...	...	...	...	...	...	...
Democratic Republic of the Congo	60,659 [a,v,+4]	75,217 [a,v,-2]	0.42% [a,v,+4]	0.48% [a,v,-2]	1.1 [a,v,+4]	1.3 [a,v,-2]	...	...
Denmark	3,766,716 [+1]	5,015,673 [w]	2.39% [+1]	2.57% [w]	703.5 [+1]	921.6 [w]	18.9% [+1]	27.5% [w]
Djibouti	...	...	...	...	...	...	...	...

Table 8: Expenditure on Research and Development (R&D) cont.

Country or region	000 PPP$		As percentage (%) of GDP		Per capita (PPP$)		GERD performed by higher education sector (%)	
	2000	2007	2000	2007	2000	2007	2000	2007
Dominica	…	…	…	…	…	…	…	…
Dominican Republic								
Ecuador	38,335 [+1]	150,309	0.06% [+1]	0.15%	3.1 [+1]	11.3	11.1% [+1]	…
Egypt	474,513 [a]	927,917 [a]	0.19% [a]	0.23% [a]	7.1 [a]	12.3 [a]	…	3.9%
El Salvador	20,051 [-2]		0.08% [-2]		3.4 [-2]		…	…
Equatorial Guinea								
Eritrea								
Estonia	81,254	318,550 [p]	0.61%	1.12% [p]	59.3	238.6 [p]	52.4%	41.8%
Ethiopia	85,282 [a+5]	106,791 [a]	0.18% [a+5]	0.17% [a]	1.1 [a+5]	1.3 [a]	14.3% [a+5]	14.6% [a]
Fiji	…		…		…		…	
Finland	4,439,726	6,320,699	3.34%	3.47%	857.8	1,197.8	17.8%	18.7%
France	32,920,326 [b]	43,359,554 [p]	2.15% [b]	2.10% [p]	556.2 [b]	703.3 [p]	18.8% [b]	19.2% [p]
Gabon								
Gambia								
Georgia	21,111	27,805 [-2]	0.22%	0.18% [-2]	4.5	6.2 [-2]	28.6%	26.8% [-2]
Germany	52,283,497	69,334,450 [w]	2.45%	2.54% [w]	635.2	839.4 [w]	16.1%	16.3% [w]
Ghana	…		…		…		…	
Gibraltar								
Greece	1,269,719 [+1]	1,845,571 [w]	0.51% [+1]	0.50% [w]	115.3 [+1]	165.6 [w]	44.9% [+1]	50.4% [w]
Grenada								
Guatemala	1,097 [a]	27,720 [-1]	0.03% [+5]	0.05% [-1]	0.1 [a]	2.1 [-1]	57.9% [+1]	23.7% [-2]
Guinea	…		…		…		…	
Guinea-Bissau	…		…		…		…	
Guyana	…		…		…		…	
Haiti	…		…		…		…	

Table 8: Expenditure on Research and Development (R&D) cont.

Country or region	000 PPP$		As percentage (%) of GDP		Per capita (PPP$)		GERD performed by higher education sector (%)	
	2000	2007	2000	2007	2000	2007	2000	2007
Holy See	...	...	...	...	...	...	...	...
Honduras	7,090	8,572 [-3]	0.04%	0.04% [-3]	...	1.3 [-3]	...	...
Hong Kong (China), SAR	830,919	2,172,836 [-1]	0.47%	0.81% [-1]	124.7	304.6 [-1]	80.2%	45.3% [-1]
Hungary	975,619 [1]	1,818,797	0.78% [1]	0.97%	95.5 [1]	181.3	24.0% [f]	23.3% [f]
Iceland	216,187	293,034 [-2]	2.68%	2.78% [-2]	769.1	990.9 [-2]	16.2% [w]	22.0% [-2]
India	11,918,734	14,901,892 [w,-3]	0.77%	0.69% [w,-3]	11.4	13.3 [w,-3]	4.0%	4.9% [w,-3]
Indonesia	337,350 [a]	347,237 [a,-2]	0.07% [a]	0.05% [a,-2]	1.6 [a]	1.5 [a,-2]	3.9%	4.6% [-6]
Iran, Islamic Republic of	2,547,891 [+1]	4,697,983 [-1]	0.55% [+1]	0.67% [-1]	38.2 [+1]	66.9 [-1]	21.9% [+1]	30.5% [-1]
Iraq	...	...	...	...	...	...	...	...
Ireland	1,220,956 [w]	2,522,464 [p]	1.12% [w]	1.34% [p]	321.0 [w]	586.5 [p]	20.2%	26.4% [p]
Israel	5,611,041 [+1]	8,817,635 [p]	4.45% [+1]	4.74% [p]	922.2 [+1]	1,272.8 [p]	15.0% [+1]	12.6% [p]
Italy	15,229,587	19,383,842 [-1]	1.05%	1.14% [-1]	264.0	329.8 [-1]	31.0%	30.3% [-1]
Jamaica	7,545 [+1]	9,780 [-5]	0.05% [+1]	0.07% [-5]	2.9 [+1]	3.7 [-5]	...	...
Japan	98,774,473	138,782,039 [-1]	3.04%	3.40% [-1]	777.5	1,084.6 [-1]	14.5%	12.7% [-1]
Jordan	60,403 [+2]	...	0.34% [+2]	...	11.9 [+2]	...	...	...
Kazakhstan	129,188	353,520	0.18%	0.21%	8.6	22.9	9.9%	15.5%
Kenya	...	...	...	...	...	...	...	...
Kiribati	...	...	...	...	...	...	...	...
Kuwait	86,810	111,357 [-2]	0.13%	0.08% [-1]	39.0	41.2 [-2]	8.1%	12.0%
Kyrgyzstan	10,234	26,037	0.16%	0.25%	2.1	4.9	...	...
Lao People's Democratic Republic	2,800 [a,-2]	...	0.04% [a,-2]	...	0.5 [a,-2]	...	12.0% [a,-2]	...
Latvia	80,377 [b]	251,175	0.44% [b]	0.63%	33.8 [b]	110.3	37.6% [b]	43.2%
Lebanon	...	...	...	...	...	...	...	...
Lesotho	1,031 [a,+2]	1,552 [a,-3]	0.05% [a,+2]	0.06% [a,-3]	0.5 [a,+2]	0.8 [a,-3]	...	...
Liberia	...	...	...	...	...	...	...	...
Libyan Arab Jamahiriya	...	...	...	...	...	...	...	...
Liechtenstein	...	...	...	...	...	...	...	...
Lithuania	172,986	495,242	0.59%	0.83%	49.4	146.1	36.5%	50.6%
Luxembourg	386,708	639,664 [p]	1.65%	1.69% [p]	885.3	1,371.0 [p]	0.2%	3.0% [p]
Macao, China	6,586 [a,w,-1]	18,569 [a,w,-2]	0.07% [a,w,-1]	0.11% [a,w,-2]	14.7 [a,w,-1]	39.3 [a,w,-2]	...	...

Table 8: Expenditure on Research and Development (R&D) cont.

Country or region	000 PPP$		As percentage (%) of GDP		Per capita (PPP$)		GERD performed by higher education sector (%)	
	2000	2007	2000	2007	2000	2007	2000	2007
Madagascar	14,752 [a]	25,862 [a]	0.12% [a]	0.14% [a]	0.9 [a]	1.3 [a]	100.0% [av,+1]	59.6% [a]
Malawi	…	…	…	…	…	…	…	…
Malaysia	1,045,028	2,085,079 [-1]	0.49%	0.64% [-1]	44.9	79.8 [-1]	17.1%	9.9% [-1]
Maldives	…	…	…	…	…	…	…	…
Mali	…	…	…	…	…	…	…	…
Malta	19,566 [+2]	57,262 [-1]	0.26% [+2]	0.60% [p]	49.6 [+2]	141.5 [-1]	58.8% [+2]	31.1% [p]
Marshall Islands	…	…	…	…	…	…	…	…
Mauritania	…	…	…	…	…	…	…	…
Mauritius	27,380 [v]	47,014 [v,-2]	0.30% [v]	0.38% [v,-2]	23.1 [v]	37.9 [v,-2]	…	…
Mexico	3,355,565	5,918,978 [-2]	0.37%	0.50% [-2]	33.6	56.8 [-2]	28.3%	27.4% [-2]
Micronesia (Federated States of)	…	…	…	…	…	…	…	…
Monaco	…	…	…	…	…	…	…	…
Mongolia	8,451	19,225	0.20%	0.23%	3.4	7.3	16.4% [+1]	12.7%
Montenegro	34,536 [+3]	72,697	0.80% [+3]	1.18%	53.4 [+3]	118.3	76.7% [+3]	80.0%
Montserrat	…	…	…	…	…	…	…	…
Morocco	522,576 [+1]	761,726 [-1]	0.63% [+1]	0.64% [-1]	18.1 [+1]	25.0 [-1]	…	52.4% [+1]
Mozambique	52,267 [v,+2]		0.50% [v,+2]		2.7 [v,+2]			
Myanmar	26,774 [u]	49,890 [u,-5]	0.11% [u]	0.16% [u,-5]	0.6 [u]	1.1 [u,-5]		
Namibia	…	…	…	…	…	…	…	…
Nauru	…	…	…	…	…	…	…	…
Nepal	…	…	…	…	…	…	…	…
Netherlands	8,533,046	10,907,528 [p]	1.82%	1.75% [p]	535.9	664.3 [p]	27.8% [b]	26.5% [p,w]
Netherlands Antilles	…	…	…	…	…	…	…	…
New Zealand	961,539 [+1]	1,189,316 [-2]	1.14% [+1]	1.17% [-2]	246.6 [+1]	290.3 [-2]	30.8% [+1]	32.5% [-2]
Nicaragua	4,693 [+2]		0.05% [+2]		0.9 [+2]			
Niger	…	…	…	…	…	…	…	…
Nigeria	…	…	…	…	…	…	…	…
Niue	…	…	…	…	…	…	…	…
Norway	2,663,930 [+1]	4,213,008	1.59% [+1]	1.68%	589.7 [+1]	896.7	25.7% [+1]	31.2% [b]
Oman	…	…	…	…	…	…	…	…

Table 8: Expenditure on Research and Development (R&D) cont.

Country or region	000 PPP$		As percentage (%) of GDP		Per capita (PPP$)		GERD performed by higher education sector (%)	
	2000	2007	2000	2007	2000	2007	2000	2007
Pakistan	303,403 [a]	2,751,785	0.13% [a]	0.67%	2.1 [a]	16.8	19.6%	26.7%
Palau	...	...	...	...	...	...	...	...
Palestinian Autonomous Territories	...	...	...	...	...	...	...	...
Panama	81,964 [b]	72,864 [-2]	0.38% [b]	0.25% [-2]	27.8 [b]	22.5 [-2]	7.1% [b]	8.6% [-2]
Papua New Guinea	...	...	...	...	...	...	...	...
Paraguay	16,259 [+1]	20,133 [-2]	0.09% [+1]	0.09% [-2]	3.0 [+1]	3.4 [-2]	40.7% [+2]	40.7% [-3]
Peru	139,027	239,000 [-3]	0.11%	0.15% [-3]	5.4	8.9 [-3]	41.9%	38.1% [-3]
Philippines	287,262 [+2]	290,819 [-2]	0.15% [+2]	0.12% [-2]	3.6 [+2]	3.4 [-2]	13.2% [+2]	21.3% [-2]
Poland	2,601,722	3,110,008 [-1]	0.64%	0.56% [-1]	67.7	81.5 [-1]	31.5%	31.0% [-1]
Portugal	1,322,623 [*]	2,754,319 [p]	0.76% [*]	1.19% [p]	129.3 [*]	259.3 [p]	37.5% [*]	29.9% [p]
Qatar	...	...	...	...	...	...	...	...
Republic of Korea	18,493,696	35,885,771 [-1]	2.39%	3.22% [-1]	395.3	746.8 [-1]	11.3%	10.0% [-1]
Republic of Moldova	22,494 [a,+3]	53,035 [a]	0.32% [a,+3]	0.55% [a]	6.2 [a,+3]	14.1 [a]	9.3% [a,+5]	11.1% [a]
Romania	502,267	1,320,839	0.37%	0.54%	22.7	61.6	11.8%	24.1%
Russian Federation	11,736,242	23,490,564	1.05%	1.12%	79.6	164.8	4.5%	6.3%
Rwanda	...	...	...	...	...	...	...	...
Saint Kitts and Nevis	...	...	...	...	...	...	...	...
Saint Lucia	...	...	...	...	...	...	...	...
Saint Vincent and the Grenadines	319 [+1]	963 [-5]	0.05% [+1]	0.15% [-5]	2.7 [+1]	8.2 [-5]	...	...
Samoa	...	...	...	...	...	...	...	...
San Marino	...	...	...	...	...	...	...	...
Sao Tome and Principe	...	...	...	...	...	...	...	...
Saudi Arabia	261,234 [+3]	273,072	0.06% [+3]	0.05%	11.6 [+3]	11.0	...	...
Senegal		16,252 [a,w,-2]		0.09% [a,w,-2]		1.4 [a,w,-2]		66.7% [a,-2]
Serbia	904,977 [a,n]	1,050,734 [a,n,-1]	2.05% [a,n]	1.50% [a,n,-1]	120.2 [a,n]	141.5 [a,n,-1]	34.5% [a,n]	47.9% [a,n,-1]
Seychelles	4,850 [a,+1]	4,519 [a,-2]	0.43% [a,+1]	0.38% [a,-2]	59.7 [a,+1]	54.5 [a,-2]	...	...
Sierra Leone	...	...	...	...	...	...	...	...
Singapore	2,538,473	4,819,151 [-1]	1.88%	2.31% [-1]	631.9	1099.8 [-1]	11.2%	23.9% [v,-1]
Slovakia	383,821	501,318	0.65%	0.46%	71.2	93.0	9.5%	25.0%
Slovenia	480,800	857,830 [p]	1.41%	1.57% [p]	242.4	428.6 [p]	16.6%	15.4% [p]

Table 8: Expenditure on Research and Development (R&D) cont.

Country or region	000 PPP$		As percentage (%) of GDP		Per capita (PPP$)		GERD performed by higher education sector (%)	
	2000	2007	2000	2007	2000	2007	2000	2007
Solomon Islands	...		...		...		...	
Somalia								
South Africa	2,250,432 +1	3,654,269 -2	0.73% +1	0.92% -2	48.9 +1	76.2 -2	25.3% +1	19.3% -2
Spain	7,780,724	17,955,014	0.91%	1.28%	193.4	405.5	29.6%	26.4%
Sri Lanka	73,279 a	116,029 -3	0.14% a	0.18% -3	3.9 a	6.1 -3	19.0% a	33.6% -3
Sudan	192,258	179,085 -2	0.47%	0.29% -2	5.8	4.9 -2	29.5%	27.1% -2
Suriname								
Swaziland	...		...		...		...	
Sweden	10,378,445 d,+1	12,357,368 p	4.24% d,+1	3.71% p	1,167.5 d,+1	1,355.1 p	19.6% +1	21.1% p
Switzerland	5,758,625	7,479,222 -3	2.57%	2.93% -3	792.8	1,011.8 -3	22.9%	22.9% -3
Syrian Arab Republic								
Tajikistan	5,545 +1	7,607	0.09% +1	0.06%	0.9 +1	1.1	3.0% +1	6.9% -2
Thailand	776,838 w	1,205,911 w,-1	0.25% w	0.25% w,-1	12.8 w	19.0 w,-1	31.0% +3	38.3% w,-1
The former Yugoslav Rep. of Macedor	54,777	33,654 -1	0.44%	0.21% -1	27.3	16.5 -1	60.2%	39.8% -1
Timor-Leste								
Togo	...		...		...		...	
Tokelau								
Tonga								
Trinidad and Tobago	15,789	27,811 -1	0.11%	0.10% -1	12.1	20.9 -1	23.2%	23.8% w,-1
Tunisia	211,393	660,607 -2	0.46%	1.02% -2	22.1	65.4 -2	35.7%	34.8% -2
Turkey	2,819,811	4,883,683 -1	0.48%	0.58% -1	41.4	66.1 -1	60.4%	51.3% -1
Turkmenistan								
Turks and Caicos Islands	...		...		...		...	
Tuvalu								
Uganda	74,807 +2	119,654	0.39% +2	0.41%	2.8 +2	3.9	1.3% +2	9.6% -1
Ukraine	1,548,267	2,780,261	0.96%	0.87%	31.7	60.2	5.8%	6.9%
United Arab Emirates	...		...		...		...	
United Kingdom	27,823,886	35,590,852 -1	1.86%	1.80% -1	472.7	588.2 -1	20.6%	26.1% -1
United Republic of Tanzania								
United States	268,121,000 z	368,799,000 p,z	2.75% z	2.67% p,z	941.2 z	1,205.9 p,z	11.4% z	13.3% p,z

Table 8: Expenditure on Research and Development (R&D) cont.

Country or region	000 PPP$		As percentage (%) of GDP		Per capita (PPP$)		GERD performed by higher education sector (%)	
	2000	2007	2000	2007	2000	2007	2000	2007
Uruguay	61,686	122,140 [-1]	0.24%	0.36% [-1]	18.6	36.7 [-1]	35.7%	36.7% [-1]
Uzbekistan	...	...	...	...	...	...	...	...
Vanuatu	...	...	...	...	...	...	...	...
Venezuela	775,282 [v]	905,892 [w,z]	0.38% [v]	0.34% [w,z]	31.8 [v]	33.9 [w,z]	...	...
Viet Nam	252,831 [+2]	...	0.19% [+2]	...	3.1 [+2]	...	17.9% [+2]	...
Yemen	...	...	...	...	...	...	...	...
Zambia	657 [+2]	3,840 [2]	0.01% [+2]	0.03% [-2]	0.1 [+2]	0.3 [2]	...	...
Zimbabwe	...	...	...	...	...	...	...	...

Notes:
a   Partial data
b   Break in series
d   Underestimated or based on underestimated data
f   The sum of the breakdown does not add to the total
i   Defence excluded (all or mostly)
p   Provisional
u   UIS estimation
v   Overestimated or based on overestimated data
w   National estimation
z   Excludes most or all capital expenditure

INDEX

Aalborg University, 150
Abu Dhabi, 25, 33
academic profession, 3, 15,
   19–20, 85–90, 132, 142–43;
   accountability and, 19;
   autonomy and, 19; bureaucracy
   of, 88–89; in developing
   countries, 85; differentiation
   of, 86; and mobility, 3, 19–20,
   89; part-time employment in,
   19, 86–87; qualifications of,
   19, 85, 86, 87–88; and research
   universities, 15, 86; salaries
   of, 19, 86, 88; and tenure, 19;
   working conditions of, 20, 86.
   See also faculty; instructors;
   professoriate; professors;
   teachers; teaching assistants;
   teaching staff
Academic Ranking of World
   Universities, 11–12, 79–80.
   See also Shanghai Jiao Tong
   University
access (to higher education), xii,
   1, 3–8, 11, 12, 14, 33, 37–49, 63,
   67, 76, 93–95, 99, 114, 117, 121,
   125, 128, 130, 156–59
accessibility, 69, 72, 93. *See also*
   access
accountability, 14, 15, 17, 19, 29,
   40, 51, 53, 69, 73, 74, 85, 88–
   90, 105, 106, 108, 157
accreditation, 53, 55, 60, 61, 101,
   113, 127. *See also* accreditation
   mills; quality assurance
Accreditation Board for
   Engineering and Technology
   (ABET), 61

accreditation mills, 59. *See also*
   degree mills; diploma mills;
   fraud
affirmative action, 37, 41–44. *See
   also* positive discrimination;
   quotas; reservation programs
African Network for
   Internationalisation of
   Education (ANIE), 28–29
African Virtual University
   (AVU), 124
Algeria, 29
Anadolu University, 125
Andalucía, 27
Apollo Group, 82, 124
Arabian Gulf, 9, 20, 47
Arab Network for Quality
   Assurance in Higher
   Education (ANQAHE), 60
Argentina, 45, 77, 135, 138, 139
Asia-Pacific Quality Network
   (APQN), 61
assessment, 17, 58–60, 88, 90,
   105–14, 134, 136
Assessment of Higher Education
   Learning Outcomes (AHELO),
   58
Association of University
   Technology Managers
   (AUTM), 148
Association to Advance
   Collegiate Schools of Business
   (AACSB), 61
Australia, 8, 25, 27, 40, 46, 54,
   76, 82, 110, 128, 141
Australian Universities Quality
   Agency (AUQA), 54
Austria, 71

42, 43, 67, 72, 76, 141, 143, 149, 151, 152, 156
research, 2, 3, 5, 6, 7, 9, 10, 11, 52, 86, 87, 88, 90, 94, 98, 106, 128, 131–44, 145, 146–49, 153, 160; capacity, 98; cost of, 65; effects of technology on, 118, 120, 122, 129, 130; and funding, 14, 68; and internationalization, 24, 25, 26, 28–32, 89; "organizational research units," 153; output/productivity, 57, 61, 69, 86; and private higher education, 80; and privatization, 83, 158; products, 14; and public good, 13; and quality, 53, 57, 68; and rankings, 11–12, 61; and relevance, 98, 160; research environment, 15–17; versus teaching activities, 98, 105, 110, 114. *See also* research and development (R&D); research universities
research and development (R&D), 135–39, 149–50
research universities, 1, 4, 6, 10–11, 13, 15–18, 87, 120, 134–35, 139–40, 148, 152, 159
reservation programs, 42–45. *See also* affirmative action; positive discrimination; quotas
retention, 46, 56. *See also* completion rates
revolution, xii, 1–3, 5–7, 8, 13–14, 20, 49, 118, 121, 159
rural populations/areas. *See* geography
Russia, 71, 109, 135

Saint Regis University, 127
salaries, 8, 18–20, 70, 86–90,

99. *See also* academic profession
Saudi Arabia, 78
science, 34, 100, 126, 135, 138, 139, 141; academic employment in, 142–43; "big science," 133, 138; biomedical science, 146; biosciences, 48; government support for, 133; human resource needs and capacity, 109, 150; life sciences, 26; and research, 14, 16; and social sciences, 141; and technology policy, 137–38; in traditional universities, 106. *See also* research; research and development (R&D); science parks
Science Citation Index, 11
Science City Initiative, 153
science parks, 152, 154
Scotland, 145
service sector/service industries, 2, 5, 18
Shanghai Jiao Tong University, 12, 61, 79–80. *See also* Academic Ranking of World Universities
Shanghai TV University, 124
Singapore, 20, 21, 25, 27, 31, 33, 89
Slovenia, 29
social class/socioeconomic status, 17, 38, 39, 42, 44, 99, 156
social mobility. *See* mobility
South Africa, 33, 46, 78, 81, 88, 124, 129
Southeast Asian Ministers of Education Organisation-Regional Centre for Higher Education and Development

technology; technology parks;
technology transfer
technology parks, 154. *See also*
science parks
technology transfer, 145, 146, 153
Thailand, 76, 80
Times Higher Education/QS, 12,
79
trade, 34, 62–63. *See also*
General Agreement on Trade
in Services (GATS); North
Atlantic Free Trade Agreement
(NAFTA); World Trade
Organization (WTO)
triple helix, 133, 146. *See also*
university-industry linkages
Tunisia, 29
Turkey, 29, 43, 78, 80, 125, 151

UNESCO Open and Distance
Learning Knowledge Base, 130
UNESCO Portal of Higher
Education Institutions, 58, 101
UNESCO World Conference on
Higher Education (1998), xi,
51, 53
UNESCO World Conference on
Higher Education (2009), 93,
95, 100
United Arab Emirates (UAE), 27
United Kingdom, 8, 27, 68, 69,
78, 82, 89, 121, 124, 128, 134,
136, 141, 149, 151, 153. *See also*
England; Scotland
United States, 1, 6, 17, 18, 19, 20,
27, 28, 41, 45, 55, 59, 60, 61,
62, 67, 68, 71, 72, 77, 78, 79,
80, 81, 82, 86, 89, 106, 109,
113, 120, 121, 124, 127, 128, 136,
139, 140, 141, 142, 145, 146,
147, 148, 149, 152, 153, 154, 156
Universidad Nacional de

Educación a Distancia
(National Distance Education
University, UNED), 125
university-industry linkages, 13,
14, 16, 139–40, 143, 146–54
University of Ghana, 125
University of Nottingham, 25;
University of Nottingham
Ningbo, China, 25
University of Pennsylvania, 152
University of Phoenix, 82, 121,
124,
University of South Africa
(UNISA), 124
University of Waterloo, 150
urban populations/areas. *See*
geography

Vietnam, 85
vocationalization (of higher
education), 96

Whitney International, 82
women, 2, 6, 37, 43–44, 48, 79,
94, 101, 126. *See also* gender
work-study programs, 150
world-class universities, 10, 13,
15, 80, 136. *See also* research
universities
World Trade Organization
(WTO), 29, 147
World War II, 5, 138

Xenophobia, 32

Zhejiang Wanli Education
Group-University, 25

GLOBAL PERSPECTIVES ON HIGHER EDUCATION

Volume 1
WOMEN'S UNIVERSITIES AND COLLEGES
An International Handbook
Francesca B. Purcell, Robin Matross Helms, and Laura Rumbley (Eds.)
ISBN 978-90-77874-58-5 hardback
ISBN 978-90-77874-02-8 paperback

Volume 2
PRIVATE HIGHER EDUCATION
A Global Revolution
Philip G. Altbach and D. C. Levy (Eds.)
ISBN 978-90-77874-59-2 hardback
ISBN 978-90-77874-08-0 paperback

Volume 3
FINANCING HIGHER EDUCATION
Cost-Sharing in International perspective
D. Bruce Johnstone
ISBN 978-90-8790-016-8 hardback
ISBN 978-90-8790-015-1 paperback

Volume 4
UNIVERSITY COLLABORATION FOR INNOVATION
Lessons from the Cambridge-MIT Institute
David Good, Suzanne Greenwald, Roy Cox, and Megan Goldman (Eds.)
ISBN 978-90-8790-040-3 hardback
ISBN 978-90-8790-039-7 paperback

Volume 5
HIGHER EDUCATION
A Worldwide Inventory of Centers and Programs
Philip G. Altbach, Leslie A. Bozeman, Natia Janashia, and Laura E. Rumbley
ISBN 978-90-8790-052-6 hardback
ISBN 978-90-8790-049-6 paperback

Volume 6
FUTURE OF THE AMERICAN PUBLIC RESEARCH UNIVERSITY
R. L. Geiger, C. L. Colbeck, R. L. Williams, and C. K. Anderson (Eds.)
ISBN 978-90-8790-048-9 hardback
ISBN 978-90-8790-047-2 paperback

Volume 14
UNIVERSITY AND DEVELOPMENT IN LATIN AMERICA: SUCCESSFUL
EXPERIENCES OF RESEARCH CENTERS
Simon Schwartzman (Ed.)
ISBN 978-90-8790-524-8 hardback
ISBN 978-90-8790-523-1 paperback

Volume 15
BUYING YOUR WAY INTO HEAVEN: EDUCATION AND CORRUPTION IN
INTERNATIONAL PERSPECTIVE
Stephen P. Heyneman (Ed.)
ISBN 978-90-8790-728-0 hardback
ISBN 978-90-8790-727-3 paperback

Volume 16
HIGHER EDUCATION AND THE WORLD OF WORK
Ulrich Teichler
ISBN 978-90-8790-755-6 hardback
ISBN 978-90-8790-754-9 paperback

Volume 17
FINANCING ACCESS AND EQUITY IN HIGHER EDUCATION
Jane Knight (Ed.)
ISBN 978-90-8790-767-9 hardback
ISBN 978-90-8790-766-2 paperback

Volume 18
UNIVERSITY RANKINGS, DIVERSITY, AND THE NEW LANDSCAPE OF
HIGHER EDUCATION
Barbara M. Kehm and Bjørn Stensaker (Eds.)
ISBN 978-90-8790-815-7 hardback
ISBN 978-90-8790-814-0 paperback

Volume 19
HIGHER EDUCATION IN EAST ASIA: NEOLIBERALISM AND THE
PROFESSORIATE
Gregory S. Poole and Ya-chen Chen (Eds.)
ISBN 978-94-6091-127-9 hardback
ISBN 978-94-6091-126-2 paperback

Volume 20
ACCESS AND EQUITY: COMPARATIVE PERSPECTIVES
Heather Eggins (Ed.)
ISBN 978-94-6091-185-9 hardback
ISBN 978-94-6091-184-2 paperback

Volume 21
UNDERSTANDING INEQUALITIES IN AND BY HIGHER EDUCATION
Gaële Goastellec (Ed.)
ISBN 978-94-6091-307-5 hardback
ISBN 978-94-6091-306-8 paperback

Volume 22
TRENDS IN GLOBAL HIGHER EDUCATION: TRACKING AN ACADEMIC
REVOLUTION
Philip G. Altbach, Liz Reisberg and Laura E. Rumbley
ISBN 978-94-6091-338-9 hardback
ISBN 978-94-6091-339-6 paperback

CPSIA information can be obtained at www.ICGtesting.com
Printed in the USA
BVOW06s2307240216

437703BV00008B/7/P

9 789460 91338